BEAT THE SYSTEM!

A WAY TO CREATE MORE HUMAN ENVIRONMENTS

Robert F. Allen

WITH

Charlotte Kraft

AND THE STAFF OF THE
HUMAN RESOURCES INSTITUTE

McGraw-Hill Book Company

NEW YORK ST. LOUIS SAN FRANCISCO AUCKLAND
BOGOTA HAMBURG JOHANNESBURG LONDON MADRID MEXICO
MONTREAL NEW DELHI PANAMA PARIS SÃO PAULO
SINGAPORE SYDNEY TOKYO TORONTO

Library of Congress Cataloging in Publication Data

Allen, Robert Francis, date.
Beat the system!

Bibliography: p.
Includes index.
1. Culture. 2. Social change. 3. Man—
Influence of environment. I. Kraft, Charlotte, joint
author. II. Human Resources Institute (Morristown,
N.J.) III. Title.
HM101.A574   303.4   79-28848
ISBN 0-07-001080-3

1 2 3 4 5 6 7 8 9 0   DO DO   8 9 8 7 6 5 4 3 2 1 0

The editor for this book was William R. Newton,
the designer was Elliot Epstein, and the production supervisor was
Teresa F. Leaden. It was set in Times Roman by Bi-Comp, Incorporated.

Printed and bound by R. R. Donnelley & Sons Company.

*This book is dedicated
to our family and friends
and to those
who lived the stories
that are told here.*

CONTENTS

Preface   **vii**

Acknowledgments   **ix**

Introduction   Becoming Free in an Unfree World   **1**

SECTION 1   **THE SEAMLESS WEB**

    PART 1   **HOW OUR CULTURES CREATE US**

       1   **Understanding Cultural Influences**   **11**

       2   **The Power of Norms**   **23**

       3   **Not by Accident Alone**   **35**

    PART 2   **CULTURES THAT DESTROY**

       4   **Individual Destruction**   **53**

       5   **Institutional Failure**   **63**

    PART 3   **PROBLEMS OF CHANGE AND NONCHANGE**

       6   **The Culture Trap**   **83**

       7   **Cultural Obstacles to Change**   **89**

       8   **A False Dichotomy and the Incongruent Culture**   **99**

       9   **The Fulcrum: It Doesn't Have to Be That Way**   **107**

SECTION 2   **CHANGING THINGS**

    PART 4   **HOW WE CAN TRANSFORM OUR CULTURES**

       10   **It Takes a System to Beat a System**   **113**

       11   **Opening the Culture Trap**   **119**

       12   **Knowing Where You Are and Where You're Going**   **129**

       13   **Instruments for Understanding Cultures and Planning Change**   **147**

v

14   Introducing Change   155

15   Making a Difference   165

16   Keeping It Going   175

17   The Normative Systems Model   181

PART 5   THEY DID IT: FOUR SUCCESSFUL CASE
          HISTORIES—AND A FAILURE

18   From Delinquency to Freedom   187

19   Migrancy Defeated   199

20   Changing the Litter Culture   211

21   Trouble in Paradise   219

22   A Program That Failed   227

PART 6   BUILDING SUCCESS ENVIRONMENTS

23   Moonshots: Uses of Normative Systems   233

24   Walking Ahead in the Sun   245

25   Conclusion: Getting Free   257

      Additional Credits   259

Appendix A   Norm Influence Areas to be Considered in Analyzing
              a Culture   261

Appendix B   Cultural Norm Indicator for Families   263

Appendix C   Cultural Norm Indicator for Organizations   271

Appendix D   Scoring Directions for Group Effectiveness Exercises Based
              on "Quiz on Reviewing Key Ideas"   277

Appendix E   A Partial Listing of Current and Past Normative Systems
              Applications   279

      Bibliography   283

      Index   287

PREFACE

This book is based on the premise that many of today's pressing societal and personal needs can be met by a systematic, humanistic, people-involving change process, one which focuses on the culture and makes use of the power of the culture to bring about improvement in the human condition. The key hypotheses we present are these:

> The cultures in which we live have an immense impact on each of us as individuals and on our institutions, without our being fully aware of what is happening to us.
>
> Our cultures are much more changeable, for better or worse, than most of us realize.
>
> By using a planned, systematic, people-involved strategy for change, we can consciously transform our environments and in that way re-create ourselves.

The concept and theory this book presents, the system it describes, and the cases it narrates are derived from over twenty years of field research and action studies. All of this material summarizes the vital core of the work we have completed thus far.

Our first professional contact with the power of the culture took place in the early 1950s, when we were studying urban delinquency environments in Eastern cities. It was here that we witnessed a tragic yet fascinating phenomenon. Black youngsters were moving north from Mississippi, Georgia, and South Carolina, and Puerto Rican youngsters were arriving from the rural areas of Puerto Rico. Most of them had never before been involved in delinquency of any sort; yet after six to eight months they were appearing in juvenile courts as full-fledged delinquents with all the skills and attitudes of the delinquent street culture. Here, indeed, was an effective training program of immense proportions, and much of it was taking place in such a way that the youngsters themselves were only slightly aware of what was happening to them.

Sensitized by this, we became aware that similar things were happening in other cultural settings. In business organizations, in government agencies, and in communities people were caught in their environments, and since they were largely oblivious of the insidious net in which they were enmeshed, they could do little to free themselves. Gradually we developed a set of assumptions about culture and a systematic process by which people could begin to contribute to their own freedom and bring about meaningful change.

It is this theory and process that we describe here. We hope that it will contribute to the humanization of culture and to the involvement of people in the solutions of their own problems. Our experience has been that it is possible for people to make positive changes in an amazingly short period of time. People who are seemingly helpless and perhaps about to "go under" and who lack the belief that change is possible have been able not only to endure, but to participate actively in reshaping the social environments which in turn shape them. The most exciting part of our work has been seeing once-skeptical people enthusiastically going about making the changes that they themselves chose, finding a freedom of self-determination that they had not thought possible.

We are moved to share these experiences and the lessons learned from them so that larger numbers of people can take whatever is valuable and make use of it to attain a greater congruence between the world that is and the world they want. We invite the involvement of groups, large or small, public or private, and of individuals who wish to help create better worlds for themselves, their families, their friends, and their fellow human beings, in what has become for us a meaningful, exciting, humanizing, and freedom-full way of dealing with change.

Despite our obvious enthusiasm, the purpose here has not been to provide a final, cast-in-concrete formulation, but rather to encourage realization that a systematic, participatory, win/win, culture-based approach to change is important and practical. At the least this volume will encourage people to examine the concepts it presents and determine their usefulness by trying them out in the world of everyday experience. Eventually we hope these concepts and models will be improved upon to help many more people to deal with the process of change in meaningful, satisfying ways.

Robert F. Allen
Charlotte Kraft

and the staff of HRI Human
Resources Institute

ACKNOWLEDGMENTS

In writing a book that addresses itself to so many aspects of the human condition as this one does, we have come under heavy obligation to many, many people who have provided time and support, good judgment, helpful suggestions, source material, hours of labor, encouragement, and personal kindness.

The authors acknowledge that Stanley Silverzweig was involved in the development and application of many of the Normative Systems projects and cultural transformation processes described in this book. He served as co-director of many of these projects, as did a number of the people listed below.

We would like to express special gratitude to Harry N. Dubin and Saul Pilnick, whose early collaborative efforts with the author at Scientific Resources Incorporated provided some of the seminal ideas that eventually led to the concepts that are described in the book; to Robert L. Chapman for his editorial suggestions; to Doris Ballantyne for her efficiency and perseverance in preparing the manuscript; and to Elaine, Judd, and Peter Allen and Walter Stein, for their personal support and encouragement.

From among the many others who provided suggestions and encouragement, we particularly want to thank Ed, Mary, and Joe Allen, Leonard and Susan Barris, Jack and Molly Bender, Allen Bildner, Ruth Conover, Richard Downey, Jack Dreyer, Barbara Drury, Sara and Arnold Harris, Michael Higgins, Jim Hunt, Douglas Boardman Kraft, Stephanie Kraft, Ralph Litwin, William Merkle, Joan, Mickey, and Bruce Mintz, Clark Olsen, Nona Rutter, Selma Salko, Leonard Schechter, Myron Scheinberg, Marilyn Schneider, Irving Stern, Marvin and Mary Sochet, and Jack Wagner.

Becoming Free in an Unfree World

The world that we have made as a result of the level of thinking that we have done thus far creates problems that we cannot solve at the same level at which we created them.

ALBERT EINSTEIN

The world we have made also makes us. Socializing influences that act upon us from birth largely determine what we are. If we could only direct our own destinies rather than remain victims of the situations that happen to exist! Then we could be truly free, purposefully making our world what we want it to be.

Fortunately, in recent years we have had substantial evidence that this can be done. Quietly, without public fanfare, people are making use of the cultural forces that have too often in the past kept them trapped. They are learning to shape the environments that shape them.

One such person was Juan, an orange picker in the Minute Maid orange groves of Central Florida, working in a racist, feudal system in the lowest stratum of the economy. Juan joined with fellow migrants and with the Coca-Cola Company who employed them and made a systematic, culture-based effort to change things. Together they wiped out the old system and built a new environment. Today Juan works year-round, owns his own home, earns a comfortable living, and provides security for his family. At Lakeview Park, Florida, he has helped to develop a new community with medical and day-care centers, schools, and libraries. Juan has dropped his role of oppressed migrant and has recreated himself by helping to recreate his environment.

The same process used by Juan and his associates in the orange groves was used by the Benson family of Montclair, New Jersey, to improve the quality of their home life. Outwardly they seemed like an ideal family, but inwardly they had many dissatisfactions. Mark Benson, an engineering consultant, had gone into business for himself with high humanistic prin-

1

ciples, only to realize later that he had begun to use hard-nosed competitive business tactics which he brought into his family relationships. He and his wife felt their old-fashioned values separated them from their children; the children felt home was a convenience, but fun and "real life" were elsewhere. Getting together through a systematic program that treated the family as a culture, the family members analyzed their own norms, committed themselves to both individual and family goals, and changed the norms of their home environment, developing an atmosphere of trust and sharing—one that supported each family member in his search for self-fulfillment.

In still another exciting transformation, the community of Macon, Georgia, did something about the destruction of its physical and aesthetic environment. People from all levels—from the mayor to the newest sanitation worker—cooperated in a culture-based project that dealt specifically with litter. In eight months they reduced litter by 25 percent. They were able to maintain and increase the reduction over the years, reaching an 80 percent reduction by the fourth year. In the process, people in Macon learned ways to work together on other community problems.

These illustrations might be tossed aside as exceptions were it not that they, and hundreds of similar cases, share a common system of planned change. They all used a culture-based approach, one which you also can use in your organizations and communities.

The most significant thing is not that these people were able to accomplish so much—we have always had saints and heroes succeeding despite terrible obstacles—but that they discovered another level of solving problems and were able to use it to make their world better. They shifted their focus from exclusive concern with the individual to concern with both the individual and the culture, and from blame-placing to working with others to change the social environment. They teach us that it is not necessary to be mired in helplessness, to give up because we think "it's just human nature," or to remain victims of tyrannical forces. They help us look at the tremendous problems that plague society and say, "It doesn't have to be that way."

The basic premise underlying these successful change efforts is that by taking a cultural approach, people can create greater freedom even in our problem-filled world. This premise is based on three key hypotheses:

> The cultures in which we live have an immense impact on each of us as individuals and on our institutions, without our being fully aware of what is happening to us.

> Our cultures are more changeable, for better or worse, than most of us have realized.

By using a planned, systematic, democratic strategy for change, we can consciously transform our environments, and in that way recreate ourselves.

(Note that the term *environment* as used in this book refers to *social environment* unless otherwise stated. The term *culture* refers to any group of two or more people sharing socially transmitted behavior patterns.)

The idea that human beings are able to improve themselves and their environment is very ancient and very durable. It is central to the myth of Prometheus and also to Freud's vision of the capacity of people to master their interior environment by gaining control over unconscious emotional forces. Until Freud's time, these forces were not considered to be open to rational explanation and logical understanding. The most basic contribution of Freud and his followers was helping us become aware of the great impact of those inner forces, making them more susceptible to intentional control. Today there is wide acceptance of Freud's idea that the unconscious influences behavior on many levels, and current derivatives of his work flourish (*I'm OK, You're OK*, transactional analysis, encounter groups, assertiveness training, personal growth workshops, etc.). Although Freud's contribution has been only partially realized, he opened the way for the exploration and understanding of hidden internal influences and formulated a system to deal with them.

In much the same vein, it is being suggested here that there are hidden external or cultural forces which also have a tremendous impact on our lives, without our being fully aware of what is happening. These forces help to make murderers out of people who might otherwise have been nonviolent, crooks out of honest men, and racists out of some who have done little more than be born into a culture caught up in destructive patterns of discrimination and prejudice.

Complementary, therefore, to Freud's effort to free people from the unconscious forces that affect their lives, we are now in a position to become more aware of the cultural forces that affect us, so that these too can become more susceptible to conscious influence and control. Moreover, it is evident now that whole groups of people can free themselves of destructive cultural ties more readily than we ever dreamed possible.

In one sense the idea behind this book is as new as Freud's was in his time. In another sense neither is new. Freud himself once was introduced to the Vienna Medical Society as the discoverer of the unconscious. He responded that he was not, that indeed the unconscious had been discovered long before his time by artists and poets, and that he was merely one person who had developed a systematic approach to studying and modifying it. Similarly, this book claims nothing new in the idea that our lives are greatly influenced by cultural factors—an idea that has been long recognized, waiting only for mankind in general to perceive it and make use of it. It is hoped that this volume will provide some new understanding of this old idea and some workable ways of using the culture's power for the cause of human freedom.

If we want freer and more enriched lives, we can gain them by consciously creating our cultures. If we want to avoid conformity and manipulation, then we must recognize that conformity and manipulation are a natural development when cultures are left unexamined. This book proposes *cultural analysis* as a way to gain greater insights into our problems and *cultural modification* as a way to gain greater individual freedom and improve the quality of societal life.

The basic premise is presented in two modes—the mode of understanding and the mode of action. The first section, "The Seamless Web," is an intensive look at the ways in which cultures create us. It shows how cultural norms work and how they destroy individuals and cause our institutions to fail. Cultural obstacles that get in the way of meaningful change are examined. Altogether, this first section is consciousness-raising, aiming at helping people become more cognizant of the environmental impact of the cultures surrounding them. It seeks to reveal the obvious as more interesting than one might suspect, and to make the less obvious more accessible.

In the second section, "Changing Things," a tested, systematic change process, called *Normative Systems,* is presented. This process is illustrated in five case histories, and further applications are suggested.

This book is concerned with formulating the lessons learned in successful change programs. One of the most important lessons is that cynicism is unproductive. Often a successful culture change starts with the belief of only a few that at first just moves things slightly, but then grows to encompass many and eventually makes a big difference. People have emerged from these experiences not only with a problem solved, but equipped with the knowledge, skills, and spirit to address further difficulties, and with the powerfully motivating belief that change is possible.

Perhaps the most amazing thing that has emerged from all the successful efforts is evidence that right now, within ourselves, we have the capacity to become creators, rather than victims, of our environments. By developing this capacity we can bring ourselves to a new level of group problem solving and personal freedom.

The pages ahead do not offer a magic cure-all for the world's ills, nor do they seek to entice people to choose the particular system described. The purpose is rather to encourage people to examine some basic assumptions that are central to their well-being and to help them create "success" environments rather than environments where they tend to fail. We often create cultures where people cannot succeed; then we blame them for failure. There are organizations in which people have to be competitive to survive; then they are blamed for their competitiveness. There are ghetto communities in which the environment disposes people to litter; then they are blamed for littering. There are schools in which the tests and grading systems are set up in such a way that many may be expected to fail; then they are blamed for failing. What we need desperately in many areas of our lives are ways to set up environments in which people will succeed. This book proposes a systematic way to do so.

Section One

THE SEAMLESS WEB

John Edward Halad

Part One

HOW OUR CULTURES CREATE US

Pale despair and cold tranquillity. Nature's vast frame, the web of human things.

PERCY BYSSHE SHELLEY

The web of our life is of a mingled yarn, good and ill together.

WILLIAM SHAKESPEARE

Chapter 1

Understanding Cultural Influences

A TRUE TEST WITH FALSE ANSWERS

Questions

Why do so many people think healthy babies, red sunsets, and Miss America are beautiful?

Why do so many people eat three meals a day?

Why do so many people drive 5 miles over the speed limit?

Why do so many people still smoke?

Why do people wear clothes on a hot day?

Do you think it's all right to "fudge" a little on your income tax return? Why?

Why are female infants so often dressed in pink, males in blue?

Do you sit at the same place at the dinner table every night? Why?

Why are certain kinds of sexual practices accepted and others not?

Does buying something make you feel better?

Do you think more is better than less? Bigger better than smaller?

Would you allow a little alcohol at a teenagers' party? Pot? Beer?

Why do we bottle and sell certain odors in order to get rid of certain others?

Why do we allow organized crime to exist?

Why do we allow ghettos and rural poverty to continue?

If we disapprove of wars, why don't we put an end to them?

Answers

It's just human nature.

Doesn't everybody?

If I did (or didn't), everyone would think me weird.

Answers behind the answers

It's what's expected.

It's what's accepted.

It's what's approved by the group.

It's the unwritten rule.

In short, it's the norm!

Gossamer thin yet tough; chameleonlike yet tenacious; largely obscure but patently knowable—this is the seamless web of the culture that awaits us when we are born, tightens its hold during our long childhood, and maintains its shaping energy for our entire lifetime. The web consists of a myriad of social influences which determine how we wear our hair, what we think is beautiful, how many meals we eat, with whom we fall in love, and countless other ways of behaving.

Try this at your dinner table tonight: Instead of sitting at your usual place, quietly seat yourself at another. You will probably get a reaction indicating you have broken an accepted pattern.

Or check your male friends' hairstyles. How many of them wore their hair longer a few years ago? And how many are now wearing it shorter, as the current fad dictates?

To be sure, where you sit or how long you prefer your hair is of little importance, but the same kind of cultural persuasion goes on in much more serious matters. Cultural influences can be matters of life and health and death. They can promote violence, destroy individuals, and undermine the goals of our institutions. There is not a problem, public or personal, in the world today that is not affected by negative cultural influences. The network is vast and energetic, a force to be reckoned with. But it can become an ally in our quest for fulfillment if we first take on the tasks of (1) understanding its composition, (2) increasing our awareness of its extent and power, and (3) examining thoroughly the various ways in which it operates. The first task occupies the rest of this chapter.

UNDERSTANDING CULTURAL NORMS

Understanding culture is a deceptively simple matter. It begins with the recognition that whenever two or more people come together over a period of time with a shared goal, they develop a culture. A cultural group can be large or small, formally structured or unplanned; it can meet regularly or sporadically, and can last for a weekend or many generations. A family, a committee, an agency, a hospital, a school, a prison, a multilevel business corporation, a corner grocery store, a church board, a neighborhood, a large city, a police department, a kindergarten room, a personal growth marathon weekend, a dormitory, a kingdom—all develop cultures, for each is an assemblage of people who in one way or another pool efforts and resources to reach a goal. The goal may be stated and even written down, or it may be unstated and unacknowledged. The real goal may be quite different from the stated goal. But, recognized or not, the common bond is there.

When people come together over time, they bring with them, or create, certain expectations regarding one another's behavior. Every culture has ways of doing things that influence its members, and these we call *group norms* or *social norms,* or simply *norms*. These building blocks of the culture are powerful forces which, when left unexamined, can become obstacles to the achievement of our potential as human beings.

The term "norm" is not new to the social sciences. It has been used generally to designate a standard or rule that states what a person should or should not say, do, or think. This book uses an expanded definition which covers unstated as well as stated standards. Norm is an umbrella term for all behavior that is expected, accepted, or supported by the group, whether or not the standards are written down, expressed orally, or acknowledged. The important thing is that the behavior is sanctioned. People are encouraged and rewarded when they follow norms and confronted when they violate them. In this way norms gather strength and eventually become profound socializing influences.

The word norm as used in this book does not refer to the *average* or *mean,* but to a standard as demonstrated in behavior. When the adjective "normative" is used, it means "related to norms." Thus, a *normative influence would be an influence characterized by socially supported behavior, and a normative workshop* is one that focuses on norms.

While this use of the word norm may be unfamiliar to some readers, even though it is well known to others, we are all quite used to hearing norms expressed in everyday language as pithy truisms or clichés:

> When in Rome, do as the Romans do.
>
> When you go to the village of the tortoise and it eats earth, you eat some, too (African).[1]
>
> Listen, you, around here everyone shoots the stuff.
>
> Why hurry? No one ever gets to meetings on time.
>
> In this county, you'd better vote Democratic.
>
> But, Mother, all the other girls do!
>
> Because everyone is.

Many norms—in fact, most of them—are unexpressed. They remain in the minds of members of a cultural group as ideas about behavior expected of them by that group. Consciously or unconsciously, they are valued by members of the group, and determine attitudes and the behavior manifested in carrying out those attitudes.

It is important, however, to distinguish between norms and values. Although there is a difference of opinion about what a *value* is, basically the term is used to speak of an abstract thing held by an individual to be of worth and enduring over a period of time. It is an idea that may or may not be carried out in behavior. It differs from a norm, which is a way of *behaving* common to two or more people. Most important, unlike values, norms are necessarily accompanied by social and/or psychological sanctions. "It is the norms, not the values, that have the pressure of reality upon them. It is the norms that are enforced by sanctions, that are subject to the necessity of action and the agony of decision. It is, therefore, the norms that represent the cutting edge of social control."[2]

SEEING NORMS

It is easier to spot norms that affect other people than to see those that affect us. Many a father has said to his teenager: "Why do you have to be like them! You don't have to do it just because your friends do." However, the father does not recognize that he is wearing the same kind of shirt and the same kind of tie as *his* friends and associates, and that he

[1] From Robert E. L. Faris (ed.), *Handbook of Modern Sociology* (Chicago: Rand McNally, 1964), p. 1.

[2] Ibid., p. 461.

gives the same kind of parties, serves the same kind of food and drink, and follows the same schedule and the same social patterns.

The farther away the other people are, the easier it is to see that they are programmed, molded, wooed into conformity. The former Eskimo custom of letting the elderly die quietly, alone on the ice floe, we can easily see as cultural. The Africans who were brought up to believe that facial scars are beautiful—we can understand that they are the victims of society—no problem! And the Oriental women of several decades ago, hobbling along on bound feet, how trapped they were in the norms of their society, how blind to freedom!

Others are influenced—in another country, another culture, another time in history. But when we look at ourselves, logic melts. "I make up my own mind," we say. But actually we stop short of the deeper truth? The tribal chief's bevy of 350-pound concubines, Rubens' heavy-hipped and plump-bellied goddesses, and the slim sex kitten of the *Playboy* center fold are all examples of culture-influenced ideas of beauty.

A generation ago, would anyone have thought, "Black is beautiful"? Or was the most beautiful Negro woman the one with the lightest skin, the thinnest nose, and a Westernized hairdo? Blacks gave in to the societal norms of the time, as the models in Black magazines back then attest— black of skin, but thin-nosed and thin-lipped and with straightened hair.

With a little observation, one can see that not only the norms of beauty, but all esthetic choices, are cultural. Why do we think that a given man is handsome? That a painting is superb? Why does that music thrill us? Why is this fabric design just right? The culture has taught us well—that certain things are tasteful and satisfying and others are not. "I don't know art, but I know what I like," people say, or "I don't have to study music to know that's a good tune." The truth is that in another part of the world, or in another culture, that good song would be raucous cacaphony and that elegant painting would be an ugly assault on the senses.

Even as you sit reading this book, you are surrounded by the evidence: The decorations of the room, the style of architecture, the clothes you are wearing, even the time of day you are reading and the choice of this book—all are influenced by the accepted, supported, and sanctioned behavior of your environment.

More important, we all are influenced by many social norms that interfere with our health and well-being. One of them is the heavy-meal-at-night norm that most of us take for granted, ignoring nutritionists' advice that a large breakfast, a good lunch, and a light evening meal would be more beneficial. Another is the imbalance of food distribution in the world: In one country people are struggling to lose weight and taking diet pills; in another people are starving.

As part of a closer look at norms, let us draw some comparisons and distinctions between norms and some of the other words we use to categorize human behavior.

NORMS AS TRADITIONS, FASHIONS, AND SOMETIMES LAWS

We often see norms as traditions, customs, procedures, precedents, fashions, fads, trends, or vogues. Laws, rules, procedures, statutes, codes, and regulations may all be norms, too—or they may not, depending upon whether they affect behavior. Values, morals, and ethics may have corresponding norms, or they may not. Let us look at some of these terms individually to see clearly their relationship to norms.

Traditions

Traditions produce ritualized behavior that persists for long periods of time, often passed down from one generation to another. They may involve norms, insofar as the tradition is actually carried out in behavior and has not become an empty form—for example, the act of shaking hands, which began centuries ago as a demonstration that neither party was palming an edged weapon. Most people do not question the act today—it is the unwritten rule, the tradition, the norm.

One of the difficulties with norms is that the behavior they foster may be repeated without purpose. The original meaning of the behavior can be lost so that the behavior seems irrelevant, and yet it continues. "Trick or treat" at Halloween, originally a religious ritual to appease wicked spirits, is a tradition whose roots have been cut off. Perhaps on some deeper level we still feel the ritual buys some time from evil forces, but for the most part it no longer makes sense. A norm like this may have served its purpose 500 or 1,000 years ago, and yet it is still acted out in behavior today.

Fashions

Sometimes we see norms as fashions. There was a time when women would not have thought of wearing their dresses short enough to show their ankles. They would have been ostracized if they had, for concealing the whole leg was the norm. However, as times have changed, there have been periods when women wore their dresses above the knee and looked strange if they wore them longer. It was what people expected others to wear and what they supported in their own behavior. Today in America a great diversity in skirt lengths may be found in any public gathering.

Overall a new norm is taking precedence: "It's OK to do your own thing." This kind of diversity in dress styles is accepted, supported, and expected by the larger culture.

Of course, fashions have always varied from one group to another. The Amish would disapprove if a woman were to show very much of her leg, no matter what the fashion is elsewhere. In this case, the norm is an expression of the value system, indicating what the group thinks ought to be.

One of the most obvious examples of the norms of fashion is the male hairstyle mentioned earlier. No longer does length of hair help to differentiate subcultures, as it did on a typical college campus of the 1960s. Then the "jocks" wore it short, and the "hippies" and "freaks" wore it long, each person doing what his subculture expected of him. In the seventies the outer culture largely accepted the new norm, and a businessman or a senator was as likely to have hair over his collar as a hippie. What was once a norm of a small subculture gained wide support.

Laws

It is important to distinguish between norms and laws, for some norms are unwritten, informal codes of behavior, while others are not even recognized. Formal written laws may also be norms, but many are not. Although 55 miles an hour is the legal speed limit, the norm is to top it by 5 miles an hour. Judges, police officers, and drivers alike generally accept this. The moderate speeders know they can usually get by.

Likewise, the idea that it's all right to cheat a little on your income tax, even joke about it, is a norm in the United States, even though the law states specifically what can and cannot be done.

Tradition, fashion, and law are familiar ways in which we categorize cultural influences. While these categories often embody norms, they are not synonymous with them. For example, traditions that are reinforced by strong norms retain their power; effective laws are also norms; fashions that are supported by the culture continue. Beyond these recognizable categories there are many kinds of behavior that are expected, accepted, and supported by the culture. The norms are unseen and unacknowledged, but are nonetheless powerful influences.

In dealing with change processes for individuals and groups, it has been found much more useful to focus on norms and certain categories of norm influences than to classify behavior by the familiar older terms such as those above. Taking all sanctioned behavior and dealing with it in categories of norm influences (as we do in Chapter 3) can produce a degree of understanding that is immensely helpful in a systematic change effort.

WHAT NORMS ARE NOT

A norm does not determine all individual behavior. Only when the individual behavior is the behavior expected and supported by the group is it a norm. Thus the sniper in the University of Texas tower who fired his gun at passersby was not acting in accordance with a norm. But it was the norm for American soldiers in My Lai to kill villagers and build up their unit's body count.

Individual habits can be, but are not necessarily, norms. For example, the automatic behavior, or habit, of brushing one's teeth in the morning conforms to a norm. But one person's habit of using salt rather than toothpaste is not a norm.

Susceptibility to norms is not a matter of personality. It is a mistake to think that a conforming person is more susceptible to norms than an independent person is. The very independence may be largely due to the norm of "doing your own thing" that gets group support.

NORMS ARE NECESSARY

It is not that we could live without norms. The multitude of socializing influences that we classify as norms is necessary because we are human in a world of human beings. Although unchecked and unexamined norms can cause us a great deal of difficulty, the total absence of norms would be more disastrous. In fact, one of the worst social conditions a group or community can suffer is *anomie,* a term used by Emile Durkheim for a breakdown in cultural structure, and often defined as an absence of norms. Under such conditions, mass homicide, suicide, and destruction are not uncommon.

Thus norms provide a part of the social fabric which ties us together as human beings. Without norms we would be lost in lawlessness and drifting futility. Without them, adult perception would be like that of the new born as William James describes it, "a blooming, buzzing confusion."[3]

One of the reasons norms are so intrinsic to the human condition is that they are thoroughly implanted during the uniquely long socializing period of the human childhood.

THE LONG CHILDHOOD

Walt Whitman wrote in *Leaves of Grass:*

> There was a child went forth every day
> And the first object he looked upon, that object he became,

[3] James, *The Principles of Psychology* (New York: Henry Holt, 1890), p. 488.

And that object became part of him for the day or a certain part of the day,
Or for many years or stretching cycles of years.[4]

One might well wonder at the strong human susceptibility to norms, which we see so easily in the child. Our responsiveness to social factors, a natural function of being human, is intensified by that peculiar characteristic of the human race—the long childhood that precedes maturity. The elephant, who lives twice as long, only takes six months to gain physical maturity; the chimpanzee, who is considered the human's nearest relative, grows to maturity in nine to twelve years. The human's years of nurturing and dependence are important factors in the influence of norms. Since young human beings depend on others for their very existence over an extended period of time, they are especially fertile ground for the implantation of cultural attitudes and behavior. As Bronowski has said:

The plasticity of human behavior . . . that is what characterizes us; in our social institutions, of course. . . . And the brain and the baby is exactly where the plasticity of human behavior begins.[5]

Because this "plasticity" is a basic aspect of humanity, cultural conditioning becomes a way of life. The conditioning may change, so that what is learned is replaced by something else, but what does not change is the fact that we depend on conditioning.

This is not a matter of conformity, but rather of humanity. The child is clearly vulnerable to the impact of norms. Basic attitudes affecting one's perceptions of oneself and of the world have cultural roots implanted in the early years. Human beings are inescapably social beings, defining themselves by dependency on others, responsiveness to the group, and the necessity of belonging.

The basic socialization is further reinforced by the enforced delay in independent decision making. Responsiveness to cultural influences is thus doubly ensured by childhood, in which the developing human being requires a long period of interrelationships with others in order to survive. Actually, this dependency continues into adulthood. Our cultures are constantly creating us, and the "long childhood" lasts all our lives.

[4] Whitman, "There Was a Child Went Forth," in *Leaves of Grass,* Emery Holloway (ed.) (Garden City, N.Y.: Doubleday, 1926), p. 305, stanza 1, lines 1–4.

[5] Bronowski, *The Ascent of Man* (Boston: Little, Brown, 1974), p. 412.

LESSONS OF HISTORY

At one time "scalps of grown [Indian] men usually brought $25 to $50 (though the colony of Massachusetts once offered as much as $100), and those of women and children half that amount."[6]

Our tendency today is to look at behavior in terms of individual pathology. How pathological, we say, to murder and scalp an Indian child for bounty! But relying on individual pathology cuts us off from a much more profound insight to be gained by seeing the cultural nature of the behavior pattern. Our ancestors treated the scalping of Indians as socially approved behavior. Scalping was accepted and rewarded.

Similar patterns can be seen in the practice of selling slaves. Men who were pillars of the community and loving fathers owned slaves and bought them like cattle in the marketplace. The slave traders were respected businessmen. Despite legal bans, they carried their human cargo across the ocean up until the Civil War. In fact, as late as 1858 slaves were imported in considerable numbers—15,000 that year. The captain in *John Brown's Body* expressed the prevailing sentiment when he deplored his work, but said: "I get my sailing orders from the Lord. . . . It's the Lord's work."[7] Today we look back in horror at the easy acceptance and glib rationalizing of these inhuman practices.

From today's vantage point we find it incredible that certain kinds of behavior were supported, expected, and accepted:

125 years ago	Blankets from the beds of typhoid victims were passed out to Indians.
120 years ago	In some subcultures in England women would enroll one or more of their infants in burial clubs, "paying a trifling premium until, after a decent interval, the child died of starvation, ill-usage or poisoning. They then collected three to five pounds by way of benefit."[8]
90 years ago	Schizophrenics were "treated by the use of cold showers and deliberately caused abscesses."
70 years ago	Suffragists were jailed for demonstrating in favor of women's right to vote.
40 years ago	Some physicians believed in "detoxification" for people with mental disorders. Organs—ovaries, gall bladders, colons—were removed to get rid of "poisons" that

[6] A. C. Parker, *The Indian How Book,* as quoted in the *Dictionary of American History,* (New York: Scribner's, 1940), vol. V, p. 37.

[7] Steven Vincent Benét, *John Brown's Body* (New York: Rinehart, 1927), p. 13.

[8] William L. Langer, "Infanticide: A Historical Survey" *History of Childhood Quarterly,* vol. 1, no. 3, Winter 1974, p. 360.

were thought to be unbalancing the mind. Four out of ten such patients died.

40 years ago   German officialdom put 6 million Jews to death.

30 years ago   Tens of thousands of people had their brains mutilated by the "ice-pick" method of lobotomy, which drastically reduced the quality of their lives.

Some day our descendants may look back on what we do in much the way we now look back on the destructive and barbarous practices of our ancestors and wonder that we allowed them. Imagine their horror at our inhuman practices of food distribution, the squandering of suburban school funds on excessive athletic facilities while teachers are laid off to save money, the ghastly treatment of multiplegics in some veterans' hospitals, the poverty of cultural institutions and human services programs in certain municipalities, our acceptance of the inevitability of violence, our reckless waste of natural resources, the welfare system's incentives for a father to abandon his family, and our acceptance of pain, misery, war, crime, and poverty! If we could be there to defend ourselves, our plea would no doubt be: "I was not the only one—that's the way everybody was back then. It was the culture!" And we would be right.

Our descendants may not understand that it is "just the way things are." Paying some people not to produce crops while others starve, killing our fellow human beings in wars, and in some cases destroying ourselves with drugs, tobacco, and alcohol are socially supported patterns of behavior in some groups, not individual pathology but cultural norms that influence our behavior without our realizing it.

What does all this mean to persons interested in individual and social change? Understanding norms and how they operate allows us to deal with our cultures so that they are no longer vast, ghostly abstractions that frustrate and frighten us. By making use of our knowledge about norms, we can dispel some powerful myths that befog reality, and we can become creators rather than victims of our environments.

Chapter 2

The Power of Norms

The most important factor for the development of the individual is the structure and the values of the society into which he was born.

ERICH FROMM

Try to imagine what it would be like if you had to decide each day what kind of clothes you would put on, where you would sit at the table—or even whether you should eat your breakfast at the table or on the floor! Imagine if you had to say to yourself, "Now, let's see, should I have the juice first or last? Should I stir my coffee with a fork or a spoon? Shall I wash this dish before I use it again? What would be the proper way to greet my spouse?"

One day would be barely underway before we would break down under the stress of trying to cope with all the decisions needed to respond to the environment. Fortunately, experience has prepared us—the norms have taught us—to react unconsciously to thousands of situations each day.

Although most of us are easily able to recognize a norm here and a norm there, few of us realize the extent to which our lives are influenced by norms. Thousands of them impinge upon us every day. Many of the things we think of as individual decisions would, in fact, not have been made if it were not for group expectations and support. And many things that we dismiss as "human nature" are not human nature at all, but norm-induced behavior.

To be aware of the power that norms have over our lives we must realize that they can be helpful as well as harmful, and that they are absolutely necessary. We could hardly live without them. The question is not whether or not we are going to have norms, but what kind of norms they will be.

". . . A MINGLED YARN, GOOD AND ILL TOGETHER"

Norms can be good influences, especially if they are freely chosen. They are constructive in the sense that they permit us to function without the necessity of thinking through a range of alternatives and their consequences in the multitude of situations we encounter every day.

But norms can also be detrimental. They can get in the way of achievement of our goals, stifle our feelings, or put limits on our imaginations. They can keep us from seeing the good choices that are possible, and they can in themselves be destructive. There is hardly a problem in the world that does not have related negative norms that contribute to its persistence.

Our history is replete with illustrations of norms whose power has hindered the achievement of stated goals. The Emancipation Proclamation was issued on January 1, 1863, declaring that the slaves of the revolted States were now free. Unfortunately, it did not end up freeing blacks from patterns of prejudice and discrimination that are even today evidenced in the continuing struggle for human rights. Similarly, the French Revolution of 1789 expressed the essence of a new faith in democracy: liberty, equality, and brotherhood for all individuals. Yet the Reign of Terror followed, its norms circumventing the goals of democracy and freedom.

Some very pertinent examples of norm destructiveness have been exposed by psychohistorians who have studied the evolution of childhood:

> The history of childhood is a nightmare from which mankind has only recently begun to awaken. The further back in history one goes, the lower the level of child care, and the more likely children are to be killed, abandoned, beaten, terrorized or sexually abused.[1]

The chamber of horrors that these researchers have unearthed is not a matter of individual actions or isolated cases. Persecution, infanticide, and abandonment were the norm.

CEILINGS ON THE MIND

Less dramatic than these, but equally influential, are norms of the past and present that limit the imagination and blind us to interesting choices. Think of the fun of dancing that the stern Calvinistic dogma forbade; the beauty of a Van Gogh painting, which his contemporaries largely rejected; the loveliness of Indian crafts and the wisdom of their folk medicine that were largely disregarded by nineteenth-century white Americans influenced by the norm of "The only good Indian is a dead Indian."

Historical failures show how people have put ceilings on what is possible. Sailors once thought that if they traveled too far, dragons would be

---

[1] Lloyd de Mause, "The Evolution of Childhood," in Lloyd de Mause (ed.), *The History of Childhood* (New York: Psychohistory Press, 1974), p. 1.

waiting for them at the end of the earth. People once thought child labor was the only way a society could survive economically. Each of these represents a limit on the human mind—easily recognizable because they existed so long ago. What kind of ceilings curtail our way of doing things today?

Currently, norms like "A man doesn't cry," "Don't show your anger in public," and "Hide your emotions so no one will know" affect emotional responses and tend to stifle feelings. Sometimes they are advantageous in that they smooth out the rough edges of social discourse, but they extract a terrible toll in loss of spontaneity, creativity, and the joy of living fully. It is now thought that they also inhibit the flow of communications between people. Yet the old norms linger on, long after they have been shown to be detrimental.

As we will explain in more detail in Part 2, the destructive power of norms can be seen in both individuals and institutions. Boys who develop delinquent behavior often do so in response to the demands of their group. To lie, to cheat, to steal, and to take drugs may be the only ways to "make it" in the subculture to which they belong. The fact that this behavior works against success in the outside world may be of little interest to each boy, for his access to the outside world is limited. He will often end up as an addict or a criminal or both—destroyed for succumbing to the norms of the group.

Most mental hospitals start out with ideals about helping people become able to care for themselves—at least that is their credo. Yet despite the devotion of many staff members, these institutions often develop norms that get in the way of independence.

Actually, much of what is labeled insane in a society is largely a matter of norms. The severity of a psychosis is judged by the ability of people to understand what is expected of them, and even the forms of mental illness are affected by the fashions of the day. Freud saw more hysteric patients in a year than today's psychiatrist sees in a lifetime. On the other hand, the depressive symptoms which are so frequently treated today were much less prevalent in Freud's time, even among the population that he worked with most closely.

THE UNIVERSALITY OF NORMS

These examples of norms give some indication of their all-pervasive nature. Not all behavior can be labeled "normative," but all behavior that is learned and is supported and expected by a group can be—and that covers a great deal.

Norms are everywhere, in all parts of the globe. Unseen, largely unacknowledged, they affect all people, no matter what their ages, occupations, or personalities. The only people whose behavior is not influenced by norms are those with severe emotional problems or great intellectual deficiencies. What we see as the strange customs of other peoples are in fact norms, supported by particular cultures. There is a Chinese restaurant in the documentary film *Mondo Cane* where dogs are on the menus (Americans shudder) and are displayed in cages so that the customers can choose their dishes. Shocking to us, but not to the people who support the custom. On the other hand, we Americans have seafood restaurants where customers can choose their own lobsters from a tank of live ones and see nothing strange in this. How shocking it must be for the Hindu—from an environment where cows are sacred—to find Americans slaughtering them and serving them on their dinner tables!

Because the human race shares many traits, we make the mistake of seeing a great deal of behavior as instinctive or innate rather than cultural. The social anthropologist Murdock lists seventy-one practices which he calls ''human universals,'' practices found in every culture. These range from ''age grading'' and ''athletics'' to ''visiting,'' ''weaning,'' and ''weather control.''[2] All human beings, no matter where they live, develop a language, have certain taboos, and formulate a religious and ethical value system. Norms determine how we manifest these universals— i.e., what specific things are taboo, what language we speak, what the age-grading system is in detail, and so on. The same thing is true of the biological functions of eating, sleeping, and defecating—what and how much we eat, when and how we sleep, where and how often we defecate, all are norm-influenced.

Not only are all areas of the world and all ages of history rife with norms, but within the individual lifetime, norms know no age barriers. We tend to think of adolescence as the time of greatest susceptibility to norm pressure, but actually all stages of life are affected. During the teens, the shift of the child's primary reference from family to peer group causes norm power to surface, and parents are frequently in despair over the outside influences on their children. However, the 6-year-old girl who plays with the dolls little girls are expected to play with and the 50-year-old executive who writes off a golf membership as a business expense because ''everybody does it'' are reacting to norm pressure just as much as the adolescent who breaks from the family.

All our lives, to an extent we have hardly begun to recognize, we are affected by norms. This happens in countless areas, including our percep-

[2] G. P. Murdock, ''The Common Denominator of Cultures,'' in R. Linton (ed.), *The Science of Man in Crisis* (New York: Columbia, 1945), p. 12.

tions, our acts of peace and violence, our political loyalties and our religious values, our personalities, our intelligence, our scientific choices, and our sexual actions.

SEEING AS EXPECTED

Whether we look at stars or stereotypes, planets or problems, our perceptions are influenced far beyond ordinary recognition by the ideas sponsored by cultural norms. Much of what we see is what we are expected to see. Students in a graduate seminar at Kean College (New Jersey) recently conducted a perception experiment as a part of a project to test the way norms can change what we actually think we see. The results were in line with similar experiments on perception done in other places[3] and revealed some surprising things about the students' perceptual choices.

Cards such as those shown in Figure 2–1 were used. Each person was asked to point out such things as the largest smile, the longest line, the circle with the most dots. But eight people who had been briefed earlier always chose the second longest line, and so on. At first, the ninth person chose the obvious answer. But each time that person (a young woman) saw that she was out of step with the rest of the group, she began to doubt her own eyesight. "Well, I guess I really need new glasses," she remarked. By the sixth round, she was doubting what she saw and beginning to vote with the group. At the last card she actually agreed that a circle with seven dots had more in it than a circle with eight dots! It had only taken fifteen minutes of group norm pressure to make her disbelieve her own perceptions.

DOING AS EXPECTED

Norms can also be a matter of life and death. Many things that are crucial—such as crime, poverty, religious and moral values, political choices, drugs, violence—are highly susceptible to norm influence. Stanley Milgram of Harvard University, in his study of obedience,[4] made this point dramatically. He led forty volunteers (American males, 20 to 50 years old) to believe that they were administering electric shocks to a "victim" who pretended great pain. The volunteers were under pressure from the research team to continue despite the pain they were causing.

[3] "Group Influences on Individual Choice," a report by students at Kean College (unpublished).

[4] Milgram, "Behavioral Study of Obedience," *Journal of Abnormal and Social Psychology,* vol. 76, 1963, pp. 371–386.

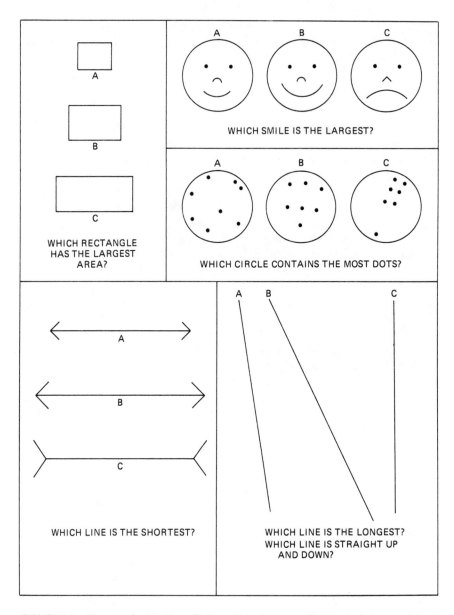

FIGURE 2-1 Excerpts from a Kean College, New Jersey, graduate seminar experiment.

The majority of the volunteers overcame humane convictions and obeyed orders to administer shocks they believed severe and dangerous.

Are the principles of Milgram's study applicable to American society in general? Paul D. Ackerman of Wichita State University analyzed our national experience in Vietnam as an "extension of Milgram's studies of submission to authority."[5] In Ackerman's "scenario" the subjects of this larger experiment were told that a war had to be carried out in a small Southeast Asian country and that they should support it. They did so, constituting the norm. Meanwhile, a large group acting as ordinary citizens, but in reality confederates of the experimenter, pretended to protest the war on grounds that it was unjust and inhumane, and a second group of confederates played the role of the Asians being bombed, burned, and shot. Ackerman's "findings" supported Milgram's thesis. The "subjects" willingly obeyed commands to destroy the Southeast Asian country, even though they really believed the Asians were suffering.

It is evident that the road to violence is paved with cultural norms just as much as was the college student's perception of dots in a circle.

VOTING AS EXPECTED

The arena of politics also yields evidence of the power of norms. The political party one belongs to, for example, depends to a large extent on the party that is supported by the social environment. When the norms change, the allegiance also changes, as is illustrated in the example below.

A group of Democrats lived in the Hudson County area of New Jersey. Their families had been Democrats for years. But when they moved out to the suburbs, something happened to their political loyalties. At first they found themselves saying they were Democrats. However, in the predominantly Republican atmosphere of the suburbs, they began to realize they were different from the people around them. Gradually they became independents. Eventually, as they joined country clubs and social organizations, that independence was not enough. They declared themselves Republican—though they really felt themselves to be independents. In this way their politics moved continually along, pushed by the norms of the environment. What happened to the Hudson County Democrats is typical. Studies of voter attitudes show that the social environment close to a person is what most influences his or her choice.[6] People are more

---

[5] Ackerman, "A Longitudinal Extension of Milgram's Studies of Submission to Authority Figures (or Maybe We Should Have Used More Deception)," in *Psychosources* (New York: Bantam, 1973), p. 178.

[6] R. Duncan Lane, "Analyzing the Social Process Underlying Group Voting Patterns," in Eugene Burdick and Arthur Brodbeck (eds.), *American Voting Behavior* (Glencoe, Ill.: Free Press, 1959), pp. 333–334.

affected by what trusted people around them are saying and doing than they are by political facts.

Though we tend to think that when bloc votes are delivered political manipulators are at work, actually the people who "deliver" the vote at the poll are the ordinary friends, coworkers, and family of the voter.

BELIEVING AS EXPECTED

Religious values as well as political loyalties are affected by cultural norms. A striking example occurred in the worker-priest movement in France forty years ago. The Roman Catholic Church, faced with the increasing loss of its working-class members, sent priests who were strong in their convictions and dedication to their vows to live and work with the men and women of the most secularized and antichurch segment of the working class. The idea was to bring the church's teachings and values to the workers—to go where they were, rather than expect the workers to come to the church. But what happened was that the priests joined the workers' culture rather than the other way around. There was a change in the values of the individual priest after he joined the workers' group. He became secularized; he took on the workers' values and behavior. The church hierarchy was very much disturbed to find that many of these man were changing their priestly ways, giving up abstinence and moderation, eventually leaving the priesthood and marrying. The individuals had quickly taken on the norms of the group they were with, despite their earlier convictions.

THINKING AS EXPECTED

Even intelligence is affected by societal norms. Jean Piaget, after extensive study of individual learning patterns, concluded:

> Society, even more in a sense than the physical environment, changes the very structure of the individual, because it not only compels him to recognize facts, but also provides him with a ready-made system of signs, which modify his thoughts; it presents him with new values and it imposes on him an infinite series of obligations. It is therefore quite evident that social life affects intelligence.[7]

Not even medical science is immune to norm influence. Scientific methods demand rigorous open-mindedness, and empirical evidence is based on accurate observations; yet norms are at work. They affect the focus of research, they influence the opening of some doors and the clos-

---

[7] Piaget, *Psychology of Intelligence* (Totowa, N.J.: Helttfield, Adams, 1966), p. 156.

ing of others, and they determine the scientist's perception of his findings. Even more basic, the high status of science itself is culturally determined.

Norms of the Western culture heavily support the physical sciences, and the result is our technological age with all its advantages and all its problems. This ascendancy of science is evident in many ways. Research grants in the physical sciences, for example, are more available than grants for sociological, cultural, or historical studies, and in recent years it has been easier to get funds for applied science than to obtain grants for pure research.

The high regard in which we hold science is reflected too in our advertising slogans. "Scientific evidence proves . . ." say the toothpaste, deodorant, and aspirin advertisements.

Within the prestigious world of science, cultural norms pervade every area of activity. The types of treatment doctors choose for their patients, for example, are highly subject to norms. As noted before, the mental health field went through a "detoxification era," followed by the fashion of new "cures," such as lobotomy and insulin therapy (which, like the removal of "toxic" organs, could cause death as well as permanently disabling side effects). The strong norm reinforced by these was the high priority placed on curing the mental disorder—a priority that put cure above the quality of life and the dignity of the patient, or even above life itself. Many in the medical profession have long been willing to risk a person's life to cure his or her mental problems.

The focus of most doctors today in strictly medical cures, and their reluctance to accept objective, verified evidence of the effectiveness of behavioral cures, demonstrates the strength of cultural norms. In *The Wall Street Journal* we find this report: "The long-term medical 'cure rate' for obesity is less than 10%; the behavioral cure rate is about 60%. Yet most physicians continue to prescribe pills and fancy diets for weight loss, when what 90% of the patients need is encouragement in learning how to eat sanely."[8]

The power of norms in the medical world is also evidenced in the way people are classified. People with mental disorders have been classified in the past as subhuman, vegetables, animals, criminals, agents of the devil, and more recently as diseased organisms. Further classifications label a person "schizophrenic," "manic-depressive," and so on, ignoring the fact that there is a total human being to be considered.

Persons with sexual tendencies deviating from the accepted norm have been subject to similar classification.

For a long time cultural norms clung to the idea that homosexuality was pathological. The increasing acceptance of nonprocreative sex as a normal

[8] James V. McConnell, in Letters to the Editor, July 17, 1978, p. 11.

part of life gradually eroded the earlier cultural attitude. In addition, considerable research disproved earlier findings about homosexuality, and finally—but as late as 1974—the American Psychiatric Association, although in a far from unanimous vote, decided homosexuality should no longer be classified as a disease.

Today other deeply held Western prejudices are evident in the reluctance of the American medical community to regard Oriental medical methods as possible alternatives. It took a long time for acupuncture to be seriously considered, and it is interesting to see how its acceptance was enhanced when it was coupled with Western technology—acupuncture machines and mechanical testing devices.

A similar phenomenon is at work among the general American public in the widespread recognition of Transcendental Meditation as a way of dealing with some stress-related problems. Its backup data on blood pressure, brain waves, and other physiological studies contributed to its early popularity as compared with other meditation techniques.

The power of norms in the scientific arena is probably most exciting, and at the same time most threatening, in the field of genetics. What we once thought of as stable genetic elements, impervious to cultural influence, now reveal a tremendous susceptibility to human influence. Recent research has shown that chromosomes can be tampered with and sex hormones increased or decreased. Simple innoculations during early pregnancy can cause idiocy or disfiguring mutations. Futurists, in both scientific writings and science fiction, warn us that our future can be ruined by a handful of genetic specialists.

Here again, the question of what we do with our knowledge becomes all-important. Uses of new expertise in genetics are just as subject to cultural norms as were uses of our knowledge of gunpowder and atomic power. After all, Nobel did not invent dynamite because he was looking for a better way for people to kill each other, and his establishment of the Nobel Prize may well have been designed in part as a compensation for the culturally determined misapplications of his invention. Likewise, the brilliant physicists who were intrigued with the mysteries of nuclear fission were influenced by the social environments they worked in. The use or misuse of the developing knowledge of genetic engineering will depend not so much upon the motives of the geneticists as on the norms of their culture.

SEX AS EXPECTED

Through the impetus of the women's liberation movement, the gay liberation movement, the so-called sexual revolution, and the general falling off of the Victorian-Puritan stranglehold on beliefs about sexual relationships, we are beginning to understand the cultural nature of sexual functioning. Some go so far as to question whether a concept of masculinity based primarily on the sex act is anything more than cultural conditioning. One writer recently expressed it this way:

> I believe that masculinist genital functioning is an expression of male power in the culture. I believe that male sexual aggression is entirely learned behavior taught by a culture which men entirely control . . . there is a sexual program promoted by patriarchy (not Mother Nature). . . . Male bonding is institutionalized learned behavior whereby men recognize and reinforce one another's bona fide membership in the male gender class and whereby men remind on another that they were not born women. . . . Men who are programmed to make genital assertions of their masculinity in erotic encounters with women know privately but well what an unreliable gauge of masculinity their genital programming really is. Far more reliable are their non-erotic bonds with other men— where power, prestige, privilege, and pride are actually gauged and exchanged, and where the culture's norm of masculinity originates and prospers.[9]

The liberation movements of today could be the beginning of a freeing process, as people make use of new awareness and change the negative norms that have held them back. Such movements could also be only slight symptomatic shifts followed by unpleasant backlash effects. We have a choice about what will happen, if we can understand the normative base from which we are working.

THE TENACITY OF NORMS

Norms are tenacious. Anything supported by the culture at large tends to hold on, whether or not there is a logical reason for it. Today our social scene is riddled with behaviors that have lost their roots—vestigial appendages that usually cause no trouble, but occasionally kick up and destroy people.

Many things start with good reason, but then go on and on—the cause obsolete, the form remaining. A case in point is the location of garages. Long after automobiles replaced horses and carriages, people continued to build garages at some distance from their houses, simply because stables had been erected a good way off. There had been reasons for that— the horse smell, the attraction of flies and mice. But it took quite a while for people to realize that there was no reason why a garage could not be attached to the house, adding considerably to convenience, especially in bad weather.

---

[9] John Stoltenberg, "Toward Gender Justice" *WIN*, Mar. 20, 1975, pp. 6–9.

NORMS, THE QUICK-CHANGE ARTISTS

Because the culture is so all-powerful and universal and is made up of such a large web of tenacious norms, it is tempting to assign it an exalted, unassailable position in the human scheme. But there is another all-important characteristic of culture that counteracts our tendency to deify it. The culture is extremely malleable. Paradoxically, the tenacious norms are also amazingly changeable.

The susceptibility of norms to quick and thorough change can be devastatingly negative. During wartime, the norms of many young American people are radically altered in training camps.

> I got drafted into the army and it made quite a big change because I was waving flags all the time that I was on my train, you know, down in South Carolina where I got my murder training. And I . . . okay, I went in there and my complete moral worth was completely destroyed . . . they had to completely resocialize us, which they were very effective at doing. I didn't agree with everything, but I went along with it. Then I was sent on to advanced genocide training down at Fort Polk, Louisiana, I wanted to kill . . . anyone, that, that wasn't, you know, completely in agreement with me. I just wanted to kill everything.[10]

The behavior of people like this who testified so movingly in the Winter Soldier investigations illustrates the culture's power—not only in sanitizing the atrocities that seemed "normal" in Vietnam, but also in permitting the realization that swept over the veterans when they returned and saw their actions in the light of the antiwar sentiment that had been building up at home. It is hard to imagine these moving tales being told in the army barracks, but in the supportive atmosphere of the peace faction, governed by different norms, the courage to speak out is more understandable.

[10] Jim Weber, Sergeant (E-5), A Company, statement from the *Congressional Record,* Apr. 4, 1971. It is quoted in John Kerry and Vietnam Veterans Against the War, *The New Soldier,* David Thorne and George Butler (eds.) (New York: Macmillan, 1971), p. 38.

Chapter 3

Not by
Accident Alone

*Some seeds fell by the wayside, and the fowls came
and devoured them up; some fell upon stony places
. . . and because they had no root, they withered
away. And some fell among thorns and the thorns
sprung up, and choked them; but others fell into good
ground, and brought forth fruit. . . ."*

MATTHEW 13: 4–8

The development of a culture is not a random event, and its norms are not
maintained merely by chance. It is not by accident alone that

Youngsters get turned off from school—and onto drugs

Our human freedoms are restricted

Health and preventive medicine are neglected while diet fads thrive and
hospital costs mount

There is only minimal concern for the physical environment

Competition is encouraged and collaboration discouraged in our society

"Violence is as American as apple pie"

A business organization lacks enthusiasm

A teenager starts smoking cigarettes

Many people won't use their seat belts

Problems may seem to pop up arbitrarily, but there are always discernible causes for behavior that persists. Sometimes these causes may be
hard to find, but they are there nonetheless, and they influence the behavior of all of us.

Of course, "accidents" do occur—the birth of a genius, the eruption of
a volcano, the chance discovery of an island or a chemical ingredient—but
these are not of themselves beginnings and do not by themselves change
the direction of a culture. The norms of a culture are brought to bear on

the "accident" and may cause any possible effect to wither away on barren ground or to be nourished and bear fruit. Accidents, when supported by the norms of the culture, become continuing patterns of behavior.

When a culture supports the change, a new norm becomes part of the accepted pattern. It was a quirk of fate that King Ferdinand of Castile had a lisp, but it changed the pronunciation of many Spanish words because it was supported by the culture. Who would not want to speak like the king?

Because there are causes behind seemingly random behavior patterns, it is worth taking a closer look at the ground upon which they grow. When the troubling areas of our social environment are put under scrutiny, they reveal certain basic dynamics, or hidden control mechanisms, that work upon all human interrelationships. What the Bible refers to as "good ground" can be expressed precisely and usefully in normative language: certain key norm influence areas determine which seeds will sprout, develop, and flourish, and which will wither away. ("Good ground" here means only fertile ground—the norms that grow there may be positive or negative, helpful or destructive.)

While there are a myriad of influences and influence areas, many can be grouped into seven areas (see Appendix A for a more extensive listing):

1. Rewards and permissions

2. Modeling behavior

3. Information and communications systems

4. Interactions and relationships

5. Training and skills

6. Orientation

7. Commitment

These influence areas usually operate in close association with one another, and in this way encourage, maintain, and extend behaviors that eventually become the norms of a given culture.

REWARDS AND PERMISSIONS

Behavior that persists in a culture is usually rewarded in some way by the members of that culture. Thus a group that cannot understand why its members are behaving as they are would do well to look at the rewards being provided.

Rewards may be monetary—like salaries, raises, bonuses, and special financial compensation—or they may be privileges and benefits. They can also take the form of recognition, status, or praise. Sometimes the rewards are admission to an "inner circle and the feeling of importance and power that ensues—as were the rewards that enticed many of the Nixon circle to go along with questionable practices. Sometimes the rewards are symbolic—a grade, an honor, a certificate of merit, an A on a report card, or a Boy Scout badge.

The ways of a culture are also supported by the absence of penalty. Many of us tend to go 5 miles over the legal speed limit because we know there is little likelihood that we will be punished. Police who let drivers go on their way at 60 miles per hour are, therefore, actually supporting illegal behavior. In addition, the legal behavior in this instance may even be penalized—drivers who do not go over the speed limit sometimes become objects of derision to their own passengers or to the horn-blowing driver behind them. Thus, with multilevel support for speeding, and penalties for not doing so, breaking the law becomes the norm.

It seems as though the culture gives us "permission" to do certain things, permission taking the form of rewards or punishments, or of their absence. For good or bad, the group acts as a permission giver for things the individual would seldom do otherwise. It is amazing how little permission it sometimes takes when an individual's personal inclinations are already pushing in a given direction. There are happy instances when a hard-nosed, authoritarian boss who has seemed "unbudgeable" softens and relates in a gentler way when given permission to do so. This might begin to happen as the result of a workshop designed to foster a more human environment within the workplace—perhaps a workshop started by the boss's superiors and actively supported by them. The boss may have yearned, underneath, to relate to his or her subordinates in a more human way. The workshop provides permission to do so, and the hard shell can begin to fall away. "Permission" sometimes means making people feel it is all right to do what they were ready to do anyway.

When behavior is disapproved and, rather than being given status, the person is taken down a peg, withdrawal of permission can be devastating. Many a culture keeps its norms in force by punishing "deviant" behavior. Supervisors who are greeted by a hostile environment when they try out some of the ideas that they have picked up at a training session are likely to soon disregard their new found knowledge.

Without looking around us very far, we can see situations where cultural rewards have had a major impact. For many years, the rewards systems in government agencies have tended to support conformity rather than achievement. People who rocked the boat were less likely to be retained and promoted, while those who went along with the existing system tended to be rewarded with regular salary increases and other organizational privileges related to seniority. In our colleges, the "publish or perish" norm has long been exerting pressure on professors to focus their time and energy on the preparation of papers for scholarly journals, rather than on improving their teaching skills. It is not by accident alone that teaching is often at such a low level.

Influences in the rewards and recognition area are among the most powerful norms that exist. In business management, for example, a company's compensation system has a major impact on what occurs there. In one Normative Systems program the top management of a large supermarket company could not understand why its executives were in continual competition with one another. Executives in charge of one sales area, such as produce, groceries, or meat, seldom lent assistance to another sales group, and often actually sabotaged its efforts. An examination of the cultural influences at work in this situation revealed that the compensation system actively encouraged this behavior, for each sales group was being rewarded in terms of its "percentage of store business." Thus there were two ways to be successful: by increasing one's own business or by decreasing the business of one of the other groups. This reward system had, in effect, helped to create the problem that the company was hoping to overcome.

Another example of the effect of rewards is the problem of finding doctors who will practice preventive medicine. Although there is a growing recognition that a healthy life-style is the biggest contributor to health, few doctors help their patients change life-styles. To do so the doctor must, in a sense, become a teacher, but doctors are not paid to teach their patients and they receive little praise in the profession for doing so. The rewards, both in money and in status, are for prescribing, for doing surgery, for *treating* illness—not for preventing it.

MODELING BEHAVIOR

Because we model what we see, modeling can be considered a form of communication in a broad sense. If you have ever taught a little child to tie a shoelace, you know the difference between verbal and symbolic statements on the one hand and practical behavior modeling on the other.

Why do young people smoke when their parents tell them not to? Recent studies show that young people are more likely to smoke if one person in their family does. Here we have the modeling influence again. And think of the further modeling they get from other young people—a much more powerful influence than admonishments not to smoke.

The same sort of thing happens at all levels of maturity. Managers in companies may say "We want teamwork," but if they are in a constant struggle with their associates and everyone sees it, little teamwork is modeled and therefore there will be little teamwork in practice. Supermarket managers who want to reduce employee pilferage but feel free to take an apple without paying for it are modeling. So are the seasoned officers whom the young police officers watch during their first ride in the patrol car. Most likely the new police officers learn more about interactions in the neighborhood on that first trip than they have learned in all their police human relations classes.

For an example of the wide repercussions that modeling behavior can have, we need only look at the Nixon White House. The norm was to excuse an excess of loyalty to Mr. Nixon by professing an extraordinary loyalty to the country: "for national security" was the umbrella term. Like all the king's men of the Watergate scandal, all of us—even those who lead more prosaic lives—are good examples of the effects of modeling behavior. We watch what our leaders do, and we follow suit; we watch people in power, and their effect on us is tremendous. And we also imitate persons who are not in power—especially our peers. An informal or indigenous leader can become as formidable a change agent as the official leadership.

These people and the total culture mold us by what they do, and that is more important than what they say. For example, we tell young people in the ghetto that education is important. Yet these same youngsters may walk by an elegant air-conditioned, marble-with-brass-trim bank on their way to a dilapidated, empty-shelved, dirty school building. What do they learn about what is important in the culture?

The strong influence of modeling can be seen in the societal problems that cause so much concern. For example, our high rate of violent crime is quite predictable if the modeling effect is considered. Despite recent examples of principled nonviolence, the main cultural tradition of this country strongly supports physical and weapon-using violence. It is modeled by authority on many levels, from the police officer on a beat to the nation's football, hockey, and comic-book heros.

A few years ago the newspapers headlined a story of New York hooligans who set a derelict on fire and threw him into the East River. Shocking? Yes, but it was found that police officers in the same neighborhood had made a practice of roughing up "bums" in the park, in full view of passersby, in order to make the neighborhood "more inhabitable."

On the highest end of the authority scale—the Presidency—violence is also modeled. This is true even of the most impressive of Presidents. People were taken aback by Malcolm X's statement on John Kennedy's assassination: "A case of the chickens coming home to roost."[1] Yet the Muslim leader was hitting on a truth, for as Americans we had long been involved in violence both at home and abroad. At the time we were supporting killing in Vietnam, giving financial backing to dictatorial for-

[1] *The Autobiography of Malcolm X* (New York: Grove Press, 1964), p. 301.

eign regimes, and letting social conditions in the ghettos wreak havoc with the lives of the poor. It is not surprising, then, that high national status is given to those who represent violence in our society. The military's presence at the Kennedy funeral—with uniforms, gun salutes, and caissons—attests to the importance of these symbols of violence and gives mute support to Malcolm X's comment. (And later, ironically, the violent norm found another victim, Malcolm X himself.)

Sometimes what we think we are communicating is quite different from what we are in fact modeling. Take, for example, the use of school grading systems, which tend to pay little attention to the child's ability and willingness to help others in the class. Instead, they stress how he or she is doing competitively, in relation to other children. Therefore the child quickly learns not to be cooperative and resists helping a friend with a paper or an answer.

INFORMATION AND COMMUNICATIONS SYSTEMS

Usually what is communicated in a given culture heavily influences what is emphasized. When information on a given subject flows within an organization, the importance of that subject tends to be reinforced. Thus, in schools we have a great deal of "information flow" on grades—warning notices to parents, report cards, honor rolls, and so on. There is little information flow concerning values, creativity, personal ethics, mental development, or progress in human relations. Unfortunately, when information is lacking, the subject, even though tremendously important to the welfare of individuals and the group, tends to be overlooked.

The organization that gives its members information on immediate profits but not information on contributions to the development of people and on longer-range profit opportunities will certainly find its members more concerned with short-range profit results than with long-range development of people and profit opportunities.

In families, children who are not told of their successes in keeping their rooms cleaned are unlikely to maintain such behavior over an extended period. And children who are not involved in understanding (at their own level) the financial situation of the family are in no position to make appropriate decisions about their own spending habits.

One company improved productivity merely by giving employees information on the productivity gains they had achieved. Another cut absenteeism by 10 percent simply by writing congratulatory letters to all who had not missed work during the preceding one-year period.

While such gains might not be long-lasting unless other influence areas are also brought to bear (such as rewards and recognition, modeling, and so forth), they do illustrate the importance of information flow in supporting positive change. The clarity of the information is important also, particularly in these days of computers. Computer information is sometimes provided in such a way that it is difficult for the uninitiated to understand it.

We have many kinds of information systems—language, obviously, but also body-gesture systems and spatial systems. All send out important messages that enter the environment and cause people to behave in certain ways.

Let us look at a most obvious form of communication—the use of words. Since words have connotations (special, often emotional, associations) as well as denotations (definitions), they are loaded with hidden forces that affect the establishment of norms.

Drinking alcoholic beverages, for example, is a norm in many parts of our society, and the way heavy drinking is described is often a function of the groups to which we belong. Hence our norm-sensitive vocabulary provides that a person who habitually drinks excessively at surburban cocktail parties "gets high," or is "tipsy" rather than "drunk." By using "soft words" for inebriation, the culture upholds the cocktail party norm.

Similarly, some individuals have tried to minimize their guilt feelings by using words like "lift" and "rip-off" for their thievery.

As Benjamin Lee Whorf pointed out many years ago, the formal aspects of our language, the grammatical patterns and word choices, affect our belief systems and the way we look at our world. The Hopi Indians see their thoughts as influencing not only their actions but the material universe as well. Their language reflects this, and it passes on the concept to children of the culture. As Whorf says, "It is not unnatural to suppose that thought, like any other force, leaves everywhere traces of effect."[2]

Conversely, concepts of the world are reflected in language patterns. The Eskimo has one word for snow that is thawing, another for slushy snow, another for hard-packed snow, and so on, whereas we have only the word "snow"—an obvious indication that what is important in the Arctic is not so important in Alabama.

We have only one word for love—be it brotherly, motherly, romantic, erotic, or whatever, it is called "love." One wonders what this says about our difficulties in solving human relations problems. Does our lack of discrimination in the vocabulary bespeak a lack of discrimination in the feelings themselves? Would creating more words for love liberate some ideas?

Language can freeze ideas, as well as liberate them. Muzafer and Carolyn W. Sherif tell us that language carries social products to individuals

[2] Benjamin Lee Whorf, *Language, Thought and Reality* (Cambridge, Mass.: Technology Press, 1956), p. 149.

"in consistent and enduring forms. . . . Once learned, words tend to have a categorizing effect on experience and behavior."[3] What often happens in our society is that we define ourselves before we act and then spend time trying to live up to the definition, instead of saying, "What do we need to do?" and then defining ourselves on the basis of what we do. For instance, an institution defines itself as a "mental hospital" and in that category does not feel it should help people get jobs, although meaningful employment might help some of the patients more than treatment.

Because of this freezing quality of language, words are especially important in any effort to rid ourselves of destructive norms. Consciously changing the language (for example, black instead of Negro) can pave the way for new norms. (Black is beautiful.) The connotations of new words are important in firmly establishing the new norms. Our concept of ourselves is intimately connected with our language.

INTERACTIONS AND RELATIONSHIPS

The nature of the interactions between people and the relationships that develop have an important impact on what occurs in a culture. Sometimes people lack adequate interaction with others who practice the desirable norms, and therefore they do not pick them up. In classrooms and communities, for example, there is often so much self-segregation in cliques that those with negative attitudes about school seldom interact with those who have more positive attitudes.

Another problem arises when relationships are on such a dehumanizing level that people tend to see each other as objects. In many migrant camps, for example, although there are many interactions between supervisors and pickers, the pickers feel they are not seen as people but as "hands," to be used for the company's purposes. Similarly, many a family, if it really analyzed its interactions, would find that most take the form of instructions from the parents to the children, or checkups on whether or not those instructions have been followed.

When relationships are built around such narrow role perceptions, difficulties often arise. In a community where most contacts between police and ghetto residents involved situations in which one was the punisher, the other the culprit, hostility existed between the two groups. When a cultural change system was applied, opportunities for more multidimensional interaction helped to break down the hostility.

Often our interactions and relationships are structured around what

---

[3] Sherif and Sherif, *An Outline of Social Psychology* (New York: Harper, 1956), p. 483.

people in transactional analysis (TA)[4] call "negative parenting." This type of "parenting" causes us to put down other people and to focus on their flaws and failures rather than on their strengths and successes. The influence of negative interactions and relationships on the development of cultural norms is considerable. R. D. Laing expresses vividly the potentially destructive relationship that sometimes exists between children and the society into which they are born:

> From the moment of birth, when the Stone Age baby confronts the twentieth century mother, the baby is subjected to these forces of violence, called love, as its mother and father, and their parents before them, have been. These forces are mainly concerned with destroying most of its potentialities, and on the whole this enterprise is successful. By the time the new human being is fifteen or so, we are left with a being like ourselves, a half-crazed creature more or less adjusted to a mad world. This is normality in our present age.[5]

Although Laing's view may be an extreme one, there is enough truth in it to warrant our attention. It is no wonder that the problem of negative parenting continues to be one that we have to deal with throughout much of our adult life.

TRAINING AND SKILLS

Few things wipe out a norm more rapidly than the inability to follow it. In a ghetto school, for instance, a great deal of time may be spent in impressing pupils with the importance of reading. But unless they can read, the exhortation is valueless and often detrimental. Youngsters who believe reading is an authentic value, yet have not been taught to read well, become even more frustrated and self-deprecating than those who never saw the importance of learning.

The same is true of supervisory norms in a business. A person may have superb technical attainments but lack training in leadership and in the human relations skills that are required for a management job. In many cases, people are given almost no training in the leadership-development area, yet are expected to step into the role when they are promoted.

People tend to do what they are trained for and what they have the skills to do. This can be seen on all age levels. For example, take a

[4] For an explanation of transactional analysis, see Eric Berne, *Games People Play* (New York: Grove Press, 1964), or Muriel James and Dorothy Jongeward, *Born to Win* (Menlo Park, Calif.: Addison-Wesley, 1971).

[5] Laing, *The Politics of Experience* (New York: Pantheon, 1967), p. 58. Reprinted by permission of Penguin Books, Ltd.

medical school which professes to encourage human interaction between patients and medical practitioners but provides its students with only scientific and technical training. Since there are few opportunities for the development of interaction skills, the physician who graduates from the school tends to be poor in that area. Likewise, youngsters who learn only competitive skills in their educational program are not likely to develop collaborative models in their adult years.

By examining what people are trained for, how the training is conducted, and how the people respond to the training, a great deal can be understood about the culture and its functioning.

ORIENTATION

As people come into a culture, they are particularly susceptible to its norms. This is true of a baby coming into the world, a new student entering a high school, or a new employee coming into a company.

Though this initial period is the most receptive one, it is typically neglected, and orientation of new people in a company is one aspect of training often bypassed. When there is an orientation program, the tendency in many companies is to use the people who are least successful—those who are not busy at other jobs—to orient new people. So it is the norms of failure that are passed on.

In a high school, for example, it was found that the most successful students were too busy studying or taking part in school activities to help new students get used to the school. As a result, the new students were actually oriented informally by the near dropouts, students who spent their leisure hours smoking in the rest rooms. Later a formal orientation committee of the most successful students was created and did a great deal to keep new youngsters from taking on undesired norms in their first few weeks at the school.

A look at the orientation process provided the key to a problem that developed in a prison culture. The administrators of the prison could not understand why the excellent orientation diagnostic setup that they had installed—which they claimed was one of the best in the country—had such a negligible effect on the major problems. Analysis revealed that the orientation-diagnostic process was so slow that prisoners were backlogged for a month in unsupervised "bullpen" arrangements. These "bullpen cultures" had become the primary orientation "program" for the institution.

Whatever the culture, the effort made to align or position people so that they can relate to the positive, helpful, and desirable norms from the beginning of their membership in the group is likely to pay off in terms of both achieving and sustaining the desired social environment.

COMMITMENT

The level of commitment, which can be measured by the allocation of time, resources, and energy, very often determines what happens in a culture. This is true of a family, a company, or a whole nation.

If the United States wants a real war on poverty, it needs to commit resources to it, as it did to the war in Vietnam and World War II. The funding even now allocated to the military (excluding veterans' benefits and services) is over 23 percent of the national budget, while only about 6 percent is allocated by the federal government for education, training, employment, and social services. The proportions say a lot about our national level of commitment to programs for helping people. While the allocations may be different at different governmental levels, it is still clear that Americans commit more resources to cigarettes and cosmetics than to solving many significant problems of our society.

We might well ask ourselves some hard questions. Who is it in our society that gets the economic commitment? Who is subsidized to the greatest extent? Not the poor people; not the low-cost transportation systems. We talk as though we were committed to a free and open economic system, but are we really? Our economic troubles today appear to be caused to some extent by these tremendous discrepancies—and to some extent by our neglect to deal with the problem of competition. It is not by chance that we have national economic difficulties.

Or consider a family. If time and energy and a large part of the family budget are committed to keeping the lawn, decorating the house, and providing lavish entertainment, the children deduce that these are the most important things. If, however, the family commits a great deal of its resources to sending a daughter to college, the level of commitment to education is evident and college becomes important.

Many a program in an agency, a committee, or a company fails because the high ideals formulated at its beginning are not backed by commitment of time and resources. What we are committed to is often what gets done.

OVERLAPPING INFLUENCES

In looking over these critical norm influence areas, we can see the interrelationships that exist. What is modeled is communicated; what is communicated is recognized; and recognition is a kind of reward. Orientation involves a lot of modeling behavior; we feel rewarded by doing things skillfully after we have been adequately trained. Training, in turn, requires an allotment of resources. These areas do overlap and blend into one another. However, special focus on each is a useful device, as we will see when we describe applications of the system.

Let it suffice now for us to see that each kind of norm influence is critical in determining what happens in our cultures, and these influences—not accidents—account for what develops and continues. Thus, if it looks as though something is happening at random and the behavior looks very strange and unusual, chances are that examination will reveal that it is what is rewarded, modeled, supported, trained for, committed to, and communicated that makes the difference. For example, we might ask why some medical students remove pages from library books and medical journals to ensure that their fellow students do not have access to them. Is it because people are naturally selfish, or does it have to do with the influences that we have just been describing? Our experience indicates that it is the latter, since the culture models the idea that being a winner is more important than the process by which the victory is achieved.

In many of the most crucial problems confronting us, all these critical norm influences are in evidence, interacting with one another to foster strong negative norms.

Even behavior that seems inexplicable and accidental is often under-standable in terms of the inner culture, or reference group, that is operating in the person's life, bringing to bear upon him or her the norm influences from these crucial areas. For example, when a delinquent youngster seems to be behaving individualistically—perhaps wearing a hairstyle that is out of place in the family or classroom, or wearing his shirt unbuttoned—it is a trick of perspective. He may not really be behaving that way on his own as it might at first appear—we are just not seeing him in the context of his reference group. If we consider his relationship to his inner culture, we will realize that the boys of his gang, whose support means the most to him, wear the same hairstyle and unbutton the same buttons on their shirts. Modeling behavior, rewards, commitment, in-teractions, and relationships are all important factors in this case.

The most dedicated religious group is as dependent on cultural support as the city street gang. Listen to Ram Dass, one of America's best-known gurus:

> Thus, when you define yourself as a seeker after sensual gratification, then you surround yourself with other people who are seekers after sen-sual gratification. When you define yourself as an intellectual, you often surround yourself with intellectuals. When you define yourself as a seeker after consciousness, you start to surround yourself with other seekers after consciousness, because in that phase being around such people really gives you a kind of environmental support.[6]

[6] Dass, *The Only Dance There Is* (Garden City, N.Y.: Anchor Books, 1974) p. 3. Copyright 1970, 1971, 1973 by Transpersonal Institute. Used by permission of Doubleday and Company, Inc.

What we are saying about norm influences applies to people who may not be in physical contact with the groups that are affecting them. When a scientist seems to be leading a strange isolated life in the laboratory or a successful artist leads a life different from that of neighbors in a rural community, they may not be receiving support from their neighbors but from the worldwide communities of scientists and artists with whom they most closely identify. While widely dispersed, their communities turn out to be real reference groups that are influencing their behavior.

Some of us are even influenced by the historical figures with whom we most closely identify. The norms of an Elizabethan scholar may be as much influenced by some things in sixteenth-century England as by to-day's standards.

So too the young people who identify with the video heroes whom they meet only through the television screen. The nature of these heroes' interactions—even to the rewards and recognition that are meaningful to the young people—becomes a part of their cultural environment.

The main point is that all of us are subject to the cultural influences that we have been examining. Unfortunately, we are often unaware of them. When this happens they have the potential for immense destruction, some examples of which we will look at in the next chapter.

But before we turn to Part 2, you might use the quiz below to check your understanding of the composition and extent of the normative web.

QUIZ ON UNDERSTANDING NORMS

The score of this true-false quiz is not important, but the answers may help to further expand your awareness of how some important cultural forces work in our lives.

QUESTIONS

T F   1. Norms are another way of talking about individual habits.

T F   2. When a group of people share an attitude or behavior, you can be relatively certain a norm exists.

T F   3. Often when we say, "It's just human nature," it is not human nature at all. What we are really talking about is a norm.

T F   4. You cannot live without norms.

T F   5. By supporting normative behavior, groups can influence members to do things that are contrary to their personal value systems.

T F   6. Norms can put a ceiling over our heads and limit our imaginations.

T F   7. A quiet, reserved person is more susceptible to the influence of norms than more vocal people are.

T F   8. The older a person is, the less he or she is influenced by norms.

T F   9. Intelligent people, by and large, tend to make a conscious choice of the norms that they are going to be influenced by.

T F 10. A person or an organization that is not in some way influenced by norms would find it pretty difficult to function effectively.

T F 11. Once norms are established, they cannot be changed.

T F 12. People tend to imitate what they see others model more than what they read in laws and regulations.

T F 13. People sometimes need permission from the group to behave in the way they would like to behave.

T F 14. One way to help yourself make personal changes is to surround yourself with people who exemplify the changes.

T F 15. Budgets often tell more about commitment than statements of purpose do.

ANSWERS

1. FALSE. It is important to recognize that the norms we are talking about are group norms. Thus norms are what most members of a group are expected to do, while an individual habit is repetitive behavior unique to one person.

2. TRUE. In our definition of a norm we said that it is what most members of the group can be expected to do under certain circumstances and what most members of the group support.

3. TRUE. For example, we sometimes say, "It's just human nature" to litter the streets or to cheat on income tax returns or to exceed the speed limit by 5 miles per hour. Actually all these practices could be changed if the "unwritten laws" were to keep the streets clean, to be strictly honest, and to drive 5 miles under the speed limit.

4. TRUE. Norms are a necessary part of the human social condition. When positive they can save us time and energy and help us to become more human; when negative, they can be terribly destructive.

5. TRUE. Recall the Milgram experiment. These people thought of themselves as nonviolent.

6. TRUE. Negative norms can hold us down without our realizing it. We tend to think many things are inevitable and unchangeable, when actually positive norms could be substituted.

7. FALSE. Research indicates that everyone, regardless of intelligence, position within an organization, age, or personality, is susceptible to normative influence.

8. FALSE. Age does not affect susceptibility.

9. FALSE. People of every level of intelligence oftentimes are not even conscious of why they behave in a certain way. For example, think of the family at the dinner table—evening after evening, sitting in the same places.

10. TRUE. There are literally hundreds of decisions we would have to make every day if we were not aware of the expected behavior, and if we did not know what the norms are for the particular group with which we are associating.

11. FALSE.   It is amazing how quickly norms can be changed. We can see it in styles—
              the length of skirts accepted one year looks ridiculous the next. Even nega-
              tive norms that seem to be embedded in a culture will respond to a system-
              atic change process.

12. TRUE.   If the law says 55 miles per hour is the maximum allowed and people do 60,
              60 will become the norm.

13. TRUE.   Group support often has a more powerful effect on behavior than individual
              needs and desires; in fact, it often determines what we call individual need.

14. TRUE.   A reference group (like a group for those who want to lose weight, stop
              smoking, or change drinking habits) provides powerful support.

15. TRUE.   What a group spends its money, time, and energy on is what it really is
              committed to, no matter what the written statements say.

Part Two

CULTURES
THAT DESTROY

Man is born free; everywhere he is in chains.

JEAN-JACQUES ROUSSEAU

The recruit (mental patient, inmate, etc.) comes into the establishment with a conception of himself made possible by certain stable social arrangements in his home world. Upon entrance, he is immediately stripped of the support provided by these arrangements. In the accurate language of some of our oldest total institutions, he begins a series of abasements, degradations, humiliations, and profanations of self. His self system is systematically, if often unintentionally, mortified.

ERVING GOFFMAN
in Asylums

. . . there were three women on bicycles, and the pilot told the crew chief and myself just to blow them away. I refused. I told them my gun was jammed, and I could not fire. They ordered me again to unjam it and do 'em in. And I refused. So the co-pilot did it with rockets. God, I thought I was going crazy! I cried. I'm not ashamed to say it. It made me sick. Then, after we got back they gave me Article 15 [nonjudicial punishment] for disobeying a direct order.

TERRY WILLIAMS
(E-4), 129th Assault Helicopter Company, 238th Aerial
Weapons Company
in Congressional Record, April 7, 1971

Chapter 4

Individual Destruction

Maybe if I were President, I could change things. Till then, I'll be like everyone else and I'll carry my orders out.

LT. WILLIAM CALLEY, JR.

Normative networks seem to be operating at random, but actually, as we have seen in the previous chapter, they make use of observable forces: rewarding, modeling, communicating, and so on. We might call these networks "programs," with the understanding that they are usually relatively *unplanned,* nonparticipatory programs, undertaken *without the meaningful involvement of people in the decision-making processes.* This involvement principle is crucial since, from the perspective of this book and the system it describes, freedom is based on an opportunity to shape one's own life.

Some unplanned nonparticipatory "programs" are relatively harmless, like those that determine our hairstyles. Others are immensely destructive, catching people up in destructive behavior without their being fully aware of what is happening to them. Whether it is the Ku Klux Klan, the Nazi party, or the racist norms of a local golf club, we can see that the cultures that surround people often cause them to behave in ways that are harmful not only to them but to the society in which they live.

Let us look at some actual examples taken from studies of normative behavior. The first deals briefly with a young man caught up in the destructive culture of a modern supermarket and the second with an innocent youngster destroyed by the ghetto culture. The third example examines in greater detail a more notorious unplanned program—the one that led to the downfall of Lieutenant Calley.

RETAIL STORES—SCHOOLS FOR CRIME

Jim Williams, a 17-year-old high school student has just been employed by the Y-Z Supermarket as a part-time cashier and pack-out boy. Jim is "a good boy," according to his parents, and "a good guy," according to his friends. He has never been in trouble in school or on the streets.

A year later, Jim is charged with grand larceny for stealing over $5000 worth of cash and valuable goods, and he faces a possible prison term. What happened?

During Jim's very first week on the job, one of the fellows wanted to talk to him privately after work. Jim expected it would be just another example of the friendliness of Y-Z Supermarket. He was not at all prepared to hear this:

"Jim, we sure are glad to have you with us. Incidentally, I don't know if anybody's mentioned it to you, but we stick together here, and we do some discounting for each other."

"Discounting?"

"Yeah, you know, I'm going to have some of my friends here tomorrow night, and I'll tell them to go through your register. You can discount some of them—you know, don't charge them for the meat, skip a few other things—keep the prices down. OK? You know what I mean?"

Jim knew what he meant but was not at all sure he wanted to get mixed up in such an activity. His friend sensed his reluctance.

"Look—everybody does it. It's not stealing. The company makes a lot of money; they expect it. We'll be doing the same thing for you, remember that."

Jim was faced with a dilemma: Should he get involved? Or should he tell his new friend he didn't want any part of the stealing? Maybe he should even report it to the manager.

Jim liked the people he was with and wanted to remain friends with them. But if he said "no" to his new friend and refused to discount, he would lose some of the friends he was in the process of making. He might even feel terribly uncomfortable about remaining part of the Y-Z "team."

After weighing the pros and cons, Jim decided to go along with the way things were in his new environment. He continued the pilferage, stealing more and more valuable goods, and finally found himself in trouble with the law.

We might be tempted to dismiss Jim's problem as individual pathology, but we can learn a great deal more by looking into the pathology of the culture he joined. The first thing we note is that Jim's behavior is part of a wider problem. Losses due to pilferage, unnecessary product waste, or destruction are a standard part of every store's bookkeeping. Stealing by employees and customers is so prevalent that management accepts it as a perennial expense, much of which is passed on to the consumer in the form of higher prices. What Jim did was join a pilferage culture and take on that culture's norms, drastically changing his values and behavior in the process. Starting from his very first day at work, he was the target of certain key norm influences operating in the Y-Z Supermarket culture. These pressures, ranging from peer-group activity to leadership passivity, brought about changes in Jim's way of relating to his job.

The reward system itself was one of these key influences. A reward for becoming part of the pilferage system was the "in" status Jim would have. The punishment for not participating, or for telling the manager, was social ostracism. This was in line with the very strong norm in our society that keeps people from thinking they should "squeal."

In the Y-Z Supermarket where Jim received his "basic training" in thievery, the management complained about pilferage but did not confront the problem candidly at the top organizational level. When the store manager wandered through the produce department, he himself often picked up an apple to eat. A bowl of fruit from the produce department sat on his desk. With his own behavior he was modeling the negative norms he wished to eliminate.

The message indirectly communicated to Jim by peers and boss alike was that pilferage was expected. Even the vocabulary strengthened the negative norms. When Jim allowed friends to take items without charge, it wasn't stealing, it was "discounting." The thief who stole the most off the shelves was known admiringly as the company's "rip-off artist."

No feedback of information from the management to the employees told about the amount of pilferage or what it meant in dollars and cents. There was no sharing of concern for the problem, only a win/lose tactic: "We'll catch you." The employees felt a strong sense of "them against us" as far as management was concerned.

One might ask why the Y-Z Supermarket allowed the stealing to continue. The management knew they had a problem. What were they doing about it? Very little. In truth, Y-Z was stumped. The company had tried the simple solution—find the culprit and arrest him. It had tried security devices to deter thievery and detect its occurrence. None of this had worked.

As a result, the "helplessness" norms were strong in the Y-Z Supermarket. The employees took pilferage as the "way things are." The management complained, but thought, "You just can't change human nature." Jim, too, took on these negative attitudes and felt himself more a victim of social customs than a free moral agent.

Jim's case—grand larceny—was an extreme that most employees don't reach. Still, a significant number do, and a large percentage are involved in lesser infractions. Interviews in dozens of retail stores indicate that 60 percent of employees go along with the pilfering norm—at first with great reluctance and anxiety, later as a matter of course. Of those who refuse to participate, many end up on the turnover list in a relatively short time, saying the company is just not their kind of place. A few stay on, cherishing their own values in the midst of great pressures to violate them. We can take little consolation in the ability of a heroic few to survive morally. As Bertolt Brecht said in his play *Galileo,* "unhappy is the land that needs a hero."[1]

DRUG-CULTURE DESTRUCTION

LeRoy moved with his family from the rural South, expecting to find a wonderful world in the North. Through an aunt, they were able to rent a walk-up apartment in the poorest section of Newark. The family of six—a mother and five children—moved in. LeRoy was a curious and friendly 13-year-old who wanted to go out on the street and meet some of the kids he saw hanging around, but his mother warned him not to. However, after a few days, he couldn't stand it. Needing some sort of social contact, he slipped out and made his way toward a group of boys down the block. He listened to their talk, hanging around the periphery of the group. He was genuinely shocked when he realized they were talking about stealing a car in order to get money for heroin. When he heard the talk, and was filled in by some of the boys, he really thought they must be crazy—stealing! Taking that stuff! When the boys asked him if he wanted to join with them, he said, "No way, man. I don't want no trouble like that."

Why was it, then, that six months later, LeRoy was a dedicated member of the gang, clever at stealing, and hooked on heroin?

The ghetto neighborhoods of Newark provided firsthand evidence of the power of a destructive culture. LeRoy was typical of the youngsters caught in its devastating unplanned norm "program." This is what happened:

When LeRoy initially met members of the street gang and turned them down, their reaction was swift—"All right, then, get out of here. We don't want you hanging around." He was clearly a threat to the good feeling and security of the group.

So LeRoy went back up to the apartment, but that wasn't much fun. After a few days, he was down on the street again, this time a bit wiser. When they asked if he wanted to help jump a guy for his wallet, he made excuses: "Gee, yeah, I'd like to, but I have to take care of my brother— my old lady won't let me out tonight." Those excuses lasted only a few times. He could see that if he was going to have any friends at all, he'd have to get into the action.

The next step for LeRoy was finding himself going along, still thinking

---

[1] Brecht, *Galileo*.

it was crazy, still thinking it was wrong, but figuring he'd have to pretend to want to do it to be allowed to stay in the group.

They stole a woman's pocketbook—and they got away with it. LeRoy's job was to watch out for police on the corner. He was complimented: "You were real cool, LeRoy. You did all right, man." Since he hadn't been caught, his anxiety was reduced, and the next time it wasn't as hard to take part. He still hadn't tried the drug himself, but he could see that the leaders of the group really liked it, and he was being urged to try it by some of the guys. He was beginning to feel accepted.

A few weeks later, a new kid began hanging around, and LeRoy, the new convert, filled *him* in. Trying to prove he was "one of the gang," he even sniffed some of the stuff in front of the new kid. It helped him get over some of his own anxieties and proved that he was supporting the group. He got the new kid to go along with the next job, and the rest of the gang let him know that they appreciated it.

Another thing was happening to LeRoy. When the gang members were talking about past deeds, he found himself boasting about the things he used to do in the South: moving three cars from one side of town to another in an hour and stealing a police car. LeRoy found his own past history was changing fast. It seemed to go along with becoming a big guy in the group. Soon he didn't even really know which of the things he talked about happened and which didn't.

So it was that in six months LeRoy was one ot the top guys of his gang, respected by the others and in trouble with the law. He was also hooked on heroin. His habit grew fast, and his need to buy more rose by leaps and bounds. Within a year he had died of an overdose. The culture had done its destructive work quickly.

THE DESTRUCTION OF RUSTY CALLEY

There have been few more dramatic examples of the destructive impact of a culture on an individual or a nation than those provided by our military experience in Vietnam. The case we have chosen is that of Lieutenant William L. (Rusty) Calley. Rusty Calley entered the army culture as an "ordinary American boy." He was somewhat tense and had a history of minor offenses, but had never displayed murderous inclinations. Something happened—and he evolved into the Lieutenant Calley of My Lai notoriety.

Any war may be regarded as a destructive normative network, but Calley's unit, Charlie Company, demonstrated vividly how certain norms can generate harmful behavior and have a tragic impact upon the people associated with them. It is illuminating to see how these norms operated within the culture of this army unit, causing its members to do things they probably would never have done if they had had a chance to examine openly the cultural norms that were influencing them.

The behavior modeled by Calley's leaders and peers strongly influenced this unstable young officer. Consider the modeling behavior of two of Calley's superiors, George S. Patton III, colonel in command of Calley's regiment, and Ernest Medina, captain of Charlie Company. Seymour Hersh reports that Patton

> would exhort his men before combat by telling them, "I do like to see the arms and legs fly." He once told his staff, "The present ratio of 90 per cent killing to 10 per cent liberation is just about right." Patton celebrated Christmas in 1968 by sending cards reading: "From Colonel and Mrs. George S. Patton III—Peace On Earth." Attached to the card were color photographs of dismembered Viet Cong soldiers stacked in a neat pile.[2]

Of Calley's immediate commanding officer, Hersh wrote:

> . . . Medina was quick to beat and terrorize suspected Viet Cong soldiers or civilian sympathizers in his attempt to gain intelligence information.[3]

Calley was especially anxious to emulate his captain, and was clearly influenced by the "enjoyment" of other members of his immediate team and by their apparent support of what was occurring. "I liked it in South Vietnam," he said later. "I knew, I can be killed here, but I could also be more alive than in America . . . I really felt, *I belong here*."[4]

The tragic paradox is that the culture in which Calley felt "more alive" was one governed by norms of death and destruction. These two incidents involving Calley's peers were among many reported in the Winter Soldier investigation:

> As they filed through a hamlet, Carter offered a "papasan" a cigarette. As the man took it, Carter suddenly began to club him with his rifle butt. He broke his jaw and ribs. Most of the company watched. Some "were mad as hell," Olsen said, but no one said anything. Nor was Carter reprimanded.[5]

> There was a tiny little form, that of a child, lying out in the field with straw over its face. It had been clubbed to death. As later was brought

[2] Hersh, *My Lai 4: A Report of the Massacre and Its Aftermath* (New York: Random House, Vintage Books, 1970), pp. 9–10.

[3] Ibid., p. 30.

[4] William L. Calley with John Sack, *Lt. Calley: His Own Story* (New York: Viking, 1971), p. 3.

[5] Hersh, op. cit., pp. 31–32.

out, the Marine that clubbed the child to death really didn't want to look at the child's face so he put straw over it before he clubbed it.[6]

People like Calley expected to be rewarded for following the leads of their military culture. Calley's subculture had some special innovations, including a reward system that particularly encouraged the kind of behavior that occurred in My Lai.

> "Many battalions staged contests among their rifle companies for the highest score in enemy kills, with the winning unit getting additional time for passes."[7]

Not only the rewards but the language itself made it easier to adopt the new, destructive ways. Euphemisms were everywhere. When whole families were uprooted and moved to fortified hamlets and their homes and fields burned if they refused, it was "pacification" or "rural construction." When this didn't work very well, the Marines were ordered to kill the Viet Cong and move the civilians out—and this was called "sanitizing" or "sterilizing" the area. The sum of dead enemy soldiers was called "body count," and many a body count was inflated with a portion of civilian victims. One didn't kill people, one "wasted" them.

The Americans who fought in Vietnam were well-oriented to the roles they were expected to take. For example, a marine described punishment and reinforcement at boot camp:

> Whenever a "boot" [trainee] used the term "Vietnamese," he would be punished—his drill instructor would punch him in the abdomen, hit him on the head, pull his hat down over his ears, or twist his nose. The purpose of this treatment was to make certain that he referred to the Vietnamese—*any* Vietnamese—only as "gooks," "dinks," "slopes," or "slants." These preferred derogatory terms received unstinting approval.[8]

In some areas training was tragically deficient. Seymour Hersh tells us:

> The average GI's ignorance of Vietnamese customs was appalling, but even more appalling was the fact that the Army's efforts to give the men some kind of understanding of what they would be faced with were minimal. The Vietnam-bound soldiers were given—at the most—only one or two lectures on the country and its people, while in training.[9]

---

[6] Testimony of Mike McCusker, Sergeant (E-5), 1st Marine Division, from the *Congressional Record,* Apr. 4, 1971. It is quoted in John Kerry and Vietnam Veterans Against the War, *The New Soldier,* David Thorne and George Butler (eds.) (New York: Macmillan, 1971), p. 52.

[7] Hersh, op. cit., p. 9.

[8] *San Francisco Chronicle,* Jan. 25, 1971. (Marine Ken Campbell describes basic training at Parris Island Boot Camp.)

[9] Hersh, op. cit., pp. 7–8.

Calley had never been told what the Geneva Conventions of War specified, and had not been given any opportunity to examine what was right or wrong in a particular situation. Further, there was very little interaction with the Vietnamese on a human level, and little chance for soldiers like Calley to see them as people. Interpersonal relations were for the most part those of soldier to enemy, and were characterized by blame placing and putting people down for their limitations.

Certainly the resources of time, money, and personnel were allocated for destruction. We couldn't take time to train Calley in the Geneva Conventions or in the handling of civilians, but we could take time to train him in the use of destructive weaponry.

All these influences put a tremendous pressure upon individuals to be destructive. There were few opportunities for members of Charlie Company—or any army culture—to think through what was happening to them. An army functions on the premise that orders will be given by a higher authority to a lower, and anyone who breaks or tries to reverse this chain of command will be punished. Within the narrow area of an upper-level strategy meeting there may be testing and feedback, but when it comes to communications between different ranks, there is virtually none.

When a program is not based on cultural influences involving the input of people at all levels, there is a tendency for the individual not to take responsibility for the decisions, at any level.

This normative way of looking at the My Lai massacre suggests that the behavior of Calley at My Lai was a direct outgrowth of the culture that existed in that time and place. He was part of a subculture nesting within other cultures, all influenced by destructive norms:

> Civilization, which has generally relied on war as a way of solving conflict throughout the ages

> Western civilization, with its particular kind of pressures upon the individual

> The American culture, which impressed upon Calley its norm that "Communists are the enemy and lack the human qualities of the rest of us"

> The military culture, which molded him with its norms of authoritative commands, obedience to orders, decision by the few, rewards for killing, and models of destructive behavior

> His martial "duty," which taught norms of "wasting" the people of Vietnam

> "Charlie Company," Calley's peer culture, which had its own special negative extremes

Considering the many cultural layers that were at work, the end product is exactly what we might expect. Our venture in Vietnam is over, but destructive normative influences are constant and pervasive, and they even now threaten the achievement of our most precious goals.

Because Jim and LeRoy and Calley were culturally conditioned to accept socializing influences and were largely unaware of what was happening to them, they easily picked up the negative norms of their respective cultures. Although we have been luckier than they in the types of norms to which we have been subjected, none of us is immune to environmental pressures that could lead us into behavior that seems unbelievable from our present vantage point. Only by becoming and staying aware of what is happening to us can we get below daily events and discover the patterns that govern our actions and limit our alternatives. Armed with this knowledge, we can take the first step toward meaningful change.

Chapter 5

Institutional Failure

The ward is a factory for the combine [which is a huge organization that aims to adjust the Outside as well as Big Nurse had adjusted the Inside]. It's for fixing up mistakes made in the neighborhoods and in the schools and in the churches, the hospital is. When a complete product goes back into society, all fixed up as good as new, **better** *than new sometimes, it brings joy to Big Nurse's heart; something that came in all twisted different is now a functioning, adjusted component, a credit to the whole outfit and a marvel to behold.*

KEN KESEY
in *One Flew over the Cuckoo's Nest*

Every one of us is affected by institutional failure. We are all too familiar with schools that don't educate, churches that place little emphasis on religious values, businesses that impede economic well-being, mental hospitals that make people less able to cope with the outside world, old age "homes" that become houses of horror, welfare agencies that degrade their clients, encounter groups that increase dependency, communes that lose their sense of community.

Our institutions today often interfere with the very purposes for which they were created. Some hospitals, schools, prisons, churches, governments, social agencies, and families, fulfill important roles and are able to help people. Many others develop harmful patterns that not only keep them from reaching their objectives, but have a destructive impact on those supposedly being served. We make changes, institute reforms, try experiments, but to little avail. We are drinking from a poisoned well—a culture caught up in destructive, dehumanizing patterns. In our large institutions these patterns are magnified, and their failures touch thousands of individual lives.

HOW DO WE KNOW THEY ARE FAILING?

If we look at the recidivism rates of prisons and mental hospitals, and if we consider the number of people who go to such institutions and never come out, it is obvious that these institutions are not making the positive changes in people's lives that their founders expected. Often they actually change people for the worse, making them more dependent, less sensitive, and more separated from the mainstream of normal life. Even those who go in for a while and are released often find their problems exacerbated. A former convict or mental patient often has a hard time finding employment and gratifying social interchanges. The student who fails has a harder time getting a job and fitting into society. Unfortunately, when we separate people from society and classify and label them, we give them an extra burden to carry rather than relief from the pressures from which they were suffering. In the process, the costs to society mount, compounded by bureaucratic structures and red tape.

In addition to the great numbers of people who are not helped, and the great costs, we know our institutions are failing because of the low level of satisfaction with their performance. They tend to attract the enmity of both recipient and donor. For example, no one, from the head of the government to the lowest-paid welfare recipient, seems to think welfare is working. No one, from the Secretary of Health, Education, and Welfare to the people who drew up the Patients' Bill of Rights, seems to be satisfied with hospitals of any type. Students, parents, teachers, and other educators are questioning the value of the urban public school. The low level of satisfaction is manifest in declining church membership, in literature about the drawbacks of the nuclear family, in treatise after treatise on why schools fail.

HERE TO STAY?

Despite this dissatisfaction, we also witness a deification of institutions. It is as though they have taken on a life of their own—an immortal life—becoming more important than the people in them. People and their needs fade in the background, as efforts are focused on achieving a smooth-running prison, a harmonious school, a quiet, efficient mental hospital.

One common reaction to all this disillusionment is to mistrust all systems and to try to "throw the baby out with the bath water." Political activists in the last decade burst into hallowed halls and burned papers, even buildings; philosophers have reacted with homage to our existential despair; novelists and playwrights have sought, in fancy, to destroy the old ways.

Hardy naturalists have, in fact, gone back to the land and tried to survive without institutions, but most people find it impossible to deinstitutionalize their lives. We therefore end up with costly efforts to patch up the old, or with the substitution of one inadequate institution for another, equally inadequate.

Is the answer to do away with institutions? Hardly. In a complex and heavily populated world, we cannot escape having institutions, nor would we really wish to. At their best they bring order into what would be a jumbled, chaotic welter of experiences, and they help us set common goals. Furthermore, we cannot do away with all the norms generated by these institutions, any more than we can do away with norms anywhere. The answer lies not in destroying institutions, but in understanding more thoroughly the normative influences within them, and then making use of this understanding to create the kinds of institutions that will be truly helpful to us.

Examining some of the patterns that tend to develop in institutions will reveal some of the crucial normative influences. While the patterns are overlapping (for instance, the overprotection pattern that so often contributes to dependence), it has been found helpful to focus attention on each as a way to see contributing norms. As we saw earlier, cultures do not develop by accident alone, but through the support and acceptance of certain behaviors.

DEPENDENCE

The pattern of dependence is so ingrained in our institutions that we tend to think of it as natural. People who are in institutions to be helped are expected to be receivers, not contributors, and what they learn from the institution is, therefore, dependence upon other people. The hospital patient, the jail inmate, or the high school student is expected to be a dependent "child," and the staff, jailer, or teacher is the "parent"—an authority figure from whom all orders and decisions come.

The client of a hospital is called a "patient," and is expected to be "patient" while doctors, nurses, and attendants do things for him and to him—often without explanation. In a mental hospital or old age home this is even more pronounced. Often clients are treated like helpless children, even to the point of being dressed like children and given nursery furniture and a kindergarten atmosphere. In a nursing home for the aged we hear, "Isn't that cute?" over and over as a nurse places a bow on an old lady's head or watches a husband and wife go into a private room for their hour together.

In mental hospitals a typical practice is to ring a bell for medication, have clients line up, and hand them their pills. Thus, when they are released, they have had no experience in submitting a prescription to be filled—so they don't get their medication and end up back in the hospital because they haven't taken it.

In our jails, the model is similar. People who are in trouble because they have not learned to make decisions are placed in a situation where they make even less use of decision-making skills. Even the smallest decisions are made for them—when to eat, when to turn out the lights, when to exercise. They become increasingly dependent on others through their jail experience, and it is no wonder that so many cannot cope adequately outside and are back in prison in a short time.

Despite educational theory to the contrary, the typical school today still encourages a dependence on the teacher's thinking, a regurgitation of information rather than independent thinking, and an overreliance on the authority of the teacher and administrator. Our public schools constitute one of the most repressive environments imaginable. Not only are action and communication constrained, but students are usually seated in rows, at desks with inadequate writing space, and must raise their hands for permission to relieve themselves. Everything is done for the teacher's (or administration's) convenience, the students are incidental.

OVERPROTECTION

Contributing to the development of dependence is the pattern of overprotection. Most institutions overprotect their clients, both physically and emotionally. Patients and students are not allowed to experience even minimum risks.

Overprotection is manifest in the design of physical facilities, especially in our mental hospitals. Though the average crisis period for a given client may be as little as twenty-four hours, a client may be kept for months or even years in a locked ward, separated as though he were a great danger to himself and others. Walls are stripped because thumbtacks or mirrors are considered risky, adults are put in cribs with sides up when it is unnecessary, and even the dishes they eat from are cold, metal, unbreakable. (Some of this overprotection is due to norms that have recently grown in power—norms that have brought increasing risk of lawsuits in an increasingly litigious society.)

Overmedication to calm the client down is another form of overprotection. This reaches the extremity of inanity when the person is awakened to take a sleeping pill.

FEELINGS DENIED

Related to overprotection is the pattern of denying feelings on the part of the staff, teacher, or counselor. People in authority are often expected to conceal their feelings from the people who seek their help. Teachers are not expected to express their own frustrations and concerns, and the teacher who reveals natural human feelings in the classroom is often considered to have lost "clout," no matter how much the situation warrants an emotional response. Generally people in authority are expected to exhibit cool, smooth, nonturbulent surfaces at all times. The analyst who has occasionally fallen asleep in his darkened consulting room while a patient is speaking to him is supposed to pretend otherwise.

NONHELPFULNESS

We observe an institutional pattern of nonhelpfulness, strengthened by the general competitiveness of our society. Patients, prisoners, or students are not expected to help each other—even though the authorities preach cooperation. Mental patients are not supposed to have any skill in relating to people; students are cheating if they cooperate by telling another student an answer or helping a student with a paper; prisoners are supposed to obey guards and not relate to one another. Unfortunately, this means that a huge untapped reservoir of support and mutual assistance is wasted, for people—especially those who share the same circumstances and feelings—are quite capable of helping one another, and in this way helping themselves as well.

SEPARATION OF PEOPLE

One of the greatest dangers of institutionalization is its propensity to separate people—person from person, and person from community. Although the very basis of human life is social interaction, the institutions we develop to improve human life too often cut people off from one another.

This tendency is particularly devastating when it affects people who are already pinpointed by society as "different." Recognizing this, some professionals have recently focused on the need for a more "normal" or typical setting and atmosphere for deviants. "In typical community life," says Wolf Wolfensberger, a leader in hospital reform, "social interaction with one's everyday contacts brings with it innumerable occasions and role expectancies that have implications to the normalizing process. Unfortunately, a person identified as deviant is often further 'dehabilitated' by being deprived of these normalizing social contacts, or by being cast into social roles where he is actually expected to act deviantly."[1]

---

[1] Wolfensberger, *Normalization* (Toronto: National Institute on Mental Retardation, 1972), p. 149.

Furthermore, separation breeds distrust, especially deplorable in any change effort or rehabilitation program, for trust and credibility are essential to change.

We separate schoolhouse from community to an extent beyond what is necessary, thereby weakening the social fabric. Here and there is a glimmer of what could be done to add a whole integrative dimension: Danish folk schools with their "cradle to grave" education, and the theatrical events and music events in some American high schools that cut across school and community lines.

In many mental hospital facilities, the norm is to cut the clients off from community and family, sometimes for long periods of time. This physical separation is often accompanied by an overemphasis on labels and classifications, which adds to the *feeling* of separation. The doctor in the mental hospital makes certain you know he is the doctor, not the attendant, not the patient.

The feeling of separation is evident in schools too. The student in a high school is labeled "special ed" or "business student." Through such labels the person gets cast in a role, and then tends to see himself in that role and to make his behavior conform to it. If the role happens to be a devalued one—such as mentally retarded or deviant—the effect is a widening of the gap between him and normal society, and as a result his behavior tends to become more and more different.

BUREAUCRATIZATION

The stratifying of people within the institution adds further to feelings of separation. People are often put on different levels within the hierarchy, and then the levels are kept apart. Destructive hierarchies develop, and there are problems of communication between the various levels.

Administrative structures for specialized functions tend to be characterized by adherence to fixed rules within a hierarchy of authority. The result is often a burden of red tape that cuts off lower levels of an institution from participation in decision making. Frequently there is a cutoff of information flow, and people who ask critical questions cannot get the answers that would help them fulfill the purpose of the institution.

The kind of red tape that one finds in a large public school, for example, with comparative reports for achievement grade by grade, drains the energy and focuses attention on competition, hampering rather than helping learning.

Many churches have a bureaucratic structure that fosters ladder climbing on the part of the clergy rather than their spiritual development.

In mental hospitals we find there are conflicts between levels—medical versus lay managers, psychologists versus psychiatrists, administrators versus nurses—but always the patient is on the bottom.

Altogether, roles are defined too narrowly in our institutions. Students must be students and may not act as teachers; teachers must be teachers and may not act as friends to students; administrators must be administrators and must not teach.

DEHUMANIZATION

All the foregoing patterns contribute to the desensitization of people. Typically, in a school or a mental hospital young teachers or nurses enter with great enthusiasm and high ideals, eager to give of themselves to help others. After a short time they are overwhelmed by what appears to them to be insoluble problems, by the demands on their time and their skills by the unbending walls of the existing culture; in the end, in order to cope, they become colder and hardened.

Not only professionals, but the people being helped, become less human, for it is part of our humanity to be givers as well as receivers. Students, welfare recipients, patients, prison inmates—all need opportunities to contribute. Yet seldom is an opportunity given. The usual thing is to categorize them as receivers, not helpers, and bypass a tremendous human quality that would aid rehabilitation.

An overemphasis on jargon also dehumanizes people. For example, a typical norm in a hospital is for nurses to refer to a patient as the "heart transplant" or simply as "room 108." This type of language transmits a hidden message: "You are an object, not a person."

REALITY UNRECOGNIZED

Another basic pattern in institutions is treatment of many real, objective problems as though they were psychological problems. A mother of eight, harassed by too much work, needing an abortion and an increase in child-care aid, is handled as a social deviant—one who cannot cope.

When a person doesn't reach the expectations of his culture, often his case is treated as a personality problem, rather than a societal problem. To a great extent this is the product of our tendency to emphasize "individualism" is our society. Actually, as we shall see in Chapter 8, true individualism goes hand in hand with cultural improvement.

MORE IS BETTER

In keeping with one of the basic normative patterns of our American culture, our institutions dance to the tune of "If at first you don't succeed, do it over and over and over again." When individual psychiatry fails to rehabilitate people, the answer is: Do more of it. If a ward is not succeeding in helping patients become better, the answer is a bigger and better ward, with more money poured into it. The result is skyrocketing costs that drain financial resources unnecessarily. Recent estimates are that we as a nation spend over $200 billion a year on health services. And the price is actually greater, for every potential wage earner who is kept in a hospital—or a prison—is not only costing us the tax dollars spent for care, but depriving the nation of the tax dollars he or she might have been able to contribute.

SANCTIFICATION

Most institutions were started with high purposes: to help people improve the quality of their lives. Unfortunately, many eventually extoll the institution above people, as though the institution were a sacred entity that can do no wrong. The individuals for whom the institution was originally created seem to be all but forgotten in the process.

We have mental hospitals with rigid rules designed mainly to keep the hospital running smoothly. We have schools where the creative child is treated almost as an enemy of the class. We have churches in which the status of the church becomes more important than the spiritual development of its members. We have some prisons that are so well run that they end up as "great" prisons, but with dehumanized inmates.

Self-perpetuation goes along with this sanctification—many institutions seem to be in existence for their own sakes, the real reason for their origin residing in the dim, dark past.

ACQUIESCENCE

Another basic pattern is "going along" with the institution. Individuals must subjugate their needs to the welfare agency, the school, the hospital—and accept the decisions and decision-making apparatus of the institution without question. The institution's enemies are one's own enemies; its friends are one's friends.

Going along means accepting and even welcoming dependence. It means accepting inferiority/superiority lines, the chief relationship being subordination to authority. Going along means avoiding relationships that are not sanctioned. This may mean relationships outside the culture, or it may mean relationships between subcultures within the larger group. Often these smaller subcultures are divided and are not expected to interact. Going along means not sharing individual visions, and it means putting down the creative persons who show their visions.

We see this, unhappily, in our schools, where creative children will express themselves in a way not in keeping with the norms of the classroom. Creative behavior is often seen as disruptive. The creative child who continues painting after the art period is concluded, is usually treated as a deviant and made to feel the weight of disapproval. So he or she learns to squelch creative impulses and go along with the classroom norms.

MYTH MAKING

All institutions have myths about themselves. Mental hospitals have a myth that they contribute to rehabilitation, rather than to dependence. Schools have a myth that they are dedicated to creative learning, rather than to keeping the children off the streets. Prisons have a myth that they are maintained for rehabilitation of lawbreakers, rather than for keeping out of society people who might cause trouble. There is a myth that family members should like each other all the time, rather than have conflicts and loyalties that sometimes separate them. Welfare agencies have a myth that they are helping people combat poverty, rather than oppressing them with dehumanizing regulations.

These myths might also be seen as manifest (openly stated) functions of institutions that people pay lip service to. The real power is in the latent (hidden, obscure) functions operating underneath. Myths persist because anyone who does not support them with lip service is put down; and anyone who does support them is approved. But behavior in line with latent functions is also supported, thereby perpetuating the dichotomy between the two.

Many churches, for example, have a manifest function of caring about spiritual needs of their members and promoting moral and ethical behavior. This is often written into a statement of purpose and alluded to in Sunday sermons and at church dinners. Churches also generally have several latent functions that are heavily supported in their activities: (1) providing social relationships; (2) giving members social status (i.e., striving to be a more prestigious church than some others in town); (3) giving vestrymen opportunities to wield power; and (4) providing a type of social control. This social control sometimes causes a focus on the "right kind of sin"—swearing, drinking, and gambling—and avoids looking into such moral and ethical matters as cheating the government or forcing business competitors into bankruptcy.

Myths surrounding typical welfare programs make it difficult for them to evolve a viable mechanism for fighting poverty—such myths as the beliefs that the poor don't want to work, that all welfare recipients are cheating, that welfare clients don't care about their families, that once people are poor they will always be poor. These myths engender rigid and unrealistic regulations and undercut the goals of the program.

NO BELIEF IN CHANGE

Probably the greatest myth of all—and one which institutions share with other types of cultural groups—is the one that says: "Things can't be changed." A hospital professional who is devoting his time to making mental health facilities more human, more normal, and more democratic recently put it this way: When people don't believe in change, they express it with one of the three S's:

Shortage of time	("We don't have time to talk to each patient every day.")
Shortage of budget	("It would cost too much money to have houses instead of wards.")
Shortage of staff	("We just don't have the trained people to try a self-medication program.")

He saw all these excuses as based on the belief that change is not really possible—excuses that invariably led to the fourth S—

Shortage of ideas and imagination

This lack of imagination puts a ceiling on the mind and keeps meaningful change from happening.

NEED FOR A CULTURE-BASED APPROACH

These destructive patterns persist in our institutions primarily because an understanding of their cultural base is missing. Certain cultural norms and norm influence areas contribute heavily to each one of the patterns. By looking closely at the negative norms that generate destructive forces, we can start to deal with them and get a handle on change.

That fourth S, the shortage of imagination, can be rectified by starting to modify specific norms. This revitalization starts with a clearer understanding of the norms in action. Below are views of three institutions as seen through normative eyeglasses: hospital, school, and welfare program. Our first example is the ward of a mental hospital.

A NORMATIVE LOOK AT THE WARD

Although all hospitals, including general hospitals, have many destructive, dehumanizing patterns, these are particularly evident in the ward of a typical mental hospital.

Picture the client. The first thing he hears is a request to give up his clothing. If he should follow his natural feelings and refuse, he is considered a problem. Then he is bombarded with questions about the most personal aspects of his life, and his support or agreement is not enlisted. If he objects to this degrading procedure, he is suspect: "Here is a guy who's going to give us trouble. He's really sick. He can't even answer our questions."

He is then put in with other people, with no introduction to the group and its habits, and without help in relating to strangers. His walls are stripped bare, giving him little chance to express his individuality in his allotted space. His hair is cut to comply with institutional practice rather than current fashion. He is asked to spend most of his time just hanging around. If he questions this, or complains of boredom, again he is considered recalcitrant or not responding well to treatment.

He is put into rehabilitation programs that have nothing to do with his interests but are determined by the facilities available. If it is ceramics week, he works on ceramics. If it is jewelry week, he makes jewelry. He gets in line for his meals, his bath, and his medication.

Picture the doctor, walking into the ward all smiles, holding his clipboard, followed by nurses, asking questions and remaining cool and objective. He may have just had a fight with his wife, or one of his teenagers may have run off; but he covers it up, smiles on, and pretends everything is well with his life.

The culture in psychiatric wards very frequently gets in the way of healing people, because the norms of that culture work against the goals. Two powerful norms are: (1) around here, patients are weak and doctors and nurses are strong; and (2) doctors and nurses have no problems; only patients have problems. The net effect on the patient is that he just can't imagine ever getting to the point in life that these "model" human beings have reached. He feels his own inadequacies more and he experiences them as abnormal. In other words, he feels more mentally ill than ever.

One of the reasons why many people are ill and in mental hospitals is that they feel they have no power over their lives. They feel they are victims, and they aren't aware that they could make the decisions necessary to run their lives themselves. The logical thing would be to teach them about their own power and show them how to use it to help themselves and their fellow patients. Instead, the norm is the reverse.

In psychiatric wards the norm is generally to treat patients as helpless and incapable of taking care of their own concerns. This reinforces their belief in their illness and can even help perpetuate it. Instead of seeing what patients can do to help and recognizing that "we are really all therapists around here," the whole culture supports the idea of patient helplessness. Doctors and nurses support and reward "cooperation," which means letting them—the professionals—make the decisions. Patients are encouraged to behave dependently. If they express a desire to get out and be independent, it is considered resistant behavior.

If a patient should say to another patient, "I'd like to help you," most likely the answer would be something like, "Who are you to help? You're sick, too." If the patient should comment that the doctor seems upset, the doctor will quickly cover up his feelings, deny them, implying by his attitude that "normal" people don't have feelings.

A patient's thoughts of suicide are considered definitely abnormal, even though "existential despair" has been standard grist for the philosophical mill since Kierkegaard's time. Later, when the patient is able to adjust to the expectations of the hospital culture, when he can contain his feelings and accept the rules and regulations, he may earn a dismissal and go back to the outside as "a completed product . . . a credit to the outfit and a marvel to behold."[2] When he leaves, he may be panicky, fearful of coping with the outside world. This is also considered abnormal, even though it is a perfectly natural reaction considering the reality of his situation.

A psychiatric ward is ordinarily fraught with norms that run counter to human tendencies. If a patient is bored and bothered by the dependence, it is considered a problem instead of a sign of possible health. If a patient feels lonely and distraught when he doesn't have a visitor, perhaps even cries, it is put on his chart as a problem. If he is interested in sexuality, that is considered a problem, for in the hospital sexes are expected to stay separate. Patients are not encouraged to see their doctors as human beings, but as superiors. Doctors and nurses call patients by their first names; patients call doctors "Doctor" and nurses "Miss" or "Mr." Complaints about food are thought to show an unwillingness to get along, though the food may actually be unpalatable, or at least different from what the patient has been used to.

There is also a norm for doctors and attendants to be considered problem-free and patients to be considered problem-full. Therapists are told it is important for them to conceal their problems from the patient, because the patient might lose confidence. Patients are supposed to have no resources; doctors are supposed to have nothing but strengths. Any difficulties the hospital has are supposed to be concealed from the patients—as though the patients are blind to the problems around them and are unaware of the strong feelings that attendants, doctors, and nurses may have. If the patient notices anger and says something, the doctor will say the patient is projecting. Though many of the doctors feel stuck in their positions and are inwardly furious that they are not out in private practice making a lot more money, and that they are blamed for all the ills of the institutions, they are expected to conceal this from the patients.

This composite picture of a culture that destroys—the typical mental

---

[2] Ken Kesey, *One Flew Over the Cuckoo's Nest* (New York: Signet, 1962), p. 40.

hospital—is not meant to describe all programs for the mentally ill, but unfortunately it touches on norms that are prevalent in many of them. The ward in Ken Kesey's novel quoted above is based on a reality that exists in many parts of this nation and the world. The conflict that gives the story such a dramatic impact is between Big Nurse, who insists on adherence to the norms of the institution, and McMurphy, who breaks the norms. McMurphy relates to people, questions authority, tries to orient himself to the new group, resists questioning, fights illogical rules (he won't take a shower when he's clean), and tries to relieve the boredom of the ward. One message of the novel is that institutions are powerful cultures that can generate negative norms capable of destroying individuals.

Light was shed on similar destructive hospital norms in Dr. Wilfred Bion's pioneering work in the training wing of a military psychiatric hospital in Britain. Bion expressed "serious doubts about the suitability of a hospital milieu for psychotherapy." Bion's groups (composed of patients) made the study of their neurotic tensions a group task instead of leaving that area to the doctors. "With surprising rapidity the training wing became self-critical," Bion reports. The men created groups for specific tasks and carried out the tasks with enthusiasm. Their relationships were friendly and cooperative. Within a month significant changes had taken place. "Whereas at first it almost seemed difficult to find ways of employing men, at the end of the month it was difficult to find time for the work they wanted to do. Groups had already begun to operate well—the wing had an unmistakable esprit de corps."[3]

It is hard to picture the usual group of psychiatric patients in terms of an esprit de corps, but Bion's work proved how quickly the "victimism" attitude could be reversed. He also reversed the second norm, that doctors have no problems, by appearing as a multidimensional person, with the usual emotions and doubts of a human being, rather than as a paragon of virtue and good feeling.

Bion's work showed that it is possible to help patients deal with real feelings and thus help them to become self-respecting, responsible people. Similar humanizing work is now being done in Canada and the United States, stemming from Wolfsenberger's "normalization" principle.

Important efforts at deinstitutionalization are presently under way also in a number of countries. In these efforts, treatment and service programs for the mentally ill are, to some extent, being developed on the community level, and people are being released from hospitals into community residential sections.

Unfortunately, the norms of our communities are such that the former

---

[3] Bion, *Experiences in Groups and Other Papers* (New York: Tavistock Publications Ltd. 1959, and Basic Books, 1961), pp. 18–22.

patients are not accepted within them, and the norms of the government bureaucracy are such that little support is being given to the community services and programs. The statement "If people are well enough to be in the community they ought to be able to pay for their own services" is not an uncommon one. And the results are understandably disappointing.

The film *Toward a Caring Community*,[4] which describes a Normative Systems approach to building caring community environments, suggests alternatives to our present bureaucratic approaches. The film and the program growing out of its use are now seeking with some success to mobilize community support for change. Patients, former patients, families, community leaders, and professionals are sitting together to map out strategies for cultural change.

These are hopeful signs that we can eventually change our attitude toward people with mental disorders, and instead of rejecting, labeling, and separating them, really help them to recreate their own lives, within the context of a caring community. This concept of a humanistic environment is further described in Chapter 23.

The mental hospital is a glaring example of institutional failure. And unfortunately, other institutions are in trouble, developing similar destructive patterns that keep them from living up to expectations.

A NORMATIVE LOOK AT THE SCHOOLHOUSE

Picture a young black youth going to school in the ghetto. He is told the important thing is education; yet he sees the man who graduated from high school delivering mail and trying to save up for a car, while the sixth-grade dropout who makes his money pushing drugs drives by in a fancy Cadillac. In the school he hears about his rights to life, liberty, and the pursuit of happiness; outside he is turned down for a job, denied access to houses in certain neighborhoods, and suspect if he gets "out of his place." If he makes it to a university, he may find his classmates stealing books from the library so that others will do poorly on the examinations. Thus, the lip service paid to cooperation is steadily undercut by the realities of the competitive world.

Incongruencies between goals and actualities nearly inundate us when we look at our school systems. Of all our institutions, the public school has probably been given the most attention in recent years—the most research, the most words written about it, the most analyses by professionals, who study, deplore, dissect, and challenge it. Yet troubles persist.

[4] A twenty-minute film presentation by HRI Human Resources Institute, available through the state of New Jersey, Department of Human Services.

Let us look at some of the most glaring incongruencies:

> We say we are teaching brotherhood and tolerance, but school experiences cause students to look down on the uneducated, the ill-spoken, the unskilled. Aren't we really teaching a divisive disdain?
>
> We postulate that American education should further democratic ideals, yet don't we use it to perpetuate socioeconomic barriers?
>
> We say we're teaching our children to be responsible citizens, but isn't the norm to teach routine for the sake of routine, discipline for the sake of discipline?
>
> We say schools are institutions for teaching skills, yet don't we often graduate students who are unskilled in reading and writing, in expressing themselves, and in analyzing critically, and who cannot even handle arithmetic at the checkbook or grocery store level?

The message derived from norm studies of educational institutions is that schools are powerful cultures that often develop negative norms destructive to the very people that the schools were established to help.

The real learning in the educational institution goes on at a hidden level. Children teach each other how to manipulate adults, how to get around regulations, how to become skillful in areas (sex, drugs, smoking, gambling, stealing, cheating) that aren't in the curriculum. The "good" students learn the right amount of conformity that will bring the reward—an A on the report card, a high class rank, admission to a college. They learn from their adult models to conform to meaningless regulations, to accept the inadequacies of the system.

When there is an effort within a school to humanize the atmosphere, it is usually focused on relationships between students and teachers; interrelationships within the staff are forgotten or ignored. So the model of vested power interests persists, undercutting efforts toward cooperation.

Though we pay lip service to the value of cooperation and social responsibility, much of our educational effort aims to keep students from helping each other. If you talk to the average American teacher about the tremendous value of having students help each other on examinations, he will laugh knowingly, for here "helping" is "cheating." But in other places, among the Navajo, for example, cooperation is an ingrained norm, and they demonstrate that it is possible to educate without competition. The Chinese, during the Cultural Revolution, were cognizant of environmental factors and did not separate mentally retarded and psychiatrically impaired children from the regular classroom. It is ironic that we, who teach democracy and brotherhood, tend to think separating them is the only way to give either group a real education.

GOVERNMENT BY NEGATIVE NORM

Turning to some of our governmental institutions, we find abundant illustrations of cultural obstacles that undercut original goals. What more obvious example is there than the Watergate scandals, the culmination of a long acceptance of negative norms that worked counter to the goals of a government "of the people, by the people, and for the people"?

To focus on a narrow but persistently frustrating governmental area, let's look at our efforts to bring relief to the poverty-stricken families of America.

Picture a mother with two children. The father is unable to get a job; the mother has to stay home to care for the young ones. They need money for food, and rent, and heat. She applies for welfare and discovers that if the father moves out, she will be eligible for one and one-third times the welfare money. He moves out. The children become ill, but she gets medicine through Medicaid. Then the mother finds part-time work and a day-care center for the children. She is offered a raise—and at first she is delighted and relieved, for it will take her off welfare. But then she discovers that the costs of the medicine her children need are far greater than the meager raise. She finds it better financially to quit the job and go back on welfare; in addition, she will be able to spend more time with her children.

National programs to combat poverty show similar forces operating counter to goals. In a 1972 study, the Brookings Institution found that the federal WIN (Work Incentive) training program was successful in getting jobs for only 27 percent of the eligible welfare population, and the failure often caused welfare mothers to become even more dependent on welfare.

The normative belief that giving people money will take away their incentive to work seriously undercuts our goal of helping the poverty-stricken. Yet the Brookings Institution study shows that this belief is fallacious. By keeping payments at or below minimum subsistence, and by making any attempts to rise above that income level both difficult and risky, our present system for "helping" the poor seems to be helping them remain poor.

ASKING THE CRUCIAL QUESTIONS

It is evident that some of our institutions share certain basic problems and basic dynamics. People involved in any institution might well ask:

What myths do we perpetuate here?

What latent functions undergird (or undermine) our work?

What chance do people have to be helpful to one another?

What chance do people have to be part of a group or team?

What chance do people have to develop independence and decision-making skills?

Are people kept from helping others?

Are people expected to acquiesce—to "go along"—without objecting or questioning?

What red tape gets in our way?

Is it the norm to consider problems as psychological rather than culture-based?

Who can express feelings?

Is the institution more important than its members?

Is it more important than those we are here to serve?

Since both institutional failure and the destruction of individuals by their environments are not new concerns, one might ask why we have not been able to mend these obvious rips in the social fabric. Many reforms have been tried, but too often they are short-lived experiments, representing one side or another of a pendulum swing. They do not build changes into the cultural fabric itself. Some reasons for this are discussed in Part 3. There we should explore problems of change and nonchange, including our blindness to the culture trap we are in and to certain negative problem-solving norms endemic to our culture. By doing so we will see more clearly how the society's well has been poisoned and how it can be made clear and healthful again.

Part Three

PROBLEMS OF CHANGE AND NONCHANGE

*. . . change rampant, change unguided and unre-
strained, accelerated change overwhelming not only
man's physical defenses but his decisional processes—
such change is the enemy of life.*

ALVIN TOFFLER

*When organizations are not meeting the challenge of
change, it is as a rule not because they can't solve their
problems, but because they won't see their problems;
not because they don't know their faults, but because
they rationalize them as virtues or necessities.*

JOHN GARDNER

Chapter 6

The
Culture
Trap

Cultural irrationality is deeply entrenched in the lives of all of us, and because of culturally imposed blinders, our view of the world does not normally transcend the limits imposed by our culture.

EDWARD T. HALL

Much has been written in recent years about the problems of change, but the problems of nonchange are perhaps even more dangerous. In both situations we are trapped in cultural norms which keep us from fulfilling our desires, but in the latter the norms blind us and render us helpless.

The chief problem of change is that things are happening fast, and we cannot handle the pace. It is not that change itself is so bad, but that we are not in control of it. The problem of nonchange is that we seem to be stuck in our stultifying ways, helpless to handle rapid developments. As technology continues to develop, our inability to alter our ways of doing things may well become disastrous.

Despite that bleak picture, this book is predicated on the knowledge, borne out in over 200 projects, that controlled change is possible, and that the stultification of nonchange is surmountable. The first step (and the subject of Parts 1 and 2) is to understand culture and cultural norms and to become aware of the ways in which normative influences operate. Now the questions arise: Why haven't people made use of the inevitable norms in a better way? Why haven't the dynamics of rewarding, modeling, committing, communicating, and so on been used more often to build the environments people want? Why don't we get ourselves out of our predicaments?

The answer lies in our relationship to the culture trap, which takes one of several forms, all of which are the result of culturally imposed blinders: (1) We may not see the trap at all; (2) we may see it but not realize its breadth and depth; (3) we may feel we are in a trap, but think there is no way out—so we don't even try; (4) we may try to get out, but use methods that are tied into negative cultural norms and don't work; and (5) we may believe that the way out is to retreat into isolated "individuality."

These blinders are all reinforced by the long human childhood. From the moment we are born, the culture starts to work upon us, getting between us and the boundless universe, foisting upon us cultural interpretations and cultural perceptions. Over a long period of time the blinders become habitual, so that by the time we are adults we don't even know they are there.

SEEING OURSELVES IN A SOCIAL CONTEXT

Even before childhood, norms have set the stage for a person's development. As Karl Marx said, social existence determines individual consciousness.[1]

It was Marx's genius that he was able to recognize some of the blinders that elude most people. He saw, for example, that the contemporary concept of freedom was limited, that it merely meant freedom for the consumer to choose between different brands, when what people really needed was to gear their lives to something other than consumption. The production of too many useful things, he said, results in too many useless people.

Although Marx focused on the economic foundation as a shaper of the social environment which in turn shapes people, to see Marx merely as an exponent of economic man is to take a narrow view of his insights. To interpret him as saying that people are basically motivated by economic appetites is an error. Marx saw modern man, so heavily influenced by economic forces, as alienated from his natural self. Basically man—natural man—is driven by what Marx called constant drives—like hunger, sex, and the need for relatedness with people and with all nature. But alienated man is driven by culturally induced appetites for material goods. Born into a social environment already geared to processes of production and consumption, people become alienated.

Marx's distinction between genuine needs and imaginary needs (or appetites), which are culturally induced, is a profound analysis of the human condition. How much of our behavior and our view of the world is determined by economic forces? How much of our culture trap is the result of the frustration of imaginary needs?

[1] Marx, *Preface to a Contribution to the Critique of Political Economy,* 1859 (Princeton, N.J.: Van Nostrand, 1955), p. 141.

IT'S JUST HUMAN NATURE

A prominent TV announcer recently analyzed the tendency of many politicians to line their own pockets and concluded, "Human nature is just naturally acquisitive." Deep in the culture trap, he was demonstrating one of the thickest blinders we have—our tendency to believe "It's just human nature," which implies that there is no choice but to go along with the norm.

Even when the blinders open slightly, and we begin to sense that cultural influences are contributing to our problems, we often don't see them as anything we can change. Contributing to this feeling of powerlessness is the emotional response of many people to the cultural force, even though they do not recognize it on an intellectual, verbal level. They feel like helpless victims of some remote and mysterious power, and they respond with resignation and apathy.

Unfortunately, the idea implied by the TV announcer is a prevailing sentiment in many quarters of our society. This "what's the use" attitude is stated in a variety of ways, depending on the setting:

"You'll never get union and management together."

"Company executives and lowest-level employees won't mix."

"A migrant won't accept a full-time job."

"Litter is the fault of pedestrians and motorists."

"Employees are always going to help themselves to items from the shelves."

"A hospital can't be run by patients."

"The old-fashioned classroom situation can't be beat."

"Boys will be boys."

"Kids are going to go along with the neighborhood—you can't expect them to do otherwise."

"You can't fight city hall."

"You can't change human nature."

Myths such as these contribute to the pervasive sense of helplessness that undercuts change efforts before they even get started. As John Dewey pointed out years ago: ". . . many of the obstacles to change which have been attributed to human nature are in fact due to the inertia of institutions."[2]

[2] Dewey, *Monthly Review,* March 1950, in George Seldes (ed.), *The Great Quotations* (New York: Lyle Stuart, 1960), p. 204.

When we examine human behavior closely, we find that very few things are innate. There is scarcely an area of our lives that is not hooked into the power of the culture. A startling illustration of this is the story of the four-minute mile. For years, runners had tried to break the record, but nobody had been able to run the mile in less than four minutes. No one believed it could be done, and it wasn't done. It seemed as though that was the limitation of the human body—until Roger Bannister came along. In 1954, Bannister ran the mile in 3 minutes and 59.4 seconds, and broke through the psychological barrier. Since then scores of runners have broken Bannister's record.

A few years ago a jury in Bogotá, Colombia, revealed cultural blinders in its judicial deliberations. Six Colombian cowboys had attacked a group of nomadic Cuiba Indians whom the range boss had invited to a meal. With guns, machetes, hatchets, and clubs they had slaughtered at least sixteen Cuibas, including women and children. The jury found the cowboys not guilty "though they freely admitted their part in the massacre. The jury accepted the defense argument that no one born and raised in the traditions of the llanos (prairies) could be expected to consider eradicating a Cuiba any more censurable than eradicating a deer."[3]

CULTURAL SCRIPTS

The secret, then, is not to deny the culture trap or to give up in despair, but to examine it and try to understand it. The "long childhood" of the human group leaves us with cultural "scripts" to play out. On the international scene there is the "united against the enemy" script, in which it is necessary to have an enemy to survive as a culture. There is the "ends justifies the means" script in which whole nations indulge in atrocious practices for "justifiable goals."

Many business organizations have a "founding fathers" script. A strong authoritarian type of founder has set patterns which become rigid and out of touch with advances in the industry.

In smaller cultures, like the family, there are such scripts as the "We Riveras never give up" or the "We Andersons are always sick" script, which families faithfully play out without realizing they are in a culture trap.

HOW WE SEE DETERMINES WHAT WE DO

How we perceive a problem has a lot to do with whether or not we are able to solve it. Our perceptions are extremely susceptible to outside influence. Almost any beginning psychology book makes this point quickly with a puzzle picture. (Is it a vase or a face?)

[3] *New York Times,* Jan. 6, 1973, p. 20.

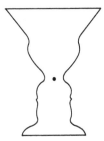

FIGURE 6-1 How much water will the vase hold? Or is it perhaps not a vase at all, but two men's profiles? Or two womens' profiles? Keeping your eye on the dot, let your mind decide. No matter which idea you choose, it will be culturally determined; our perceptions are influenced by cultural factors. (*Adapted from E. Rubin.*)[4]

We can easily see in an example like this that our perceptions are determined by what is put into our minds. This is a little more difficult to see when we are up against emotion-laden problems in real life, but it is just as true. Perceiving a problem in one way, because our culture has taught us to, can prevent us from seeing it in another way. Thus, alternatives are cut off.

For example, the burn rate is a national problem, usually thought of as a problem of medical treatment. A project in Massachusetts has gone further and conceptualized it as also a behavioral problem, and reduced the burn rate by 20 percent. One important area was burns from match play by children ages four to seven. Good results were attained by investigating multiple factors (fascination with fire, false beliefs that clothing

---

[4] The Danish psychologist E. Rubin is credited with developing this classical demonstration of variability in perception with the same stimulation. If you keep your eye fixed on the black dot, you will find the reversal does not depend on eye movement. For a more recent illustration of cultural blocks to understanding, try this riddle:

On a dark and stormy night a boy went for a ride in a car with his father. The father lost control of the car and was killed in the accident. The boy was rushed to the hospital unconscious and was wheeled right into emergency surgery. The surgeon took one look at the boy and said, "I can't operate on this boy. He's my son." How could this be?

The answer to the riddle is that the surgeon is the boy's mother. (What was the norm that got in your way when you were trying to think of the answer?)

protects the skin from flame, the limits of fine motor control in children), and by using creative educational strategies in which learners identify the problem and address the key issues. The project already shows promise of affecting the national picture in this safety area. It teaches us that *the way in which we conceptualize a problem determines how we will try to solve it.* Too often we conceptualize from our cultural stereotypes, thereby blocking off our minds from alternative solutions that might be easier, quicker, more effective, and more long-lasting.

GREAT PEOPLE AND CULTURE

Another blinder is our belief that while most people are helpless victims of society or fate or natural tendencies, there are a few great men and women who can change things—because they can stand apart, untouched by the culture. Not so. Great men and women, like all of us, are tremendously influenced by their cultures. For example, although Sigmund Freud made a tremendous contribution to society, he was more culture-bound than many other scientists. He was so caught up in German nationalism that the World War I defeat threw him into depression, and his attitude toward women so reflected the whole culture of his time that he was unable to be objective about them. Today, women's liberation forces take Freud to task for having projected his male viewpoint on the psyches of women.

Abraham Lincoln is another case in point. He has been hailed as a great emancipator and an outstanding example of the individual who stands apart from his time. Yet Lincoln's idea of freedom for the "colored people" was unbelievably limited. He hated slavery and felt it was both morally wrong and contrary to the country's self-interest, but his views on equal employment, education, and political rights for blacks would, by today's standards, put him far to the right of George Wallace.

Someone might reply, "But Lincoln would be different today. He was liberal and radical for his time, and he would shift his ideas in the light of today's culture." This is exactly the point. We are all—great and small—shaped by the norms of our day and often "helpless" in relationship to them—until we begin to remove the blinders.

If we don't see this—if we still regard Lincoln as individuality personified, Freud as an isolated genius, Leonardo da Vinci as an artist out of tune with his times—then we are still caught in the culture trap. The lesson for each of us is: Despite their genius, the great men and women of the world are, like us, products of their cultures. Because they have more in common with ordinary people than with superhuman beings, they can provide practical guides to our own behavior. Instead of despairing as we compare our own meager gifts with theirs, we might better conclude that we, too, can do a great deal more than we thought possible.

Chapter 7

Cultural
Obstacles
to Change

In a profound sense, each one of us is booby-trapped
by the patterns within which we were socialized.

ROBERT THEOBALD AND
STEPHANIE MILLS

Perhaps some day we will look back on our handling of human problems and the problems of change in our society in much the way we now look back on our primitive ancestors dancing around a fire calling for rain, and we will see that certain archaic ways of approaching problems are constantly blocking us without our even realizing it. If cultures are as pervasive an influence on human life as the previous chapters suggest, it should not be surprising to find that our very efforts to deal with these cultures are "booby-trapped by the patterns within which we were socialized."

When a problem arises, it is common practice to seek someone to blame, rather than to decide what to do about it, to confront the opposing forces rather than to develop solutions, to look for a simple solution, and to do all this with a burst of energy, but without adequate data or skills. This is normal behavior—literally, behavior based on norms.

CULTURAL NORMS OF BLAME PLACING

Who did it?

Who is responsible?

Who caused the riot?

Who failed to plan ahead?

Who is keeping workers and management from getting along?

Who is embroiling us in foreign wars?

89

It is common practice in our culture to try to find out who is at fault. More than that, blame placing is expected and accepted behavior. So we're talking about more than the individual act here; we're talking about the *expectation of blame placing,* which is a strong norm in our culture. The idea is, of course, that if we find the culprit, we'll solve the problem. Unfortunately it doesn't work that way. When we get rid of one drug pusher, another takes his place. Exposing Teapot Dome does not avert Watergate. When voters reject a president who presided over a war, they find it does little to stop the next war. On a scale varying from the minute to the infinite, this disappointment occurs over and over again.

It isn't always the person at the top who bears the brunt of the Blemish Game (as blame placing is called in transactional analysis). Often the person who gets blamed is the victim himself. When our consultants analyzed the litter problem in three large American cities, they found the person most often accused of littering was the ghetto resident, who got poor service from the sanitation department and who lived nearest to the major sources of litter. So we have a case in which the greatest victim gets the least help and the most blame.

We also seem to believe that if we get rid of the victim, everything will be fine, although the victim is rarely the cause of the problem. We imprison the drug user, arrest the prostitute, fire the department head for low productivity, and chastise the litterer, all to very little effect.

This impulse to find the culprit and change him is part of our tendency to think of problem solving in terms of the individual, as though personality or character traits were the key to the solution. Our Western tendency to worship false "individuality," as we will see in the next chapter, contributes heavily to this norm.

Not only do blame-placing activities fail to solve problems; often they make them worse. People do nothing about changing themselves when they feel others should be doing the changing. ("After all, it's their fault!") In addition, time wasted on useless polemics builds up frustration and the feeling that "nothing can be done."

An important fringe defect of the Blemish Game is the building up of hostilities between the blame placer and the blamed. These ill feelings make it even more difficult to find answers. Even when valid and obviously justified, blame placing is counterproductive. Consider the effect of: "You people are always late. You're holding up the whole meeting." Feelings bristle and get in the way of finding a solution. The tardiness continues, and perhaps even grows worse.

When we blame others, acting authoritatively and condescendingly, we are indulging in what transactional analysis terms "negative parenting." (The negative parent ego state, the judging and nurturing aspect of our inner selves, is active when we are telling others what they should do or what they have done wrong.) Typically, this negative parenting arouses the "rebellious child" in the other person, who gets angry. Pointing the finger is as little likely to help solve social problems as scolding a juvenile delinquent is to solve the problem of delinquency.

Culprit chasing also stems from the belief that finding the responsible person is the first necessary—and perhaps the only—step toward solution. The culprit is seen as the "cause," and the idea is that his or her removal, rehabilitation, or conversion will bring about the desired effect.

Blame placing is only one version of a naïve belief in single causation. We look for a single cause for a difficulty, instead of looking at the network of causes—the hidden normative system—that engenders the problem. Is a man a drug addict because someone gave him the money to buy the "stuff," or because someone saw him taking it, or because nobody stopped him? Is another man convicted of drunken driving because someone gave him his paycheck, because the liquor dealer sold him whiskey, because drunken driving is against the law, or because his father and mother drank?

Are any of the answers (or the questions) in this game of one-shot solutions really helpful in solving the problem?

CULTURAL NORMS OF WIN/LOSE

A second widespread norm that interferes with problem solving is our tendency to devote so much energy to win/lose problem solving. The scolding parent versus the rebellious child is the prototype for hundreds of win/lose situations that we set up. Management/labor, employees/supervisors, teachers/students, black/white—there are so many of these conflicts that we tend to think that "it's just human nature" to develop "solutions," in which if one is to gain, the other has to lose.

However, the more we think in terms of coming out ahead of the other person, the less we are able to see solutions that enable *both* of us to benefit. The net result of a succession of win/lose confrontations is a futile, lose/lose environment.

THE CULTURAL NORM OF SIMPLISTIC SOLUTIONS

A third and very common norm is an undue reliance on simplistic solutions. "All we need to do is spank the child. . . ." "All we need to do is allocate some funds. . . ." "Love will solve everything." We have been taught since childhood to answer questions in a simplistic, univariate way. A child is asked, "Why did you do that?" when she has been involved in a complicated phenomenon that would take a veteran psychoanalyst hours and perhaps even years to unravel. Yet the child is expected to come up with a single cause. If she says, "I don't know," she may be punished—and the next time she'll find a simple answer. Because we have been brought up with these reductionist explanations, it has become a cultural norm to seek simple solutions in which only one variable is considered.

"Let the Boy Scouts do it" has been one of the simplistic approaches to reducing litter. The mayor of one of the pilot cities said at the outset of a Normative Systems program, "Oh, yeah, we have Boy Scouts who do that for us all the time. Every spring they come and they clean up certain areas." Yet actually the Boy Scouts, who had originally been highly motivated to clean up, started to refuse to do it. Their mothers and fathers were getting tired of seeing their children cleaning up after everyone else, and tired of seeing the ground littered again in two or three months. It was not until analysis revealed the true cause of litter and the cultural approach was taken that the problem abated.

The simplistic approach is a strong norm in the business world, as anyone reading the current business magazines can testify. Job enrichment, or improved productivity, or morale boosting may be the current thing. A typical pattern is: The company president goes to a conference, hears about a new idea, and brings it back. Then the company lives with the new idea for three or four months; there may be a lot of activity and even some results, but in three or four months the company returns to the old ways.

The same kind of norm is found in many professional organizations. Sometimes it takes the form of consulting a succession of specialists. "Let's listen to what the psychologists say," then, "What do the sociologists say?" or "Ask the industrial engineers," etc. Meanwhile, the frustration builds up as each new "solution" fails to erase the problem.

Many of the single-solution ideas are good ones, and there is nothing wrong with them per se, but they do not take hold. The reason is to be found in a basic premise of behavioral science: Most, if not all, human behavior is multiply-caused. Yet most lay people and many behavioral scientists continue to attack problems with single-variable, simplistic solutions: "Ban the bottle." (But what do we do with the other 88 percent of the litter remaining when all the bottles are gone?) Punish the marijuana smoker. (But what about the next pot party, and the next, when peer cultures support use of the drug?)

Often the simplistic solution has been preconceived, and the analysis of the problem is distorted to fit it.

Despite the fact that this has happened over and over again in our constant struggle with the problems of delinquency, poverty, war, drugs, and crime, we continue to rely on simple solutions because doing so is a cultural norm. Like Cinderella, we rely on one touch of the magic wand. Unfortunately, simplistic solutions give only fleeting solace; then reality settles in, and we find ourselves staring at the cinders again.

THE CULTURAL NORM OF THE CRASH PROGRAM

Crash programs are initiated in a burst of energy and enthusiasm but do not induce commitment to sustained change. Their failure can cause an even more pervasive feeling that nothing can be done. The pendulum swings forcibly back; the problem is made worse rather than better. We see this happening with dieting. Typically, people try new diets with determination and dedication, and often, they do lose some weight; the trouble is that once the dieting period is over, the weight comes back, perhaps with a few extra pounds. Over the long run the effort has to be chalked up as a failure, and often leads to the feeling that "I just can't do it—it's my nature to be heavy."

What happens is that once the dieting period is over, people tend to swing right back into their old eating patterns. The usual story is a gradual increase in weight over the years. The same pounds are lost over and over again. The type of crash program may change—calorie counting, fasting, the Scarsdale diet, the grapefruit diet—but the pattern is the same, and each failure destroys our confidence that we can really reduce.

THE CULTURAL NORM OF HELPLESSNESS

A fifth solution-thwarting block lies in another direction—our error of feeling that if we can't work on everything at once, we can't do anything. The cultural norm of helplessness is fed by the failures of quick solutions, crash programs that waste energy and resources without results, and blame placing that ends up in win/lose confrontations. After a while people don't believe they can accomplish anything, and they may even feel their leaders are helpless to change things. Recently workers were overheard talking about the top management which had just been completely overhauled. "What's going on up there?" one employee asked. The answer was: "Oh, nothing, the chiefs are just changing their blankets again."

This feeling that no one can really do anything is one of the biggest hurdles to overcome at the beginning of a new change effort.

THE CULTURAL NORM OF PROCEEDING UNINFORMED
AND UNTRAINED

A sixth common obstacle is a proclivity for acting on the basis of inaccurate or insufficient information, or without necessary skills.

A tragic example of the destructiveness of this norm is the overprotection of clients in mental hospitals mentioned in Chapter 5. The hospitals are acting on the wrong information—that patients need always to be protected from themselves and from each other—and they set up conditions that actually inhibit the patients from becoming autonomous, independent persons.

Another thing that often happens is that information comes from only one or two segments of the organization, or simply from wishful thinking. Since change programs tend to evolve from the information available at the outset, if no information is available about some realm in which change is needed, that aspect will be overlooked and the change effort will be doomed from the start.

It is obvious that when *a solution* is based on incorrect information, or *an effort* is made without enough information, there is not likely to be any lasting effect. Yet a startling number of change programs are launched on the basis of meager and inaccurate information.

A similar attitude applies to the development of skills and techniques to carry out change programs. Solutions may look good on paper, but if people aren't helped to develop the skills needed to carry out the ideas, there is little chance of success.

Our cultural norm of placing values and aspirations on a high plane and ignoring the skills needed to realize them frequently affects supervisory success. People are hired as supervisors because they have proved themselves in other areas, but too often they are not trained to run meetings, set objectives, handle discussions, or exercise the supervisory skills necessary in their new jobs. Some who fail end by saying, "All that's not important"; others simply feel inadequate and inferior. In either case an opportunity for growth and development has been lost.

THE CULTURAL NORM OF "LET GEORGE DO IT"

A seventh obstacle that impedes change is the tendency to allow a few people to make the decisions. No matter how good the intentions, decisions which do not sufficiently involve the people affected by them often lead to disastrous results.

The fate of the League of Nations is a case in point. Woodrow Wilson was inspired and dedicated, but lack of involvement on the part of the people and Congress spelled defeat for American participation in this first major effort at international cooperation.

On a smaller scale the same thing happens in family, civic, and business situations. "Let George do it" is a common committee disease. "Father knows best" has proved its trouble-making power with many a teenager. "Why should I make a plan for next year?" the teacher asks herself. "The administration will change everything over the summer." Democratic decision making is an ideal to which we pay lip service but too often ignore in favor of quicker decisions by a few.

When changes happen quickly and people feel they cannot control what is happening, they are sometimes willing to give up power to trusted authorities. However, we live in a time when the old authorities are being questioned, undercut, or even demolished. So the scariness of "future shock" is not so much that change is happening too fast, as that it is happening out of our control—and even out of the control of those we trust with our survival.

Furthermore, we may develop such a sense of failure or helplessness that we permanently replace our own judgment with that of trusted authorities. An alarming disposition toward nonparticipation already cuts through all facets of societal life, affecting problems from the familiar to the cosmic. Therefore, if a change effort seems to be bogging down, or perhaps never getting off the ground, it is important to ask, "Are the people whose lives will be changed *really* involved in the change process?"

"PROMISES, PROMISES"

"Promises, promises!" How many times have we heard that phrase spoken in disgust—usually when it is obvious that an expected change process has not worked. It is a common fault in our society to make unsubstantiated promises. Many programs are heavy on promises and state their goals in such abstract terms that results cannot easily be measured.

When promises are not fulfilled and results are not visible (even though they may be there), the heavy clouds of disillusionment are difficult to disperse. The high hopes that were built up by the war on poverty are a good case in point. The promises were many; the results were small. The deflation of hope led to a deep disillusionment and even greater distrust of the whole system of government.

FOCUSING ON THE INDIVIDUAL

When things go wrong in our society, we tend to look to the individual for the cause and to treat the individual. The emphasis on personal counseling and psychotherapy, for example, led us to think of women's depression as an individual problem. Not until the women's liberation movement made us conscious of the ways in which women were forced into roles and trapped in stultifying patterns were the cultural aspects of the problem seen. Treating the culture freed many women from feelings of depression.

The whole idea of relying on personal counseling to remedy the problems of the ghetto is one that keeps us from examining the actual roots of such problems. Treating the ghetto culturally, i.e., helping people to change their own social environments, might well do away with much of the need for treatment of the individual.

A startling example of what happens when we shift our sights occurred in the Appalachian region a few years ago. A number of people were afflicted with a strange disease—one that caused depression, lethargy, loss of energy. It was so prevalent it was given a name—the Appalachian syndrome—and grants were awarded to study it and find a cure. The study found, not too surprisingly, that the problem was unemployment, a pressure from the outer environment rather than a disease from within. Once jobs were found, the symptoms disappeared.

This cultural norm of looking for individual rather than cultural causes is based on an overemphasis on the individual at the expense of the group. It stands high on the list of cultural norms that prevent people from achieving what they want and will be explored further in the next chapter.

THE CULTURAL NORM OF LOSING CLARITY

Finally, it is a norm in our society to start a change effort without a clear idea of where we *are* and where we are *going*. Many efforts begin without a clear analysis of what the problem is. As a result, assorted people have various ideas of what is to be done about it. For example, in many high schools, new curricula or scheduling procedures are imposed from the top, without adequate understanding on the part of faculty and students. When this occurs, the implementation is likely to leave much to be desired.

Even efforts that get off to a more fortuitous start often bog down later as the waters are muddied by a diffusion of goals, unspecified tasks, and a hazy idea about what the process is and where people are in that process at any given time. Too often in organizations "clarity of purpose" is a hot topic in opening sessions, only to be dropped later.

A RAIN DANCE IN THE DESERT

Change programs based on any one or a combination of these common cultural blocks are about as effective as a rain dance in the desert. Yet they are common in our business and social organizations. These negative norms don't all apply every time, and there are others, not mentioned here. However, the ones discussed are among those that most frequently frustrate attempts to solve problems or change things.

CURRENT RAIN DANCES (NEGATIVE NORMS)

"Pass the Buck"—Fix the blame instead of the solution.

"The Win/Lose Waltz"—Confrontation in 3/4 time.

"Starting with the Last Step"—Surefire disappointment with this simplistic number.

"The Patchwork Pavane"—Popular patches include *Pass a Law, Educate them, Get Tough, Love Everybody, Take It Easy, Write a Memo*.

"If You Can't Do Everything, Don't Do Anything"—A slow blues number, a helpless moan.

"The Stumble-Bum Gavotte"—No skills or training necessary.

"The Grand March of the Philosopher Kings"—Only a few dance; most people must watch from the sidelines.

"The Promises Polka"—Often coupled with the "Getting Ahead Gambol." Both consist of one step forward followed by two steps backward.

"The Solo Hustle"—An individual dance; the dancers are oblivious to the rest of the people on the dance floor and to the need for partners.

"The Muddy Waters Mazurka"—In this number, the dancers cannot see where they are, where they are going, or how they are going to get there.

Chapter 8

A False Dichotomy and the Incongruent Culture

An animal is either social or solitary. Man alone as-pires to be both in one, a social solitary.

J. BRONOWSKI

A society may be termed human in the measure to which its members confirm one another.

MARTIN BUBER

Probably the most insidious and least-recognized concept that keeps us enmeshed in the culture trap is the false dichotomy between the enhancement of ourselves as individuals and the enhancement of the groups and communities to which we belong. Too often we feel we need to make a choice between individual freedom and independence on the one hand and group involvement, participation, and responsibility on the other.

A choice either way is unnecessary and unproductive, for no matter which we choose, we leave out something very important to human life. Choosing individual self-development to the exclusion of group needs or choosing to perpetuate the system (institution, government, or group) to the exclusion of individual needs and rights keeps us from solving some of the most troubling problems that plague people. Either choice deludes us into believing that we have found the answers when we haven't. Extreme emphasis on individuality leads to a false sense of freedom and autonomy, when in effect we are being controlled by culture. On the other hand, extreme emphasis on the group leads to blind allegiance and conformity—the antithesis of freedom. So either way we are left in the culture trap, victims of unseen or little understood cultural influence. Yet the myth that we must make a choice between our own interests and the group's interests is deeply ingrained in our culture.

THE MYTH OF THE ISOLATED I

Writer Joyce Carol Oates comments: "One of the holiest of our myths has always been the unique, proud, isolated entity of the 'self.'"[1] In recent years particularly, the Western world has stressed individual psychology as the way to self-fulfillment. Our American dream is the autonomous person, the unique "man for all seasons," who is able to stand isolated from society and its shortcomings and to retain his integrity through inner strength. We have devised psychologies and experimented with psychiatric techniques based on the building up of egos. People are urged to "be themselves." Our emphasis on individuality is so great that it has become a myth undergirding much of our modern thought and behavior. The more fragmented our society has become, the weaker our institutions; and the less reliable our social structures, the more we have clung to our belief that we must foster individuality. We feel the way to have freedom is to declare loudly that we depend on no person.

Freedom itself is a worthy goal—to be autonomous, to have control over our lives, to be molders rather than victims of the outer world. The danger here is that we delude ourselves into believing we have achieved individuality because we have set ourselves apart. Like Narcissus, we are so focused on ourselves that we lose the world.

A DEEPLY ROOTED BIAS

The roots of this new narcissism go deep. The cult of individualism has been highly valued in our culture for a long time. Christian teachings made each person "precious in the eyes of the Lord." After ages during which socioeconomic conditions enforced facelessness in the multitude despite the theological doctrines of personality, the Renaissance watered and fed the idea of uniqueness. From those times until now we have the tragic hero who maintains his integrity and dignity in the face of cultural pressures. With the rise of the "common man" and the coming of democracy to Western Europe and America, belief in sturdy individuality spread to all classes of society. The pioneer struggling against the wilderness, and later, Horatio Alger's heroes making their way up success ladders, symbolized our traditional belief in "rugged individualism." Just about everyone gave lip service to America's belief in everyone's *right* to a fair share of the benefits of society.

These rights, of course, have truly equal effect only when the effect on others of our individual wish fulfillment is weighed in the balance. An extreme emphasis on individuality, by itself, leads to selfishness and self-

---

[1] Oates, "The Myth of the Isolated Artist," *Psychology Today,* May 1973, pp. 74–75.

indulgence. Though we rightly fear excessive conformity, solutions like Ayn Rand's, that "man must act for his own rational self-interest,"[2] for example, lead to a devastating separation of human being from human being.

What would our society be like if we continued toward this extreme? Colin Turnbull asks this question in *The Mountain People,* his study of the Ik, an African tribe which lost its humanity.[3] In less than three generations the Ik deteriorated from a peaceful, prosperous society of hunters into scattered bands of hostile people bent only on individual survival. The deterioration of human values in the Ik may seem remote to us, but it can serve as a reminder of what could happen if we don't awaken to our own biases.

THE OTHER EXTREME—CONFORMITY

The false dichotomy also leads people to make the opposite choice—blind allegiance to the group. There are those in our society who argue for higher levels of uncritical responsiveness to the requirements of the culture. Such arguments are usually disguised by such labels as patriotism, national interest, organizational pride, and loyalty. When an extreme position of this kind is taken, personal freedom is set aside to enhance the well-being of the group. The mesmeric hold of the Charles Manson "family" or the Jim Jones cult on the wills of its members, is horrible testimony to the results of an extreme "group-enhancement" position. On a lesser plane, the Nixon White House, where experienced public servants put their own group's needs first, demonstrates how people can abrogate their individual values and resolutely interfere with those of others.

We have had enough experience with conformity in our society to cause us concern about losing our freedom to some type of "groupthink." Masses of people went along with the Nazi horrors in Germany, and other masses tacitly went along with the American intervention in Vietnam. Milgram's frightening experiment (see Chapter 2), in which ordinary people knowingly administered electric shocks to other human beings, shows how easily we can be led to act contrary to our individual moral tenets.

Our concerns about conformity and manipulation are valid, but they tend to distort our perspective on group involvement, participation, and responsibility. Further, they tend to swing us over to the other, equally dead-end, extreme—thinking that we can somehow go it alone without the help of others. But a real sense of community is not groupthink; a respon-

---

[2] Rand, *The Virtue of Selfishness* (New York: Signet, 1961), p. x.

[3] Turnbull, *The Mountain People* (New York: Simon & Schuster, 1972).

sive member of a culture can be social without conforming. As Martin
Buber points out:

> The fundamental fact of human existence is neither the individual as such
> nor the aggregate as such. Each, considered by itself, is a mighty abstrac-
> tion. The individual is a fact of existence insofar as he steps into a living
> relationship with other individuals. The aggregate is a fact of existence
> insofar as it is built up of living units of relation. The fundamental fact of
> human existence is man with man.[4]

We need to enhance both the I-interests and the we-interests of society
if we are to solve basic human problems and achieve true individuality.

MAN THE SOCIAL SOLITARY

The twofold basis of humanity that Buber calls the "fundamental fact of
human existence" is defined in terms of biological needs by Jacob
Bronowski. He points out that animals are either social, like ants, or
solitary, like the bear or moose, but a person is both, "a social solitary
. . . a unique biological feature."[5] Bronowski illuminates the essential
double foundation of the human character in his discussion of two basic
needs: the need to be different and the need to be like other people.

Our current stress on individuality is, then, based on a real human need.
Within this need to be different lies the emotional magnetism of the idea of
freedom, more particularly that aspect of freedom that emphasizes our
uniqueness. We want to stand out in a crowd, to have a special niche of
our own. But obviously, this impetus can get us into trouble when it
carries us to extremes. For then it is running counter to another need just
as basic and ingrained, the need to be like other people.

We want to be like others. This side of our nature welcomes the influence of outside forces, because the influences that determine us serve to
emphasize our relationship to others. We long for relatedness, which we
sometimes call a "sense of community" or "sense of belonging," or
sometimes "love" or "intimacy."

Starting from infancy we find out who we are through our interactions
with others. We define ourselves and know that we are human through the
other human beings with whom we come in contact.

Our expanding sense of self is built on expanding options among ways
to behave. When we are with a group we relate to others and gain identity
through the interactions. In a circle of trusting friends, for example, there

[4] Buber, "What Is Man?" in *Reality, Man and Existence*, H. J. Blackman (ed.) (New York:
Macmillan, 1965), p. 232.

[5] Bronowski, *The Ascent of Man* (Boston: Little, Brown, 1974), p. 441.

is more freedom, less inhibition, and a feeling of being more of a person. Relationships with others are freeing experiences. The core of the problem is stubborn retention of that idea that somehow individualism rules out relatedness.

The few recorded cases in which infants were cut off from human relationships prove the point dramatically. The anthropologist Ruth Benedict reports on abandoned children found back in old Roman days. They had maintained themselves in the forest and were so different from other human beings that they were thought to be a distinct species, a kind of gnome that people seldom ran across. The Roman who discovered them could not conceive that these half-witted brutes were born human, Benedict says, and described them as "these creatures with no interest in what went on about them, rocking themselves rhythmically back and forth like some animal in a zoo, with organs of speech and hearing that could hardly be trained to do service, who withstood freezing weather in rags and plucked potatoes out of boiling water without discomfort."[6]

In normal circumstances, the need for relatedness is firmly embedded in the human consciousness through a long nurturing period. By adolescence our need to be with others and to be like others is firm, but we usually shift our allegiance to our peers. No matter how much independence from one group or another we achieve, the basic need to be part of some group continues throughout life; and when others don't see or treat us as one of them, at least to the extent of respecting our rights as human beings, we experience a loss of freedom.

Conversely, when we see or treat others as different, as "strangers," trouble can ensue. Strangers or foreigners are not seen as like us; therefore we fear them and either avoid or attack them. In times of war, we harp on the idea of the "stranger"; the "krauts" or "gooks" or "Japs" become our enemies.

In peaceful times, the unfulfilled need for others often manifests itself in loneliness and alienation. The elderly in the nursing home, the disabled in city apartments, and people alienated in jails and mental hospitals are tragic testimony to an unsatisfied human need and the sometimes brutal ways in which we frustrate it. The family doesn't meet the need because it is smaller than it used to be, and people aren't attached to it as long. Churches tend not to meet this need as they once did. The mobility of the population results in cities and towns made up of strangers and casual acquaintances.

Today evidence of this need is seen in the tremendous interest in

---

[6] Benedict, *Patterns of Culture* (Boston/New York: Houghton Mifflin, 1934), pp. 12–13. Copyright 1934 by Ruth Benedict. Copyright renewed 1962 by Ruth Valentine. Reprinted by permission of Houghton Mifflin Company.

"community" at the grass roots level. People are showing their need to relate well to others on more than a superficial basis. In the past few years we have had a mushrooming of encounter groups and special-problem groups; not only is there Alcoholics Anonymous, there are Parents Without Partners, singles clubs, Smokenders, the Fortune Society for ex-prisoners, consciousness-raising groups for women—you name your problem, there is probably already a group. Communes have sprung up all over the country. Experiments in extended families and other forms of small-group living are taking the place of the nuclear family for thousands of people. There is evidence of a need for a sense of community even within businesses and other large organizations.

Probably the most extreme and poignant evidence of this tremendous emotional need is a current movement to start groups for people who are dying and want to be with others who are dying. They feel their last days will be lived more fully if they are in contact with others who can truly share their point of view and recognize their feelings.

ABANDONING THE TUG-OF-WAR

So we human beings struggle with the need to be different and the need to be alike, the need to be concerned with individual enhancement and the need to enhance the group. We have engaged in a tug-of-war in which neither individuality nor social concerns can win. Actually, both concepts are vital for us today.

If we abandon the tug-of-war and think of these two seemingly contradictory aspects of the human condition as forces moving in the same direction, some interesting things happen. When the individualistic position that stresses a search for autonomy and the group-involvement position that stresses a feeling of belonging are treated equally, it turns out that they are not exclusive. Not only can they work well together, they cannot work healthfully in separation.

When both concerns are met, the individual gains greater freedom, and the society becomes more flexible and more helpful to its members. For when people show concern for the freedom of others and a responsibility toward the group's interest and well-being, each individual has more options and more services and facilities to draw on. Likewise, when individual freedom is strengthened, the culture will not be stuck in a stultifying rut, but will change to become more responsive to the needs of its members.

MAN A PART OF CULTURE

In our struggle to isolate "self" from "other," we have blinded ourselves to some important truths: We are products of our point in history; knowledge, skills, and abilities have been passed down to us from others; we operate within a framework of cultures and support groups. As Oates tells us, "The consciousness of any man is an objective event in nature . . . It is not the private possession of the individual just as the individual is not 'his' own private possession, but belongs to his culture."[7]

She points out that we accept this objectivity and impersonalism for scientists: "If there were not a massive cooperative venture among totally unconnected people in this process of establishing truths, all of science would be chaos—simply the expression of isolated individuals, deluded into believing that each is 'original' and 'creative.'"[8]

The same thing is true of great geniuses, who seem to have recognized their work as "massive cooperative ventures," though the rest of us have difficulty in giving up the idea of their isolation. As we saw earlier, great geniuses are actually very much products of their times. On close examination they turn out to be not originators, but synthesizers. As Alfred North Whitehead said: "Every great idea originated with someone who was not the first to think of it."[9]

To go beyond the false dichotomy, individuals need to become aware of the forces impinging upon them from their culture and aware of their own inner reactions and strengths as well. Perhaps as a culture we are ready to go beyond both "rugged individualism" and American chauvinism. Perhaps soon, by embracing both aspects of our social/solitary existence, we will be better able to respond to Bronowski's challenge to "assume the task of being human."[10]

[7] Oates, op. cit., p. 75.

[8] Ibid.

[9] Whitehead, *Modes of Thought* (New York: Macmillan, 1938), p. 81.

[10] Bronowski, op. cit., p. 436.

Chapter 9

The Fulcrum:
It Doesn't Have
to Be That Way

It was the best of times, it was the worst of times, it was the age of wisdom, it was the age of foolishness, it was the epoch of belief, it was the epoch of incredulity, it was the season of Light, it was the season of Darkness, it was the spring of hope, it was the winter of despair.

CHARLES DICKENS

Fulcrum: A position, element or agency through, around, or by means of which vital powers are exercised.

The American Heritage Dictionary of the English Language

In the opening lines of his momentous novel of the French Revolution, *A Tale of Two Cities,* Dickens reminds us that the good and bad can and often do, arrive simultaneously at a given moment in history. Today we are living at just such a moment. We are experiencing "the best of times" and "the worst of times." Our world seems to be coming apart, and yet in some ways we are coming closer together.

We live in a moment of history charged with rapid technological and cultural changes, which may be either a boon or a disaster for society. On the one hand, we suffer from what Alvin Toffler calls the "dizzying distortion brought on by the premature arrival of the future."[1] On the other hand, this era of cataclysmic change holds within it tremendous opportunities to move ahead in ways that were never before possible.

The previous chapters established that the dehumanizing patterns of our culture must be disrupted if we are going to effect meaningful change, and proposed that such disruptions can present positive opportunities for further change.

[1] *Future Shock* (New York: Bantam, 1970), p. 11.

Change seldom takes place unless someone or something has sufficiently upset things first. The upset may be a demonstration or a sit-in, a boycott or a prison insurrection. Whatever form the disruption takes, it presents an opportunity for needed change. Cesar Chavez and his followers in the California vineyards made the nation see that farm workers had been denied the rights of other citizens. Similarly, marches on Washington, demands by the counterculture, riots in Attica, burnings in the ghettos, confrontations on Southern buses and in restaurants—all these forced people to see problems that had been ignored or buried previously.

Disruption, however, does not always lead events forward, and may even lead them backward. After the French Revolution, the Revolutionists perpetuated the repressions of the former tyrants. After the Attica riots, there was little prison reform. Disruption can set the stage for change, but the change is by no means automatic. There is the need also for a fulcrum—an "element by which vital powers are exercised."[2] Today that element is available in the power of the culture. The unplanned, disastrous "programs" of Part 2 showed that cultural influences can have a negative effect. In the pages ahead we will see how, in planned programs, these same normative influences can be dynamic forces leading to greater freedom for people.

Now that we have shaken up the old categories and taken on some new ones, we are ready to turn the tables. Every one of the obstacles that we usually put in the way of change (see Rain Dances, Chapter 7) can be turned from a negative into a positive force, and those forces can work toward the changes we want.

[2] *The American Heritage Dictionary* (Boston: American Heritage Publishing Co. and Houghton Mifflin, 1969), p. 531.

Section Two

CHANGING THINGS

'A FIRST FOR JERSEY'

welcome helping hands

Custor

From Delingu

PEOPL

The

Of

St

How

GAIN

hite

he

black

Foo

BEAUTIFUL

Reader's Digest

Migrants

No More

grant W

City Teacher Aides

Find Some Children Lack Adequate Care at Hom

SUNDAY NEWS, MAY 7, 1967

Keine Rolle für Unbeteiligte

Eine Erwiderung zu dem Aufsatz von Martin L

An den scharfsichtigen Beobachtungen Lakins zur

schenmenschliche Beziehungen

THE QUIET

The Story of a

Small Miracle in

American Life

ATLANTA

Journal and Const

ANDREW RKS,

NNETH ROGERS, Photograp

How To Reach

New

wor

Food

A Ne

Cha

Food

Harris

Silent Majo

WALL STREET JU

Part Four

HOW WE CAN TRANSFORM OUR CULTURES

More and more, we dare to struggle for a society promoting both rational planning and democratic control.

DAVID GORDON

The world and its meaning are always negotiating with one another, with experience as the go-between.

GEORGE HOMANS

The problem of society is to nurture the creative urges and put down the destructive ones.

ERIC BERNE

Chapter 10

It Takes
a System to
Beat a System

I must create a system, or be enslaved by another man's.

WILLIAM BLAKE

If we view society's problems from the vantage point of the limited individual self, it seems almost impossible to do anything about them. The culture with its unplanned and largely invisible "programs," determines much of our lives, as we've seen, and often it seems like a mighty giant against whom we, like the Lilliputians attacking Gulliver, send tiny arrows that bounce off harmlessly. But it *is* possible to vanquish this giant and bring about the changes we desire. The way to conquer the "system" is with another system—one of our own choosing and in our own control.

Denial of the "system" will not rid us of it. We have tried closing our eyes to problems many times in the past (Hitler, discrimination, pollution, organized crime). Pretending that these negative norm patterns don't exist does not make them disappear. Meaningful and lasting change requires two things: first, a recognition that we are caught in a "seamless web" of culture, and second, use of that culture to change it.

Fortunately the steps needed are much more discernible and accessible than many have thought. The "rules" of social behavior may not be as clear as those of the natural sciences, but they exist nonetheless. The haphazard profusion of norms and norm influences that determine a culture can be understood. It is possible to use their power to solve problems and bring about change.

A NEW USE OF WHAT WE KNOW

The planned, rational harnessing of the power of cultural influences has been too long neglected. In this regard we might well take a lesson from the physical sciences, which have discovered methods of bridging the gap between wishing and actuality. The ascendancy of technology is testimony to their success. The moonwalk of 1969 was not the result of new understanding alone, but of the ability to put this understanding to work systematically. Why not a moonshot for human problems?

The concept of Normative Systems grew out of a great deal of prior work by sociologists, anthropologists, and social psychologists, and it pulls together many threads from diverse disciplines. What is new, however, is the systematic and humanistic *use* of what people already know. This approach seeks to simplify complex cultural systems and make them understandable—and therefore changeable.

The approach is based on the premise that normative influences are pervasive in virtually all situations, and so if we can get below the daily events and discover the patterns that govern our actions and limit our alternatives, it will lead to greater understanding and, ultimately, to greater freedom.

A PEOPLE-OWNED PROCESS

The primary task, no matter what the application, is to help the people in a group adopt a system of managing themselves and determining the future course of their culture. A key concept of Normative Systems is a planned program owned by the people affected by it. This prevents the program from becoming a straitjacket for enforcing conformity. The rational planning approach is inseparable from democratic control.

Not only is democratic control essential to long-lasting success, but the actual feeling of ownership is important. It helps people take on responsibility, helps defeat the feelings of helplessness that so often plague change efforts, and leads people to a greater sense of control over their situation.

This concept of ownership has two vital aspects: It must be genuine, and it must be felt. If it is merely felt without being genuine, the program is manipulative. If it is genuine, but not recognized as such, attitudes of helplessness will prevail. But if the participants really are in control—and know it—meaningful change can result.

A great deal of effort needs to be devoted to ensuring that the program and the reasons for it are understood by all the participants. This is not easy to accomplish, for people often are more interested in getting on with it than in understanding what it is they are getting on with. Experience has shown that aimless effort of this type can have a very negative impact on both short-range and long-range effectiveness.

The ownership concept, with its stress on responsibility and cooperation, operates in all phases of a Normative Systems change program. From the very first step, when the culture is analyzed, people begin to understand, relate to, and control the program. This self-direction continues throughout all phases. Once internal capability is developed, outside guidance is no longer necessary.

A GENERIC MODEL EVOLVES

The Normative Systems model itself has undergone many refinements through the years, primarily to simplify it and make it more practical. Once people understand the model thoroughly and apply it to a change effort, they are able to use it in other settings to tackle other problems.

The simplified version of the model shown below presents the four interrelated phases that are always included, regardless of the specific objective of the project.

When expressed in terms of the questions that need to be answered, the four phases look like this:

Phase I   Have you found out just what your problem really is and decided what you want to happen?

Phase II   Have you helped others concerned with the problem understant the cultural impact of what is occurring and involved them in planning steps toward change?

Phase III Have you put the agreed-upon objectives into daily practice, keeping track of results as you go along and rewarding everyone for his or her progress?

Phase IV   Have you rechecked what you have done and kept your mind open to new factors that affect it?

Phase I, analysis and objective setting, consists of fact-finding and study to ensure that the change program is based on sound information and is heading in the desired direction. In this phase a conceptual analysis is made of the culture, the key norm influences affecting the culture are identified, tentative objectives are set, and materials are developed for use in Phase II.

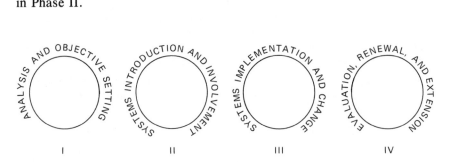

FIGURE 10-1 A simplified version of the basic Normative Systems model.

Phase II, systems introduction and involvement, introduces the system to the people most directly affected and involves them in the change process. Participants consider their alternatives and usually have an opportunity to try out the desired culture in a workshop or other high-involvement situation. With this experience, they begin to develop the belief that change is possible, and they learn the basic elements of the system that will guide the change process.

Phase III, systems implementation and change, involves systematically modifying relevant subsystems of the culture and adding new subsystems as needed. During this phase the group works with four key elements of the culture: (1) individual members; (2) work teams or peer groups; (3) leadership groups; and (4) the formal policies, practices, and structures of the organization or group. Specific change programs are usually required for each of these four elements, with each program directed toward modifying the norm influences that have previously been identified. Norm changes are reinforced and reviewed for effectiveness as the group puts them into practice in its day-to-day activities.

Phase IV, systems evaluation, renewal, and extension, provides an opportunity for a periodic, systematic review of what has been, and what remains to be, accomplished. In response, the change program is renewed, modified as appropriate, and extended to other problem areas, ultimately evolving into an ongoing, open-ended, dynamic force for creating successful cultures.

FROM RIGIDITY TO FLUIDITY

The four phases of the Normative Systems change program are interrelated and sometimes overlap, so that one phase is being introduced while the prior phase is still under way. Moreover, as other people become involved, they usually shed new light on the problem and add to or modify the initial objectives. In addition, different levels of an organization may be in different phases at the same time.

No matter what level is being introduced, such a program involves a lot of hard work. Properly conducted, though, it can bring about meaningful change much more rapidly than most people anticipate. Moreover, the changes, once achieved, can be sustained and built upon. The ability to build upon past achievements is an important side effect of successful programs. Once learned, the four-phase process can be used to deal with whatever problems and concerns arise.

Thus, embracing Normative Systems concepts means more than merely substituting a rigid new form of orthodoxy for the old, one cultural trap for another. The new system should have a responsiveness and fluidity that the old system lacked.

Certain guiding principles have been developed for using the model, and they provide an essential foundation for successful change strategies. Since they apply to every step of the change process, let us look at them before proceeding to discuss each one of the four phases in greater detail.

Chapter 11

Opening the Culture Trap

Human behavior is predictable, but, as in physical science, accurate prediction hinges on the correctness of underlying theoretical assumptions. There is, in fact, no prediction without theory . . .

DOUGLAS MCGREGOR

Probably each of us can remember times when change programs that were introduced with high hopes and much fanfare ended in failure. They started well, but the culture trap closed in on them, and soon it was back to "business as usual." If we compare these failures with effective change efforts (those that accomplished what they set out to do, and sustained that accomplishment), we find that the difference most often lies in whether or not certain key principles were followed. These principles involve pivotal norms of planning, implementation, and change, and they act as guides throughout the change process.

When people have been successful in changing their cultures, it has been the norm for them to:

1. Involve, right from the outset, those most directly affected

2. Operate on the basis of sound information

3. Apply systematic strategies and tactics

4. Be clear about objectives, plans, and tasks

5. Look for win/win solutions without placing blame

6. Be oriented toward results

7. Build in culture-based, sustained commitment and follow-through

So important are these seven principles that many programs have failed because just one of them has not been taken into account. If they are dealt with adequately, however, the change effort is much more likely to succeed.

As you read through the description of these principles, you might keep in mind a past change effort with which you are familiar. Ask yourself how the principle applied in that case and what effect it had upon success or failure. That done, you might use the checklist at the end of this chapter to ask yourself some special questions about particular change programs in which you may be involved now or in the near future.

1. INVOLVEMENT OF PEOPLE

It is hard to imagine a change principle more essential, yet more neglected, than the involvement of people in the changes affecting them. Well-intentioned programs regularly flounder because they are carried out *for* a group rather than *by* it. You hear about this daily: An expensive community youth center is closed down by vandalism a few weeks after its opening, with the lament, "Kids just never appreciate what is done for them." A philanthropist can't understand why the modern sculpture foisted upon a Midwestern community is not appreciated by the townspeople. The local housing authority can't comprehend the litter and graffiti that mar their new low-income housing project.

From the outset the successful change effort needs to aim not only at involving people but at making involvement the norm—the expected way of doing things. The Normative Systems process encourages, develops, and rewards participation at all steps. The people directly affected help analyze the existing culture, take steps toward its improvement, put changes into daily practice, evaluate their efforts, and carry out renewal actions.

Because the diagrammatic model of the change process is presented early in the program, people always have an overview of exactly what is occurring. They can see where they are and make a clear and reasonable estimate of the outcome.

The excitement and enthusiasm of change come from full participation in the process. In a business or industrial setting, on-the-job experience with new norms is emphasized, rather than isolated training programs; in a school setting, new norms are tried out in the classroom; etc. When norms are changed on the spot in this way, then checked and evaluated periodically, the change effort is more likely to produce lasting results.

Another aspect of involvement is the interaction of people as total human beings, rather than as objects, possessions, or roles. This means developing fuller relationships than people ordinarily do in an office or a classroom, for instance. If we see each other as multidimensional persons, rather than as the "boss," the "mayor", the "gang leader", the "teacher", or whatever, we will be more likely to treat each other as people rather than as cogs in an organizational machine. At the beginning of a change effort, and at regular intervals thereafter, it is worthwhile to provide opportunities for people to share aspects of themselves outside those roles in which they are ordinarily cast. This can speed up the problem-solving process, forestall role-related conflicts that would impede the change program, and help people find mutually beneficial solutions rather than placing blame, finding scapegoats, or playing psychological games with each other.

At the heart of all these people-involvement norms is the principle of democratic, as contrasted with authoritarian or specialist, control. If a consultant is involved, he or she is merely part of the process, rather than the determiner of what is to occur.

The principle of people involvement is not based simply on ideological and humanitarian notions. Practically speaking, people simply won't believe in an effort unless they have an opportunity to plan it, experience it, provide feedback, and develop a sense of ownership about it—a conviction that it really *does* belong to them, and that their decisions are listened to. Slick, packaged programs, presented to people "whole hog," have little chance of making a lasting impact or of resulting in meaningful action. But true involvement is the backbone of motivation.

Participation is much more possible than is generally recognized. Community residents who have traditionally been the recipients of services can become the providers of services when they are given the opportunity, and even children at the elementary school level have found it possible to successfully organize and administer total change programs with only minimal adult support.

2. USING SOUND INFORMATION

Complete and accurate information must be gathered from all pertinent segments of the organization or group before the targets of change are chosen and before the change program is designed. As we have seen, there is a tendency in our culture for change programs to be guided by hunches or wishful thinking rather than by sound information. Our cultural norms emphasize the development of solutions even before we have clearly identified the problems. Thus, in one change program that dealt with drug use among teenagers, the assumption was made that all teenagers were involved in direct drug use. However, a later study revealed that less than 5 percent of this particular group were directly involved, and so the nature of the program was changed.

A similar insight was gained from an analysis of child labor among migrant workers. This revealed that low worker income and lack of child-care facilities were the problem, rather than parental attitudes as had previously been surmised. Greater parental productivity and adequate child-care facilities made the "insurmountable" problem quite easy to solve.

Three kinds of information are needed for developing target goals. The first is "hard-line" data—factual, quantifiable data that can be used to measure progress. In a business organization these data might cover cost-effectiveness, absenteeism, and profits. In a school they might include test scores, the percentage of students who completed a particular program, and the number who used the knowledge gained.

The second type of information is programmatic—that is, facts about the extent to which proposed actions are being carried out.

The third type of information is cultural, covering what the norms are, how strong they are, what is actually happening in the organization, as contrasted with what is supposedly or officially happening. This third type of information deserves special emphasis, for it is the one most often neglected—largely because of the difficulty of "getting a handle" on the culture. But with the development of norm instruments, it is just as possible to get detailed, useful, cultural data as it has long been to get data on costs and profits.

3. SYSTEMATIC STRATEGIES AND TACTICS

The complexity of problems having to do with human relationships requires a systematic and fully integrated approach to change. To deal successfully with such problems, a group must deal with a number of variables simultaneously, and at all levels of an organization. Once this is understood, the group will attack the most complex problems from several directions at once, keeping in mind the cultural context in which the problems have arisen.

As we have seen in Chapter 7, what happens too often is that we deal with one variable, and when the effort fails, we feel that nothing can be done. Actually, a great deal can be done in most cases. The systematic approach, in which all the important variables are under scrutiny at once, can get us past the barrier of helplessness. Usually there are several key pressure points in a change situation at which effective work can bring about the desired change. The way to success is to attack problems intelligently and systematically, working on the important pressure points in a coordinated way.

4. CLEAR OBJECTIVES, PLANS, AND TASKS

From the very beginning, it is important to have specific, achievable goals clearly stated and clearly perceived by members of the organization or group. Similarly, the plans and specific tasks that are developed later on must be well understood.

In successful cultures the purposes are kept constantly in view as the change process develops and work gets under way in installing and sustaining positive new norms. People in one department or one segment of the culture share their objectives with one another and have an opportunity to receive help and feedback. In the course of this process, objectives may be modified, or people's perceptions of them may be sharpened.

One important technique that contributes to the clarity of objectives is thinking of them in three different aspects similar to the three information levels: first, performance objectives involving specific results, second, objectives concerned with establishing certain programs or subsystems, and third, objectives relating to changes in underlying cultural norms that will sustain the gains that are made. Many organizations deal adequately with the first two, but ignore the third. (A prime example of this is found in many companies that try out zero-base budgeting. Certain performance objectives are established, forms are filled out, and programs are instituted, but the old norm of providing "cushions" is still in use, and the budget is actually made out in the old way and then made to fit into the new forms.)

5. WIN/WIN SOLUTIONS

A fifth principle calls for the development of win/win (as contrasted with the usual win/lose) solutions, such that *all* the individuals and groups in an organization or culture stand to benefit from the proposed changes.

If we face conflicts with the attitude that solutions beneficial to all parties may be found, it is surprising how often a win/win outcome will emerge. Instead of thinking in tug-of-war terms, it is useful to think in terms of a grid, such as the one that Blake and Mouton[1] have popularized in managerial circles, in which both sides work toward achieving the goals of both. Such grids can be used by any two protagonists—management/labor, work team/supervisor, delinquent teenagers/counseling staff, litterers/litter victims, migrant workers/company executives, and so on. Instead of focusing on their differences, both parties use the grid concept to achieve a wider focus, on both individual and group benefits. It is surprising how often two once-hostile parties find their basic goals are really the same.

Problem confrontation without blame placing is constructive in a well-

[1] See Robert R. Blake and Jane Srygley Mouton, *The Managerial Grid* (Houston: Gulf Publishing Company, 1964).

conceived norm change program. When all parties are encouraged to deal with problem behavior as it is related to norms, there is minimum risk of arousing personal defenses. It is easier to take this criticism: "The norm around here is to arrive 15 minutes late to a meeting. Can we change it?" than it is to take this: "You guys are always holding up the meeting."

Tied to this more constructive approach to problem solving is avoiding the usual undue focus on what *others* can do, instead of what we can do together, to bring about change. Most problems require that each individual examine his or her own behavior in relationship to the group's objectives. People are more likely to do this when the focus is on achieving results and modifying the culture, rather than on finding out who is to blame for what has occurred. This tends to free energy formerly wasted in win/lose confrontations, and to spark enthusiastic movement toward change. Therefore, it is productive to shift from creating environments where people cannot succeed and then blaming them for failure, to creating success environments that will help people become winners.

6. RESULTS ORIENTATION

The win/win posture is supported by an orientation toward results. If we focus entirely on what we would like to have happen, we often get caught in abstractions and unfulfilled promises. If we focus on results, however—on what we actually *do*—the excitement of achievement begins to feed on itself.

Continuing emphasis on results not only replaces empty promises; it also replaces the negative norm of blame placing. Finger-pointing behavior is bypassed when the orientation is toward accomplishment and concrete results. The negative norm of helplessness is also undermined, for the realization that something is being accomplished spurs people on. Attention can be paid to excellence and to solving the next part of the problem; there is a feeling of being in control. Many people don't really think change is possible, but they can be convinced that things can happen when they actually see some results begin to appear.

Successful change programs set specific measurable short- and long-range goals that everyone agrees will constitute satisfactory cultural change. The short-range goals need to be ones that can be achieved in a reasonably short period of time and that will lead to early, visible results.

The long-range goals are also clearly defined, for mere "activities" that aren't framed in the larger context are, in the long run, as disappointing as meaningless promises. Both immediate and continuing actions are planned. Early success in modifying a culture motivates continued efforts.

Visibility of results is a crucial factor. In effective change programs, results are regularly and promptly reported in a manner that people throughout the organization can understand. Results that do not have naturally high visibility can be highlighted by good feedback and information systems.

Reports on results have the greatest impact when they are positioned in the larger framework of agreed-upon objectives and are seen as progress toward shared organizational goals. Data about accomplishments, if fed back regularly, will keep people in touch with progress toward objectives and give confidence and support to those who initially became committed to work toward change. They also help convince the skeptical.

7. CULTURE-BASED, SUSTAINED EFFORT

The successful change process, whether it is being considered by a small work team in industry or by a whole city, is the result of a culture-based, sustained effort. If we really want to change, we must commit ourselves to something that is going to extend over a long period of time, and the culture itself is going to have to be involved in the change process. (In fact, it is usually better not to start programs at all if we are not prepared to continue them.)

The case histories in Chapters 18 to 21 provide ample evidence of the far-reaching and long-lasting changes that can be made when the culture is adequately dealt with, when the effort is continually supported, and when renewal experiences sustain the commitment and involvement of all groups.

A CHECKLIST FOR CULTURAL PRINCIPLES

The seven principles of cultural change just presented are not all-inclusive, but adherence to them has made a major difference in the development of many successful change programs. Norms built around these principles play a key role in bringing about and maintaining change. Because they are of immense importance, they should be checked throughout the change process. People find that these principles gradually become almost integral parts of their lives, affecting their success in many kinds of groups, and in their interactions with individuals as well. The following questions can be used to check on whether or not the guiding principles are in operation:

1. ARE PEOPLE INVOLVED?

Are the people most directly affected by the program fully involved in the process?

Do people understand enough about what is going on so that their involvement is meaningful?

Do we know each other well enough as multidimensional people to work together effectively?

Are the purposes of the project agreed upon?

Are feedback opportunities available, so that people can provide input and find out what is going on as the program progresses?

2. IS THERE A SOUND INFORMATION BASE?

Do we have the facts necessary for making our decisions so that the program is not based on mere wishful thinking?

Have the facts been adequately checked for accuracy?

Does our information base include a clear understanding of the culture?

Have we communicated this information to all levels of the culture?

In what aspects of the problem would more information be helpful?

3. ARE SYSTEMATIC STRATEGIES AND TACTICS USED?

Are we dealing with a number of variables rather than concentrating on one?

What key norm-influence areas need to receive the most attention just now?

Are we working on these key norm-influence areas in an integrated, coordinated way?

4. IS EVERYTHING CLEAR?

Have we spelled out clearly three types of objective—performance, programmatic, and cultural?

Have we checked to see that everyone concerned perceives these clearly?

Are our plans clear to all the people involved?

What are the specific tasks set up to carry out these plans?

Does each department and/or segment of the culture understand the objectives, plans, and tasks of the others?

5. ARE WE TRYING FOR WIN/WIN SOLUTIONS?

How much time do we spend on finding out who is at fault?

Have we tried to devise solutions that would benefit all parties?

Have the win/win possibilities been communicated widely?

Does my own behavior reflect the new norm?

6. ARE WE ORIENTED TOWARD RESULTS?

Are we focusing our attention on results rather than just on activities?

Are these results measurable and visible?

Is there an opportunity for immediate accomplishment to spur us on?

Can we fulfill the promises that are being made?

Are the accomplishments publicized so that the group as a whole gets information on them?

7. IS IT A CULTURE-BASED, SUSTAINED EFFORT?

Have we committed ourselves to this effort for a long period of time, or is it a single-shot crash program?

Do we have definite renewal efforts planned and scheduled into the project?

Do people at all levels of the organization understand that the change effort is an ongoing one?

Are we treating symptoms or underlying normative patterns?

Chapter 12

Knowing
Where You Are
and
Where You're Going

ANALYSIS AND OBJECTIVE SETTING

PHASE I

How does one begin a change process? The first step is analysis, and the second is setting objectives. Obvious? But too often these steps are left out. Ineffective change programs may omit this phase for any one of a variety of reasons. Being objective about situations of which we are a part is not so easy as being objective about faraway places. In some ways we know more about the aboriginal cultures of Australia and the South Sea Islands than we do about our own.

Sometimes these steps are left out purposely by unscrupulous leaders. Tyrants don't want people to examine their values or set goals. Widespread understanding of human factors is dangerous to dictators, but crucial for people who want to run their own lives.

Sometimes impatience may cause the omission. We are often so anxious to "do something" that we just jump on the current bandwagon and hope. This frequently happens in schools, where new ideas about learning and classroom management are tried without involving students (or even teachers) in either analysis or goal setting, and without trying to help them understand what the changes will mean to them. Likewise, certain misapplications of sensitivity training leave out the analysis and objective-setting stage, plunging people into highly charged experiences with little preparation and little attempt to help them understand what is happening.

Ignoring the analysis and goal-setting steps squanders time, energy, and resources. Even more devastating in the long run is the feeling of frustration that follows these failures. The "helpless-victim-of-society" attitude grows, and the next change effort is made even more difficult.

CULTURAL VIEW A NECESSITY

In any analysis, dependable information is a prerequisite to meaningful change and long-lasting results. In Normative Systems the information must include, or yield, an understanding of the culture and its impact on what is occurring—particularly an understanding of the problem area as it is related to cultural influences. A realistic analysis starts by asking questions like these: "Why is this behavior happening here?" "Is it an individual or a group behavior?" Or, more specifically, "Do the neighborhood norms support dangerous skateboarding?" "Does everybody *expect* organized crime?" "Does the culture support drunken driving?" "Do these medical norms make sick people sicker?" If the answer to questions like these is yes, the problem is cultural, and the approach to change should be cultural.

An analysis that is not culture-based is likely to treat problems as a matter of individual behavior, missing one of the key reasons for the bulk of human actions—the support of the group. This happened a few years ago during an attempt to rehabilitate delinquent boys. On the assumption that delinquency was an individual problem, the emphasis was placed on one-to-one therapy. Afterward the social scientists noticed that as soon as a supposedly "cured" boy went back to the streets, he reverted to delinquency. Since the problem lay with the street culture, not with the individual boys, the answer lay in treating the culture itself.

"UNCOMMON ANALYSIS" VERSUS "COMMON SENSE"

By an "uncommon analysis," we mean one based on profound realities rather than on what often passes for common sense—merely noting the negatives. Unfortunately, much analysis is not based on sufficient cultural data or on a real understanding of the data available. Instead, it is based on fallacious, easily held, and often repeated "commonsense" beliefs.

This type of "analysis" skims the surface, taking note of what is wrong but not looking for the underlying reasons for it.

There are programs for reducing drug addiction based on the common-sense idea that if we educate young people about drugs, addiction will stop. The actual result is that the youngsters become educated drug users. The drama and mystique of the drug culture are often enhanced in the process, and so the problem becomes more widespread and harder to combat.

With juvenile delinquency, the approach that "makes sense" on the surface is to take misbehaving youngsters away from their street gangs and into a controlled environment where they can be taught to behave in a disciplined way. What is not understood is that the principal thing they learn, both on the streets and in the controlled environment, is conformity. Put back into the delinquent street culture, they promptly adhere to its rules.

A useful analysis is not only wide but deep, plumbing beneath surfaces, taking soundings to disclose the latent reasons under manifest negative behavior. It aims for a deeper understanding of a phenomenon that originally existed only as a description or negative judgment of behavior. For example, many times organizations will come up with the observation "We have no teamwork." The reasons given will be dead-end ones—that people just don't like to work together, or that it's a competitive world and one has to be tough to survive. People tend to neglect the further observation that those who try to practice teamwork in the organization are often penalized, while those who do not are rewarded.

Another frequently observed negative is the one called a "communications breakdown." Very often, this exists simply because someone does not consider good communications to be in his or her best interest. It may be a physician who needs poor communications between patients, and between patients and staff, in order to retain his own status and economic power. It may be a union leader who believes any highly involved union member could be a threat to her position. It may be a company executive who sees personal advantage in keeping "his" people uninformed.

The people who make an analysis, therefore, need to get behind the behavior itself and ask such questions as: "What need does this behavior meet?" "What is being rewarded and modeled?" All the crucial norm influence areas come into play here to help supply the answer to "Why?"

PARTICIPATION IS IMPORTANT

The study of a culture may be conducted by either outsiders or members of the organization, and by either professional change agents or lay persons with special training and competence. The choice of the most appropriate persons for a specific cultural analysis will depend upon such factors as budget, project size, time, and availability. A combination of internal and external personnel is usually desirable. The insiders can provide necessary peer insights, and the outsiders can provide greater objectivity and a freedom from cultural myopia.

Wherever circumstances make it possible, analysis is made with the participation of the people who are part of the culture to be changed, and who will take part in the problem-solving effort. It is particularly useful for people to analyze themselves because this gives an added impetus to the change process. When people take an objective look at themselves, the feeling of "ownership" of the change process develops early, and the analysis step sets a solid base for meaningful involvement later on.

The positive results of youngsters' participation in analysis were evident in a youth center in a depressed factory area. Formerly, individuals who disrupted a gathering were banished from the center for about a week. They usually did not return, but got into worse trouble outside. In reviewing the rules, the youngsters decided that most disruptions were caused by temporary hot-headedness, and that a brief cooling period was all that was necessary. Now, if someone disrupts a meeting, the leader will say, "OK, John, let's take five." And most of the time, five minutes is all it takes—and the boy returns to take part in the group activity.

ALWAYS A SYSTEMATIC REVIEW

Piecemeal analysis usually results in piecemeal solutions. When we look at only one portion of the problem, we are likely to come up with simplistic solutions which have little chance of long-term success.

Any social problem is influenced by hundreds and even thousands of variables. As a result, analysis often appears to be an insurmountable task. However, it has been our experience that social problems can be approached and analyzed as systematically and thoroughly as those of the natural sciences. It is not necessary to deal directly with all the variables: key pressure points can be selected for in-depth analysis. Every culture has certain key influence areas that have a major impact on that culture. These seven have proved to be particularly instrumental:

1. Rewards

2. Modeling behavior

3. Information and communications systems

4. Interactions and relationships

5. Training

6. Orientation

7. Allocation of resources

Sound familiar? They are; they were discussed in Part 2 in terms of their negative effects on unplanned programs. Here, though, they reveal their usefulness in positive, planned programs for achieving freely chosen goals.

In addition to these seven influence areas, there may be others in any given project that the group feels it is essential to examine. The first step of the process provides this opportunity. (See Appendix A for an extended list of influence areas that can be considered in making an analysis.)

Selecting key pressure points might seem to be a job for the experts, but experience has shown that the people affected are capable of doing this themselves. After the use of basic questions and checkpoints, examination of data without preconceived notions, and open discussion of problems by the group, the key pressure points usually become quite obvious.

The Analysis of Rewards

As we have seen, people do the things that they believe will get them what they want, whether it be status, money, recognition, or personal satisfaction. This is the basis of "operant conditioning" and behavior modification. While the Normative Systems approach rejects the manipulatory aspects of some forms of behaviorism, it does recognize the basic value of the idea of reinforcement by reward. Cultural support itself is a reward that reinforces a behavior.

At the outset of a cultural change program, both positive and negative reward and reinforcement systems are reviewed. Such things as commendations, bonuses, compensation systems, and public praise are noted, as well as discharges, rebukes, and other disciplinary practices. It is also important to recognize that people may be ignored or even punished for behavior that contributes to the achievement of organizational goals, either because the behavior is not noticed or understood or because the goals of the organization are obscure.

Effective change programs will support positive behavior consistently and constructively and confront negative behavior, so that desirable norms will be strengthened and undesirable ones will be weakened or eliminated. It follows that a good hard look at actual practices in the confrontation of negative norms is important to the analysis. What is confronted in a culture, and how, can have an important impact. Often the strength of a norm can be determined by the willingness of the people within the culture to confront a violation of that norm. For example, wearing clothes is a strong norm, and 99 percent of the time that clothes are *not* worn in public, the behavior is confronted.

Formal systems of rewards and confrontation are exceedingly important, but so are informal rewards and confrontation systems. Penalty systems are sometimes not obvious. For example, the penalty for putting out garbage for pickup in the ghetto may very well be a blow on the head as the person walks down a darkened hallway or staircase. Hardly anyone would send his 12-year-old child to put the trash out if it is going to endanger his life. "Air mailing" it out a window is safer. (And since others are also "air mailing" trash, why not?)

Conversely, what seems like a punishment may be a reward. The Collegefields study (see Chapter 18) showed that the authorities thought they were penalizing the boys when they sent them to court. To the boys, however, it was an exciting event—their "day in the sunshine"—i.e., a rewarding experience.

What actually constitutes support? Abraham Maslow's hierarchy of human needs indicates that once the basics of food, shelter, etc., are met, human beings want safety and security, then a sense of belonging and love. When those needs are satisfied, they want self-esteem and self-respect. Finally, they want self-actualization—that is, a fulfillment of their potential.[1] The most appropriate reward depends upon where the individual is in this hierarchy. When a person's needs have been met on one level, additional rewards on that level are unlikely to be useful. (As you rise from a feast, the prospect of an additional dinner just then is not likely to be very motivating.) Much of our effort to humanize technology and to make our institutions viable rests upon rewarding the *real* desires that underlie human behavior.

An analysis of the rewards system might raise questions like these:

What behavior is supported by recognition and prestige?

What are people rewarded for?

What behavior is confronted? Ignored?

Are there hidden penalties for a given type of behavior that need to be taken into account?

Are people noticed and rewarded when things are going right or only noticed when they do things wrong? (Do we parents spend most of the time scolding? Do we teachers emphasize corrections and mark only what is wrong on a paper? Do we supervisors notice employees only when something is not done right?)

What kind of results get a payoff around here?

Is it who you are or what you are that really counts?

Are we overlooking opportunities for rewards?

[1] Maslow, "A Theory of Human Motivation," in Richard J. Lowry (ed.), *Dominance, Self Esteem, Self Actualization: Germinal Papers of A. H. Maslow* (Belmont, Calif.: Wadsworth, 1973), pp. 154–165.

Modeling Behavior

To analyze modeling behavior we need to look at all levels of the organization or community and determine whether people demonstrate the behavior they seek. In hierarchical groups—businesses, schools, communities, and even families—the top leaders are pacesetters, and therefore their behavior needs to be examined first. It does little good to tell children "Smoking is bad for you" if one of the parents smokes, or that "Reading is great!" if the parents never crack a book.

We saw this disparity in a hospital. Nurses and attendants were resentful of the orders to wear masks and gloves in the rooms of patients who were in "germ-free" isolation—not because they didn't want to help the patients, but because the doctors who ordered the gloves and masks did not wear them themselves. When the doctors were made aware of the effect of their own modeling behavior, they changed and the resentment vanished.

It is important to be aware not only of our negative behavior but of how our positive behavior may be misconstrued. A store manager once took a package of cigarettes from the stand, intending to pay for them. Just then he was called to the back of the store, and although he paid for them later, the modeling influence on employees was established, and "free" cigarettes became an inadvertent fringe benefit.

The mass media constitute another frequently overlooked source of unsuspected modeling that may be affecting behavior we are trying to change.

Some questions that might be asked in an analysis of modeling behavior are:

> In view of the goals we have set, what kind of behavior can we model that will be in keeping with the way we want things to be?
>
> What kind of behavior is currently being modeled?
>
> Are we modeling what we are asking of people in the organization, community, or group?
>
> Which people are likely to have the greatest influence, and what model is their behavior presenting?
>
> What are the key reference groups to whom we look as sources of information about the most effective ways to behave?
>
> Are there ways our program can involve these groups in the modeling process?
>
> Are there ways in which our behavior might be misconstrued by others?
>
> Are the mass media modeling behavior that influences the success of our change effort? If so, is there something we can do to offset or correct the effect?

What Is Communicated?

In analyzing and setting objectives for change projects, it is essential that the existing communication and information systems be carefully reviewed. The information communicated within an organization—regarding old norms and new, the results of new behavior, the change process itself, and the group's objectives—has an important impact on what is occurring there.

In an elementary school, analysis showed that though teachers were eager to foster good human relations, the information flow chiefly concerned grades and individual accomplishment. The students were given no information on how well they were doing in helping one another. In a retail chain store, the information on profits tended to stop at the store manager level. As a result, there was little interest in or recognition of the importance of profitability below that level.

The way information is communicated also has an impact on the culture. In successful change programs there is information flow on high-priority items, and people recognize the importance of two-way communications. They communicate clearly, making sure their messages are understood; they listen carefully to one another; and they actively seek out ideas and opinions.

Questions to ask in analyzing information and communications systems include:

What kinds of things are reported regularly and in detail?

In what area is there the most information flow? The least?

Who gets the information provided by our organization? Who does not?

Will anyone ever know when something happens to improve the situation? How?

How will the results be presented? Will they be noticed?

Is it a norm for people, including the leadership, to freely communicate with members of the group at all levels?

Do people sometimes hold back information from others in order to maintain their own positions?

Is it a norm for people to be "politic" or "diplomatic" in information sharing rather than to communicate and share information openly?

Do mixed messages sometimes cause confusion?

Do people seem to need more information than they have in order to do a good job?

Is it the norm for people to practice two-way communication or do we have a lot of one-way communication?

Is it the norm for people to seek out the ideas and opinions of others?

Are we emphasizing the things we need to emphasize in our information and communications systems?

Interactions and Relationships

The interactions and relationships between people in a group, organization, or community setting have an important bearing on the planning of change programs. Where positive interactions and relationships are limited, there may be serious blocks to problem solution and cultural improvement.

Often people have inadequate interaction and relationships with others who could be contributing to the normative objectives of the change program. Thus students and professors frequently have little contact with one another although a goal of the college may be to enhance the students' abilities in research and scholarly dialogue. Parents are constantly telling children what to do, how to do it, when, and sometimes why, although a family goal is to teach responsibility and self-discipline.

Differences in time viewpoints sometimes have an important effect on interactions. Young people view time differently than adults. The company cleaning crew may view twenty-four hours as an interminable time between the discussion and the execution of an idea, while the management group may consider two or three weeks too short.

Physical space and physical facilities also have an important impact on people's interactions and relationships. Sometimes desks in an office are placed facing each other; then people talk and don't get their work done. Sometimes the desks are too far apart, so that people feel isolated and don't relate well. College departments are usually housed separately and have little contact with each other, making it necessary to devise special interdepartmental programs.

Additional insights into interactions and relationships may grow out of the analysis of such things as role definitions, ideology, power patterns, or social stratifications.

In analyzing this norm influence area, questions like these might be asked:

What opportunities do we have for interacting with one another?

What opportunities do we need if we are to have a positive impact on one another?

Are there things we can do to improve the effectiveness of our relationship patterns and change those that are working counter to our objectives?

Does an "open door" policy exist so that all members of the group or organization can be in contact with the leadership when they find it necessary?

Are there opportunities for people at all levels to initiate behavior?

Are suggestions for change made in an objective, nonjudgmental way, or is there a lot of blame placing and negative "parenting"?

What could we do to improve interaction and relationship patterns which could contribute to our change objectives?

In a school: Do members of the administration listen to the teachers and the students—and to each other?

In a family: How much time is given to conversation *not* concerned with instructions and chores?

In a business? Do people feel a "we" relationship between themselves, the management, and the company, rather than an "us-them" relationship?

The Training System

It is obvious that training is needed when a new piece of machinery is added, a new career is chosen, or a new class is to be taught. What is not obvious, however, is that when things go wrong in the realm of human interaction, they may not go right until people learn how to deal with them effectively.

An analysis of what training people do and do not receive can often help in the planning of a change program. A large accounting firm spent millions of dollars annually on technical (accounting) training and only a few thousand on supervisory training. A review of supervisory norms revealed that the supervisors were excellent accountants themselves but could not supervise the work of others. Greater emphasis on supervisory development was clearly in order.

In a family it may not be quite so obvious that training and development are important, but their absence may prevent the family from being the kind of group it wants to be. In analyzing its norms, one family found that it needed more skills in human interrelationships. There was constant bickering, blame placing, and defensiveness. The daughter, a college student, offered to help them learn the skills of TA, which she had studied in her psychology course, and the family found that learning this skill helped them to change the factors that were causing problems.

Perhaps an even more important concept in this influence area is the need for cultural support of the training that takes place, and ongoing cultural support for the new skills that have been acquired.

Since this is often a hidden and neglected influence area that blocks people from reaching their goals, it is important that the analysis uncover it with some penetrating questions and observations. As examples:

Are the training programs we now have working?

Are they being supported by the culture?

Is there a particular kind of training that would help us meet our goals?

What skills are lacking?

In college: How often are colloquiums on new teaching techniques held? Is the faculty really given opportunities for further training?

In a business: Do employees receive the training they require, and is this training the responsibility of each manager and supervisor?

In a medical school: Are doctors trained to teach patients preventive medicine? Is there a course in life-styles or stress or preventive medicine?

Orientation

Understanding the process by which people are oriented to the norms of the culture is crucial to planning an effective change program. When the formal and informal orientation system can be brought to bear on the goals of the change program, a great deal can be accomplished.

When this does not happen, the informal and unidentified orientation process can signal contrary norms to new organizational members. In a pharmaceutical company, for example, analysis revealed that new employees were being oriented to negative work norms by having to spend a great deal of time waiting around during their first two weeks in the company. By the time they began work, the "high-productivity" norms that had been mentioned in the formal orientation sessions had become something to talk about rather than something to achieve. Similarly, in a retail store, new employees were found to be oriented to negative norms during coffee breaks, during gripe sessions over lunch, and in behind-the-counter asides. Norms of blame placing, pilferage, and "get the best of the customer" were being perpetuated.

Setting up an effective orientation program also provides a mechanism for seeing that new organizational members have a chance to contribute to the organization's cultural input. Often, the change process itself can be introduced during the orientation, and the ideas of new members can be solicited. This provides the direct benefit of inviting new people to help in the change process and generates new ideas as well.

Characteristic questions that can contribute to analysis of the orientation process include:

Are the orientation approaches that we are using helping new organizational members become part of the change process?

Are the right things being communicated by the orientation process?

Are the formal and informal orientation processes linked with one another?

Are the people most in contact with new members those who exhibit the positive behavioral norms, attitudes, and work habits?

Are new people left to sink or swim in learning what goes on in the culture?

Since the time when a person enters a new culture is one of the most teachable moments, is sufficient emphasis given to the orientation process?

Allocation of Resources

Whatever the problem, an analysis of the resources devoted to solving it is helpful. We say we want changes, but unless we allow time and allocate financial and personnel resources for them, there is little chance that we will achieve them.

A few years ago, the Human Resources Institute analyzed sanitation in a supermarket. The problem was an important one that affected the health of customers as well as the shelf life of the products. Everybody in the supermarket chain talked about sanitation, and if you listened to the discussions alone, you would think it was the most important thing in the supermarket world. But analysis revealed that there was really no commitment to sanitation. None of the workers had schedules that allowed time for cleaning the machinery in meat departments or for cleaning out cases. It all had to be done during the workers' "free time," which was nonexistent.

Lip service and actual commitment to a project or change can be distinguished by looking closely at the money, time, and work force actually allotted for it. Analysis in this area has a double payoff: (1) we find what our true commitments are so that we can change them if we wish; and (2) we find out whether we are really backing our change effort with adequate resources.

Here are some typical questions to ask:

What are we spending our money on?

What is the budget?

How much time do we spend on the things we value the most?

How much time is allowed for this project or activity?

In a business: Are employees given time during working hours to do this?

Is attention paid to utilizing people's best talents?

In a school: Are children really given the time and resources to develop creatively? How much time? When? What material aids do they have?

In a family: If the family wants "togetherness," is it putting aside time in which to do things together?

DEALING WITH THESE INFLUENCES

Obviously, these norm influence areas do not have the same relative significance in every setting. Some may be more important than others, depending on the situation. In one group, the rewards system may be exceedingly important; in another, the allotment of resources may be crucial. If all the areas are examined, however, the chances are that none of the key influences at work in a given situation will be overlooked.

Although it is not necessary to bring about changes in all influence areas simultaneously, it is advisable to make sure that those most important in a particular project are accounted for early in the analysis and objective setting. This will help us find the key to what the group really supports, accepts, and expects of its members, and begin to reveal why certain strong norms persist.

As we pointed out earlier, many of the influence areas overlap. We have separated them here because focusing on them one by one in a systematic effort is usually helpful in planning an effective change program.

SOME FURTHER AREAS FOR ANALYSIS

The preceding list of seven crucial areas is, of course, not exhaustive. There may very well be other influence areas that should be considered. These include those related to the change principles that were presented in Chapter 11 and those related to the special goals of the particular change program. Among the change principles, the norms of involvement and noninvolvement, results orientation or lack of it, and constructive problem solving or blame placing are often highly important.

The typical methods used by a group of people to handle change need to be brought into the open. One revealing question is: "What is the process for making a change?" The predisposition might be to say: "We do this every year whether we want to or not—here we go again!" So the attitude is one of "this too shall pass," and there is little receptivity to change. In some organizations so many experts examine the problems and write reports, with the final result a mere shifting of the hierarchy, that the employees are continually expecting to lose their jobs.

Regardless of the influences selected, the primary characteristic of a useful analysis is that it is culturally oriented in a systematic way. If it has looked beyond individuals and determined what the social influences are, and has dug beneath the manifest goals to determine the underlying forces at work, then there is a good chance that it will provide an effective informational background for the other phases of the change process.

SETTING OBJECTIVES

Clarifying and setting objectives actually starts along with the analysis of the culture, for as behavior is examined, goal setting begins. From the first discussions it will be evident that some norms are detrimental, others helpful. However, the major focus at first is not on judging, but on merely observing and recording the behavior that is occurring, and attempting to discover the "why" behind it.

Once this is accomplished through a systematic review of the crucial influence areas, we can ask: "What do we really want around here?" (Not yet, "How will we get it?" That will come later.) Sometimes it is difficult for people to respond positively to this. Some, blocked by their own cultural blinders, will tend to be cynical and ask, "What's the use of dreaming? That never will be possible." But it is essential that we conjure up the vision of the kind of an environment we want. Only then can we measure the gaps between what is and what could be. Only then can the objectives of the group be set.

There are a number of ways of conjuring up that vision. Sometimes it can be done merely by focusing on what we really want, with no holds barred. Sometimes project teams have developed tape-slide shows picturing what the culture would be like if the desired changes were made. Writing a scenario about the future is a creative technique that can be used by either a group or an individual. People simply put down just what they want the culture to be in the near or distant future. At this stage, it is important to focus on what is desired, rather than on what is thought possible. Later the answers can be used to explore the extent of the normative gap.

An interesting variation is to invite group members to pictorially illustrate their "dreams" regarding the desired culture. Sometimes such visualizations help people break through the language barriers that separate them.

Like analysis, preliminary objective setting may be accomplished with the assistance of outsiders, but those most directly affected should always be involved. If it is not participatory in its initial stage, then it must be reviewed by the group members and modified by them in the opening workshops. It is essential that members of a culture understand and identify their own objectives before trying to bring about change.

Involvement of people in setting objectives helps to ensure that the program or project is keyed to a shared purpose. It is exceedingly important that all levels of an institution or an organization—all the people who will be affected by the changes envisioned—help in setting the goals. Very often the changes an organization thinks it wants are drastically modified after the data gathering is completed.

In a business, preliminary goal setting and action planning often require the development of performance standards and objectives for both management groups and work teams. The purpose is to assess areas where change is needed, to establish priorities for change, to set specific, measurable goals in each change area, and to tailor Normative Systems to the needs and development of each group or department.

The objectives of the project must be clearly stated initially, for they become the basis for future action. Failure to clarify objectives during the first phase often results in later problems of implementation, achievement, and evaluation. One helpful way of establishing objectives is to ask what project achievements would satisfy the group within a specific period. The more measurable the objectives are, the more they can contribute to the project plans and evaluations.

Three levels of objectives are set:

Level I   Performance objectives (highly measurable data)

Level II   Programmatic objectives (installation of systems and programs)

Level III Cultural objectives (setting of positive cultural norms)

The first level covers improvement of operating results, such as (in a business) increased productivity or increased sales.

Level II involves installation and/or updating of certain significant subsystems and programs. It may be, for instance, a revised program or a new compensation system.

Level III involves modifying norms that are affecting organizational achievement: Which norm influence areas are most crucial? Which of the norms need to be reduced? Strengthened?

Excerpts from the objectives of some projects show how the three types are distinguished:

A HEALTH PROGRAM

Level I   To increase the life expectancy of people in the organization by helping them decrease smoking, lower alcohol consumption, and reduce weight

Level II   To install or make available certain systems and programs that will make the organization more effective in achieving its overall objectives and the objectives of the project

Level III   To modify the cultural norms that negatively influence individual health practices

A PUBLIC CLASSROOM

Level I   To improve student reading skills and to raise the average reading level of the class

Level II   To install systems and programs that encourage progress toward the above objectives

Level III   To modify the cultural norms (both within the classroom and within the students' family and community environments) that influence motivation and the acquisition of reading skills

A CORPORATION DEPARTMENT

Level I   To increase the productivity of the department without impairing product quality

Level II   To install improved systems of orientation, skill training, and supervisory development

Level III   To modify the norms within the department, particularly those affecting teamwork and open communication

MEASUREMENT OF OBJECTIVES

To the greatest possible extent, specific measurements are set up for evaluating project achievement growing out of the three-level objectives. When the measurements are clearly understood, the project has a better chance of staying on target and of correcting any deficiencies that may develop. Each type of objective has its own unique measurements:

Level I objectives   Quantifiable data

Level II objectives   Action tracking

Level III objectives   Cultural norm indicators, organizational perception inventories, and field observations

Short-range as well as medium- and long-range goals are needed. Since the achievement of measurable results is a powerful incentive, short-range goals and quick victories can be tremendously encouraging. Long-range goals are necessary for sustained cultural improvement, of course.

Here are two illustrations of the kind of measurements that were employed in actual normative system improvement programs.

In a supermarket company these measurements were used:

Level I   Quantifiable data: Shrink will be reduced by 2 percent in nine months and to less than 1.5 percent in eighteen months.

Level II   Action tracking: Within one year every employee will be involved in an effective shrink control program. Within one year every department and store manager will be rewarded for effective shrink control.

Level III   Cultural Norm Indicators: Individual groups and departments will measure their modification of crucial norm influence areas, using norm profiles.

In a warehouse distribution center these measurements were applied:

Level I   Quantifiable data: Productivity will increase from 117 pieces per hour to 150 pieces per hour.

Level II   Action tracking: Work team meetings will be held regularly by each of the work groups: a regular communications bulletin will be launched, and all supervisors will take part in a leadership training program.

Level III   Cultural Norm Indicators: Within one year, the gap between existing and desired norms will be reduced, particularly as they affect productivity and positive interrelationships between workers and management. An organizational perceptions inventory will show a positive response to the installation of the leadership program.

AS PHASE I ENDS

At this point in the process, people are aware of both what is and what could be. If the analysis has been well conducted, they are now operating from a sound information base and the organizational change program can proceed. If organizational members have had an opportunity to be involved in the process, the basis for organized teamwork has been developed. If tentative short- and long-range objectives have been set, the groundwork has been laid for an effective measurement process.

If, on the other hand, there is more to be done, it is important that the task be completed either before or in conjunction with the subsequent phases. Proceeding without the proper foundation of a Phase I analysis is *likely* to be disastrous.

Through the Phase I process, the group actually begins to get a better grasp of the realities of its culture. While it does not rush in to change things helter-skelter, it does have the motivating force of a model of what it wants its future behavior to be. There is usually a surge of hope in the group at this point, as it realizes that the normative systems approach may lead to some meaningful changes—changes the participants had not thought possible.

Chapter 13

Instruments for Understanding Cultures and Planning Change

I have made a ceaseless effort not to ridicule, not to bewail, nor to scorn human actions, but to understand them.

SPINOZA

The total concept of systematic, participatory culture change requires instruments and techniques that can make it possible for people to examine and deal with the environments of which they are part. The instruments range from interview protocols to observation schedules and from brief questionnaires to comprehensive survey instruments.

A Normative Systems project usually starts with interviews, in which individuals talk about the organization and its problems. From there it moves on to observations of specific groups. Then a quantifiable questionnaire is used to survey the organization. These and other data-gathering instruments yield material that can be used in the construction and use of the primary instrument, the *cultural norm indicator*.

The main concern is to find the best combination of instruments suitable for the particular project. Different projects require a different series of instruments, though the basic methodology is similar. However, a norm indicator is usually the backbone of the analysis and objectives-setting phase.

NORM INSTRUMENTS

Some norm instruments useful in analysis and goal setting are described below. These can be used in the analysis and objective-setting phase, and often are part of the Phase II workshops as well. Still later, they can be used for evaluation and renewal.

The cultural norm indicator is a survey instrument that helps people

147

identify current norms in key influence areas. The statements in a cultural norm indicator define behavioral situations which help to expose key norms. People are asked to indicate their agreement (strongly agree, agree, do not know, disagree, or strongly disagree) with such statements as these:

As I see it, it is a norm around here for people:

to feel enthusiastic about what they are doing

to get regular, constructive feedback on how they are doing

to blame other people for their own mistakes

to feel they can succeed only at the expense of other people

to have a clear way of measuring results

(A complete cultural norm indicator for families and one for organizations can be found in Appendix B and Appendix C.)

If a project is undertaken for which a norm indicator does not exist, one can be developed as part of the data collection process. The form of existing indicators can be followed, though the groupings and norm items will vary according to the category. Thus, if a tennis team wanted to analyze itself as a culture, it could make up a special indicator appropriate to its needs.

A supermarket concerned with high personnel turnover, poor work attitudes, and excessive shrinkage developed items for a norm indicator that covered such critical matters as organizational pride, customer relations, honesty, security, performance, planning, involvement, profitability, cleanliness, supervision, results orientation, and communications. Norms in all these areas were put into the indicator and used throughout the store to analyze the situation and set objectives. The validation of items in a cultural norm indicator is accomplished by comparing the responses received from successful organizations with those from the less successful. A cultural norm indicator, when properly designed, can be used in any size or type of group and throughout all levels of an organization.

The Norm Profile

By combining into a total response pattern each individual's response to a norm indicator, it is possible to evolve a *norm profile* which graphically shows what the organization or group is like. The difference between the group's realities and its desires can be visually depicted.

In Figure 13-1 we have the norm profile of a family; and in Figure 13-2, two profiles from industry contrasting a less successful and a more successful organization.

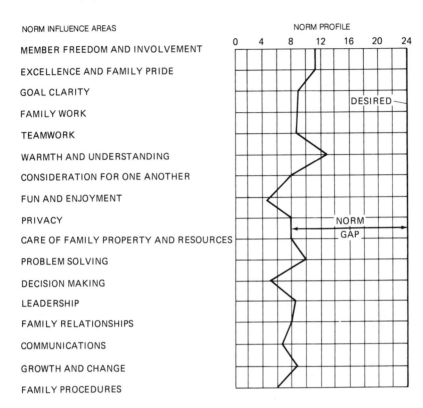

FIGURE 13-1   Norm profile of a family. As a result of discussions about their norm profile, this family decided it needed to work on a number of different areas. Together they worked out some short- and long-range objectives that would help them bridge the gap between the kind of culture they had and the kind they really wanted.

ADDITIONAL DATA COLLECTION INSTRUMENTS AND TECHNIQUES

Although a cultural norm indicator is the basic tool used in most normative systems change projects, there are a number of others.

The organizational support indicator asks people to indicate the level of support that they perceive within the organization for particular behavior. The basic question is, "How well is our organization doing in providing positive, constructive, and consistent support for the following behavior and organizational goals?" Respondents are asked to indicate on a five-point scale whether the organization is doing very poorly, poorly, fairly well, well, or very well in supporting the behavior.

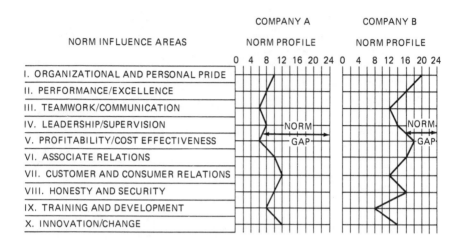

FIGURE 13-2 Norm profiles for two businesses. We can contrast the low profile of Company A with the much better profile of Company B. Company A has severe profit problems, and the primary causes, as implied by the cultural norm indicator, lie in supervision and teamwork functions. While Company B is doing well, there is obviously still a good deal of room for improvement, particularly in the areas of training and development.

The reference group indicator identifies the various reference groups that are used by individuals and groups to determine the acceptability or unacceptability of behavior. Since there is such a large number of potential reference groups on any given subject, this instrument can help to identify the most important to take into account. The questions are usually asked in reference to specific organizational concerns, such as "Who in the group would be most listened to on the subject of X?" As the reference groups in a particular culture tend to be consistent over a period of time, the results of this indicator can be valuable in planning change.

The cultural values inventory is used to help isolate an organization or group's values. Sometimes there is an interesting and important discrepancy between the cumulative score of the individuals in a group and their perception of the culture's values. For example, in a white neighborhood, 90 percent of the people may say they would not mind having a black neighbor; yet each person believes that the neighbors would object.

The emphasis here is not on telling people what values they should have, but on helping them discover what their values and the values of the culture *are*. People usually discover that they have more alternatives than they had realized.

The normative description inventory (NDI) is used to help determine targets for change efforts. It consists of a series of negative and positive norms listed in specific categories. Respondents are asked to indicate both the desirability of the norm and the extent to which it is or is not a norm in the group or organization in question. Use of the NDI is a way of getting people to look more closely at key norm influence areas. The norms themselves are usually highly descriptive and are frequently written in the language patterns of the organizational members.

The normative support and confrontation inventory helps to determine the pattern of support and confrontation that exists within an organization. It is designed to reveal people's ability to confront constructively those norms that they consider negative and to support the others. It also identifies which norms are most likely to be supported and which confronted. In one version respondents are asked to indicate what they think most other employees would do in each situation when confronted with a specific behavior. That is, would they openly encourage the behavior, approve of it and say nothing, not care one way or other, disagree but do nothing to discourage it, or disagree and openly discourage it? One gets more candid responses by asking what employees would do, rather than what the individuals themselves would do.

The organizational perception inventory (OPI) is designed to uncover people's perceptions of how the organization is functioning in key cultural areas. It provides a measure of how people feel about the organization and about the various organizational programs and activities. The number of items included will vary according to the purpose for which it is administered, but a basic OPI has been developed which can be tailored to specific organizational needs.

The role classification instrument is an aid in analyzing the role expectations of the culture and in helping individuals and groups to see the roles or the conflicting roles in which they have placed themselves.

This instrument helps people to see and understand that the expectations of the culture cause people to define themselves in certain ways. Role expectations are analyzed through a series of unfinished statements, such as, "A parent should . . ." or "A student should. . . ." The respondent finishes the statement, and the results are compared, combined, and discussed.

The role expectations of the culture may stand in the way of meaningful change unless they are exposed, so that they can be either modified or used as positive forces in the achievement of the desired culture.

Interviews can be formal or informal, individual or group. They provide us with insights needed to understand the organization and the cultural influences at work within it. There are a number of different types of interviews:

> *General exploration interviews,* conducted with a cross-section of organizational members, provide an overview of general organizational concerns from which more specific interview possibilities can be developed.

Focused-theme depth interviews are conducted with selected individuals from various organizational levels to explore specific concerns in depth. The questions may be designed to provide information about the perceived effectiveness of a specific organizational program, and the recommendations people offer for its improvement, for example.

Exit interviews with people leaving the organization can often be helpful in providing access to individual perceptions.

Group interview discussion sessions can provide input that is hard to generate in individual interviews. The dynamics of the group often spark people to respond more incisively.

Highlight tapes are another possibility. Interviews can be tape-recorded with the consent of the participants and the tapes used to spark further discussion. Dramatic impact sometimes results from editing and combining the tapes of a number of interviews, keeping material that has been repeated independently by several people and therefore represents a more generally held perception.

Observation techniques range from casual, informal observation to highly structured studies. Those most commonly used are:

Unstructured field observations, which are especially useful in the beginning of an analysis. Much can be learned about the organization by just being observant and open-minded, getting the feel of the environment. These observations can later be checked more systematically to ensure their validity and reliability.

Focused field observations are actually constructions of a situation in order to observe people's responses. For example, in a litter reduction project, a staff member littered in front of a policeman to see whether he would confront the behavior. (He did not.) In a campground, a site was left heavily littered by a group of "picnickers" who had been instructed to do so. Observers then talked to the people in adjoining sites about their reasons for not confronting the litterers.

Participant observation involves having the analyst assume a participatory role in the organization as though he (or she) were a member of the culture being analyzed. Sometimes the observer participates incognito, but usually his identity is made known to members of the culture to prevent them from feeling that they are being tricked or spied upon. In either case, his presence as a participant rather than as a mere observer usually makes it possible for him to obtain normative information that would otherwise not be so readily available.

OTHER POSSIBILITIES

The techniques described above have proved useful in a number of Normative Systems projects, but other techniques can be used or created as the need arises. As examples:

A look at book usage records in a library can be much more revealing than looking at the cards in the library catalog.

Furniture and its arrangement can be indicative in offices as well as in living rooms. Is it hard or soft? Imposing or inviting?

The wear and tear of a rug in front of pictures in a museum can tell more about the popularity of certain paintings than a survey.

Pictures and tape recordings can be extremely revealing about what is important in a culture. Moreover, presentations of this material provide opportunities for gathering further information. Discussions about norm influences can take place while the observations are being made and recorded, while the presentation is being assembled, and during meetings where the results are shown.

There is an almost unlimited number of data collection possibilities. The more people can be involved in the development and use of the instruments, the more likely the project is to be successful.

Chapter 14

Introducing
Change

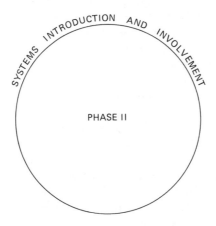

SYSTEMS INTRODUCTION AND INVOLVEMENT

PHASE II

As part of Phase II, all the people most directly affected by the change program have an opportunity to try out the kind of culture they desire. New norms are best introduced in an intense way—and for this a workshop type of setting is frequently helpful.

People are often reluctant to try new norms in a familiar setting, where the old norms are still at work. People sometimes need an occasion—a happening—to free them from traditional behavior. A Normative Systems workshop—in which they can begin to create new ways of working together—is such an event. These are highly charged sessions in which people are introduced to new normative alternatives in a somewhat intense way under the guidance of a specially trained person. At the same time the workshops create environments of active cooperation in which change can take place. As they begin to experience elements of the kind of culture they are trying to create, people develop a belief that modifying the culture is possible. In large organizations the workshops usually begin at the top, then continue downward through all levels. Usually people participate as members of functioning work teams, and the workshops range from one to five days in duration. Here is a description of an actual workshop, one of a series of employees of a division in a large company. Only the names are fictitious.

NOTES FROM A NORMATIVE SYSTEMS WORKSHOP

It is 8 A.M. Two circles of chairs are set up around movable tables. There are five informal, handwritten charts on the wall plus a flip chart, ready for use. Jim and Michael, the "trainers," are putting an agenda at each place. People begin to filter in, picking up coffee at a table near the entrance. There is a slightly discernible apprehension. One of the secretaries expresses her misgivings over coffee. "Last year I went to a two-day workshop on women's awareness, run by somebody else," she says. "I got all psyched up, but when I got back to the office, my boss said, 'O.K., let's get back to work.' I had a feeling his conscience was salved and that was all."

The consultants begin the program by introducing a top executive of the company, who tells the group that they are part of an ongoing organizational effort and that the company is committed to the Normative Systems approach. He talks of his own participation and encourages theirs. The men and women in the room are attentive—this is the "big boss."

The executive leaves with a promise to look in on the meeting later. Then Jim and Michael take turns in giving a brief overview of the normative change process. Michael shows them a model—four circles representing, respectively, analysis and objective setting, introduction, implementation, and renewal. He tells the members that task forces have been organized in the eight areas listed on a chart (such as "internal communications," "effective relationship with external division," and "rewards and recognition"). Today's participants are invited to join any of the task forces or to suggest additional ones.

Michael talks about culture and norms. This group, he says, is a culture with norms of its own. Today it will be working on the first of the three steps—understanding, identifying, and changing the norms of the organization. Members of the group are attentive but skeptical. One almost sees the thought written on their faces: "It sounds good, but maybe it's just talk." Michael quickly shifts into a discussion that involves them.

"How many of you wear your hair longer this year than you did five years ago?" he asks. Most hands go up. There is one rebel: "I wear my hair this length because I like it," he says, "not because anyone else does." Michael assures him, "There are some people who do, but many people wear it longer because it's the norm." The belligerent, not getting the argument he expected, is silent.

Michael continues: "Norms can be a matter of life and death." He talks about My Lai and Nazi Germany, and the rebel challenges him again: "It's genetic. Take people like the guys at My Lai—they've got a screw loose; that's what. I won't buy this norm thing." Again, Michael does not rise to the bait: "It is true some people have genetic defects," he says. "However, it is also true that these men were like most of us here." Again he undercuts the rising argument, but makes clear his point about culture influences.

"Try an experiment at home," Michael suggests. "Try sitting at a different place at the table and see what happens." He warns that norms are not individual habits, but behavior supported by the group.

Jim asks the people to work in two groups for a few minutes to come up with some examples of norms. Each group is asked to choose a secretary. The one woman in one of the groups is immediately chosen—and refuses the job. When the two secretaries report to the full group, they tell of such remarks as: "I cook the steaks on the barbecue; my wife does the indoor cooking—it's the norm."

After a lively discussion of norms at home, in the office, in the bar, and so on, there is a coffee and juice break. The participants seem glad. They are not bored, but they aren't buying this yet. The remarks still express skepticism: "All that work I could be doing back in the office!" "Do you think it will do any good?" "Well, at least it's a day away from work." There are some gripes about job situations.

Returning to their tables, the participants take an individual test on norms and discuss their answers. The purpose is to see that people understand the concepts and to help them realize that the group working effectively together can be better than individuals working alone. Surprisingly, the test is not nearly so easy as it first seemed, and only one person in the room has all the *true and false* answers right. They argue about one of them: "Adolescent groups are much more susceptible to norm influence than are adult groups." (False). Michael explains that because adolescents are in a period of their lives when they change a lot of norms, they may seem more influenced, but actually others of all ages are no less influenced.

In discussing one of the answers, Jim explains the important relationship between people and productivity norms within an organization and suggests that a cultural change program in a business organization is probably going to have to deal with both issues simultaneously if it is going to be effective.

The consultants keep everybody with them as far as the process is concerned, maintaining a sense of openness about the program. A tape developed from the analysis interviews is played—company people talking frankly and critically about their work environment. Jim tells the group that the tape is not just a record of facts, but a record of people's perceptions of the facts; that it is not isolated opinion, but that each voice represents many others that spoke of similar concerns. After the tape, there is a feeling of excitement in the room, for the tape has been openly critical of the organization. "The top execs ought to hear that," someone says. "They have," Michael answers. There is a murmur around the room. For the first time, there are signs that the initial skepticism is being eroded.

The afternoon session starts, the combined group questions the consultants: "How successful are you with your normative program?" Jim answers frankly: "Maybe 65 to 70 percent in the last five years, 75 to 80 percent in the last two—we're improving." He explains that success is hard to measure because the process is ongoing and becomes internalized in a company. He reemphasizes the importance of understanding norms and gives out a pamphlet in which a number of employees have written pluses and negatives about the organizational environment. He gives the participants time to read and digest it, and then asks them to take it home to edit. In a week the edited versions—with ideas added—will go to a task force. "It's your document; it's a working document," he says. "We want your input." There is immediate interest, and some work is done on the spot.

Jim asks the participants, "How would you describe your work environment?" For answers, he gets, "I think it's a good atmosphere," followed by, "Hell, let's tell it like it really is." Jim reassures people and promises anonymity; then he divides the group in two to work on the document. The comments as they work are surprisingly candid. The participants seem genuinely concerned. Jim and Michael keep them focused on norms rather than on blame placing or finding fault with individuals. They also keep them focused on what they really want the environment to be like, rather than on what they think is possible.

Jim explains a model designed to help people look at the norms of relationships. He talks about this as a way of getting to know and trust each other a little better. He points out how important it is for people to get to know each other as people, rather than as functions or objects. He asks that each person in the group who cares to, share something likely to be helpful to the others in getting to know him or her better, as a whole human being. One man speaks out, "O.K., I'll tell you some things about me—I'm a nice guy." Michael chides him gently and gets the group into something more meaningful. "It doesn't need to be earthshaking," he says, "but something that will help us to get to know you better." A younger, long-haired fellow then volunteers an account of his past experience with drugs—how he managed to get free of them and how important this is to him. Another talks about how she is not altogether comfortable in groups and around other people, and how she is trying to overcome that but still has a long way to go. Still another talks about his children: how proud he is of what they are accomplishing and how he just couldn't take it if something happened to one of them.

At the end of the sharing session they talk a few minutes about how it feels to be open with others in an open discussion. Michael then explains some guidelines for feedback that can be useful in any meeting, ways to offer constructive criticism and praise, and ways to make it clear to the other person that you are speaking from your own perceptions and not pronouncing judgments. The group practices the rules, role-playing some problem situations they meet at work, and providing feedback for two group members (one of whom is a supervisor) who request it. The feedback goes extremely well, and the people seem genuinely pleased with this new skill they have developed.

The afternoon ends with a game in which the two groups vie for some mythical financial gains. The game is fun—fierce competition arises. The participants realize that win/lose situations become lose/lose for everybody. It is a sobering ending to the day, for it shows how quickly we can put aside our lip-service values and erect barriers. Michael points out that in real life the walls are even harder to break down.

The next day is devoted to beginning the change process. Michael talks to both groups about the Normative Systems change principles and about the next steps in the change process. The objectives of the program that had been developed by previous groups are reviewed, clarified, and added to. Somewhat surprisingly, few changes are recommended. The objectives that were chosen by the previous group are highly similar to those that the group would have chosen for itself, and the few additions and changes in wording that are suggested will be passed on to the goal-setting and planning task force that has been appointed for that purpose. One member of the group volunteers to serve on the overall organizational committee.

When the group has reviewed the goals, Michael discusses the four pivotal areas to be considered in the change process: the individual, the group or work team, the leadership, and the organizational program, policies, and procedures.

The group begins immediately to consider the changes that will be necessary. "What we have to do" has to a great extent replaced "what they have to do".

The company executive who opened yesterday's meeting stops back for an informal report on progress. The group is positive and constructive in its suggestions. Members are still somewhat reluctant to be as open with the executive present as they had been without him, but even this is recognized by one of them and shared with the executive and with the group: "It's going to take us a while to get used to the new way of doing things."

After the executive leaves, there is a general air of optimism. Michael cautions that the process of change is now only beginning and that a good deal of hard work lies ahead. The group members appear to recognize this fact, even while they sign up enthusiastically for the task forces that particularly interest them.

At 5 P.M. on the second day the participants leave, stimulated by the hope that improvements may be possible and feeling that perhaps this time something will come out of an effort to make some needed changes.

GROUNDWORK FOR CHANGE

Those who have experienced the workshops are given an opportunity to participate as coaches, trainers, or co-trainers in later workshops. This further involves them in the process and develops the important sense of "ownership" of the change program. It also lays the groundwork for later self-renewal efforts, for only by internalization of the skills can the organization have a truly self-renewing program.

In the initial workshops, people from each echelon of the organization are helped to achieve an understanding of normative influences and a realization of themselves as cultural groups. Through "sharing" exercises, they begin to see each other in a multidimensional way, apart from the roles they have been playing on the job or in the group. This personal sharing very quickly demonstrates what a more open, more trusting environment can be like.

Whether a workshop is a one-, a two-, or even a five-day experience, it usually has several "highs." The first occurs when people hear the tape on which their peers talk frankly about what is wrong in the organization. In an industry setting, this is a tremendous boost, for often they have had their ideas and feelings for years—now they hear these same ideas being openly stated, and often the boss is sitting there listening to them.

A second high often occurs when the leadership personally demonstrates how much it is committed to the program. This frequently involves admission on the part of executives that they need to change. When the boss says, "I know I haven't been treating people as I should, but I'm going to begin right now to do things differently. Maybe I won't be perfect, but I can do better," employees often begin to realize that change is possible.

Another high occurs during the sharing and feedback exercises, when people begin to understand that it is possible to develop new and more positive norms in relationships with one another; norms that will bring them together on a warmer, more human level; norms that they never before thought possible within the environment.

VARIATIONS OF INTRODUCTIONS

The workshop in a business setting just described is only one of a number of different ways of introducing the system. These range from one- to five-day workshops carried out by professional change agents to informal two- to four-hour discussions led by a group member with little prior training or experience. Materials are available to assist in this process, including a film series and self-instructional modules that can be used by group members without outside help.

Whatever method is selected, it almost always focuses on these steps. First, *understanding the culture*. In this step participants have the opportunity to gain an understanding of the immense impact of the culture upon their lives and of the possibility of bringing about change. Second, *identifying the existing culture and the desired culture*. Here people take a closer look at their culture in order to identify what currently exists and what they want to achieve. Organizational members are helped to focus on the norms they want and need if they are to be successful in reaching their objectives. Third, *initiating the change process*. This step consists of planning the change steps that will be necessary. Systems manuals are available when more extensive change programs are planned. In less extensive programs, the various change influences are reviewed and specific action steps developed.

The illustrations below present excerpts from accounts of the systems introduction phase in three quite different settings:

A family unit: From the beginning I made my family aware of the nature of my project. I discussed the Normative Systems process with my husband to introduce the whole idea to him. We had a number of discussions over a period of several weeks. The family took the family norm indicator and through use of our normative profile we had a chance to examine which cultural areas were affecting us adversely. We then had a chance to plan some changes that seemed to us to be important. Some of these were immediate changes that we have already put into effect. Others are going to take us some months to institute. We have set up a system for keeping track of what we are doing. We recognize that we still have a lot to accomplish, but that we are off to a pretty good start.

A new company: The initial introduction to the system took place in a three-day meeting of the nine newly chosen managers. The seminar began with a description of Normative Systems and an explanation of the key role these managers would play in beginning to create a new culture. Films and other audiovisual aids were used, as well as exercises designed to clarify some major issues. Each person shared his preliminary objectives for the company, listing them in three categories: performance, programmatic, and cultural objectives. Revisions and clarifications were made, and some of the objectives were hotly debated. Another element of the seminar was an interpersonal involvement situation focusing on a series of interpersonal exercises to help people break out of the more common stereotypes of their relationships to one another. Additional objectives having to do with relationships were added to the list. A presentation was made on factors that influence the development of cultures, and each of these factors was reviewed in terms of what specifically would need to be done in setting up the new company.

A Lifegain health practices change program: In the room were thirty people broken into groups of ten, each group consisting of a cross-section of people from the company. They came together as part of a Lifegain culture change program designed to help people change their health practices. The seminar began with a description of the impact that the health cultures have upon health practices. It included feedback on an analysis of the organization that indicated it was supporting a number of negative health norms ranging from pushing high calorie, low nutrition foods in the cafeteria to encouraging the misuse of alcohol at some of the company functions. Members moved on to looking at their own health practices and goals. There was a chance to build relationships that would make it possible for people to be helpful to one another. They were invited to join task forces that had already been established in such areas as the cafeteria, stress, smoking, nutrition, and exercise. A plan was discussed for making a partially worn pathway around the parking lot into a jogging trail. People left the meeting with a sense of hopefulness and a feeling that they could work together to make the situation better for all of them, and also with a realization that the achievement of changes would be up to them and that they would need to take responsibility for their own bodies.

The workshop event, in whatever form or setting, stresses many of the new norms that the group wants, such as seeing and treating each other as people, feeling good about oneself and one's group relationships, sharing ideas and feelings, listening to one another, and working toward solutions amiably.

The workshops have been very effective in giving people something from which they can measure change. We often hear phrases like, "the way we've been since that first workshop." In a real sense, there is a shared vision of the new desired organizational culture, and the workshop becomes the image of the ideal, a peak cultural experience that is not easily forgotten or readily dismissed. With this experience, people begin to develop a belief that change is, after all, actually possible, and they learn the basic principles that will guide the process.

REVIEWING KEY IDEAS

At this point, the Normative Systems approach suggests a review of some key ideas. The following true-false quiz is typical of what is used. It might be useful for readers to answer it before taking a look at Phase III. Since the merit of the quiz lies in what a person learns *after* taking it, we suggest that when you check your answers, you take time to read the comments accompanying each answer.

QUESTIONS

T F 1. "Positive norms of change" is another way of saying effective normative principles of change.

T F 2. Decision making is more efficient if fewer people are involved.

T F 3. When a new program that looks really good comes along, it is important to begin right away before you lose your momentum.

T F 4. Understanding the Normative Systems process is more important than achieving results in a particular change effort.

T F 5. When problems get better overnight, the chances are they will get worse overnight too.

T F 6. When you are trying to change things, it is a good idea to pinpoint one "problem" influence area and concentrate on improving it first.

T F 7. You can't please all the people all the time when it comes to making improvements.

T F 8. Once you have reached your goal in a certain problem area, you shouldn't have to worry about it for a while.

ANSWERS

1. TRUE. We have described them as norms because it is useful to see them as patterns of behavior which already exist, in their positive or negative forms, in the daily operations of the organization. It is important to understand that the way people are accustomed to approach change may interfere with the success of the change effort. Where such negative norms exist, the organization needs to adopt more effective patterns of behavior.

2. FALSE. Decisions may be made faster, but they probably will not be successfully implemented. When people are involved in the decision-making process, they have a stake in helping to make the decision work. That doesn't mean that everyone has to agree before a decision is made. It means that all the people affected by major change decisions should contribute their experience to the change effort.

3. FALSE. Many programs fail because they are based on incomplete or incorrect information. A thorough, systematic study of *what currently exists* is the first step in trying to bring about change.

4. FALSE. The Normative Systems approach is important only insofar as it produces successful results. The people involved in a change effort should always keep their goals in sight.

5. TRUE. This is why we emphasize systematic change strategies. Sometimes a simple solution (like a supervisor's decision to be more considerate) will improve things for a while, but if it is to continue, it will have to be systematically supported and reinforced by the culture.

6. FALSE. Problems do not exist in isolation. If you have a problem, such as "involvement" or "motivation," the chances are that you will not solve it without dealing with other influence areas as well. For example, "rewards and recognition," "follow-through," "organizational policies and procedures," and perhaps several others will have to be considered. Before you can successfully attack any one problem area, you have to be able to see how it is related to the whole culture.

7. TRUE. But you can make sure that plans for change include features which will be welcomed by each of the different interest groups in an organization. This is called building win/win solutions, and it is one of the reasons why problems are more easily solved by attack from several sides at once.

Every person may not like every aspect of the change effort, but each will see that he or she has much to gain.

8. FALSE. Few things worth changing will change permanently on the basis of a crash program. It is all too easy for the old negative norms to come back when no one is looking. Successful change programs provide for ongoing evaluation and renewal of effort as needed.

When you work with a group, you might do a group effectiveness exercise with this quiz. (See Appendix D for the scoring table.) It usually demonstrates clearly that a group working effectively together can arrive at a higher score than individuals working alone. In a mature group, people listen to one another. They have an investment in getting the best answer, rather than in being the best individual answerer.

Chapter 15

Making a
Difference

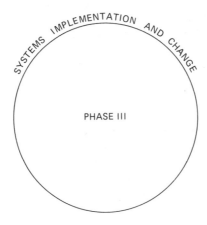

As we make choices in Phase III, we begin to see the difference between knowing and doing. Real freedom rests in not only seeing alternatives but acting upon them; behaving in new ways, making new things happen, changing things, doing what we consciously choose to do rather than what we are driven to do by unknown forces. Earlier we envisioned new norms and whole new patterns of norms, and now in Phase III we convert these dreams into action.

We may begin to close the gap between knowing and doing in a variety of ways. In the family, we might find we are practicing "togetherness" not only by making plans and decisions together but by having fun together—going on a picnic, attending a political rally, giving a party. In the neighborhood we might hold a skateboard contest in which safe practices are rewarded as well as skills and speed. While there is an almost unlimited variety of possible activities, depending on the setting, some general guidelines for Phase III change efforts have been found helpful.

PUTTING NORMS INTO PRACTICE

Some norms begin to change during the first two phases (analysis and introduction of the system), but significant change requires a systematic modification of key norm influence areas in day-to-day action. It is here, in the third phase, that the change effort is either reinforced or extinguished.

Quite often a whole organization goes through the first two phases of change and then never applies itself to the task of systematically supporting the new behavior it has decided necessary. When the consultant leaves, everything crumbles. The training program may be inspiring, but once it is over, people slip back into the old ways.

This usually happens because norms and norm influences have remained unchanged *within* the culture. If nothing is done to modify the group's day-to-day rewards, resource allocation, and so on, the old ways are likely to reassert their influence. There has to be a way to put the changes into practice, to support the new behavior day-to-day. That is what will make the difference.

The normative systems method of doing this involves four key elements of the culture: the *individual*, the *group*, the *leadership*, and the *formal policies and programs of the total organization*.

The basic principles of change are emphasized in all four of these key elements. Efforts are made to see that they are understood and put into practice at all levels of the organization. Moreover, they must be reviewed periodically to be sure they are in use. For example, if a group should pay lip service to the need for win/win solutions, and then propose plans in which one department is in a win/lose race with another, the change program could be disastrously undermined.

In all four areas, the people go through a sequential process of understanding and identifying positive norms, setting goals, putting the positive norms into practice, and reinforcing the changes by recognition and review.

What about groups (like the typical family) that are too small to contain subcultures? All four elements need to be dealt with nonetheless. A family can examine the role of each individual member in the changes sought, what the family as a group is doing to carry out the agreed-upon objectives, what the leadership role is and how it is being carried out (not only by the parents but by the children), and, finally, whether family rules, traditions, procedures, etc., are working for or against its goals. (For example, if the practice is to watch television during dinner, this is cutting into the time for talking together.)

Let us look at the four elements separately and see what can be done to implement change in each one of them.

INDIVIDUAL DEVELOPMENT

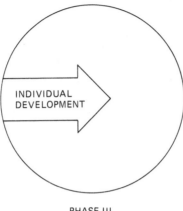

PHASE III

The individual is one of the most important ingredients in any culture. After all, it is each person's feelings, emotions, actions, and reactions that foster, and often initiate, group action. Therefore it is important that individuals be able to focus upon themselves and that they have the help of the rest of the culture in doing so.

When individuals first join a new culture, the orientation process impresses upon them the importance that other members of the culture assign to setting normative goals and to each person's participation in the process. As each continues, he is helped to develop skills that can be useful to him. What is involved is not an event, but a process. Individuals participate in setting their own goals, get help in achieving them, are corrected when necessary, receive rewards for their achievements, reset their goals, and move on to new ones. What the individual wants can and should be related in a meaningful way to the goals of the group if each is going to be completely successful. That done, win/win situations can be planned for both.

In businesses, a cultural approach integrates individual development within a performance planning and review process. Too often either organizations have no such process or the one they have is destructive—the employees being told only when they do something wrong. Sometimes a perfunctory once-a-year review is called a "performance appraisal," while actually more than a single event is necessary for sustained change. Performance planning and review need to be an ongoing process through which people can be continually informed about where they stand. It can be a way for individuals to evaluate, plan, and replan their work effort in coordination with their supervisors and their teams, with constructive feedback an essential ingredient.

Although Normative Systems programs provide the individual with whatever help he or she needs to overcome obstacles, they also emphasize the individual's ability to take on greater personal responsibility. Progress in meeting this responsibility is also reviewed periodically, recognized, and rewarded. Therefore, the program leads individuals to a greater measure of control over the changes that they have decided will be beneficial to themselves and the group.

GROUP DEVELOPMENT

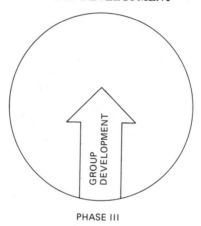

PHASE III

Cultural change requires the ongoing investment of time and energy on group development. When a family, for example, has given each individual member his due, there is still something more to be done—focusing attention on the family unit itself. "How are we doing, as a family, in working toward our goals?"

Our cultures are full of groups. These can be formal parts of the organization (as work teams and executive boards), or informal cliques and peer groups with no official status. For instance, a typical high school has formal groups, such as classes, the school board, the student council, and the English Department, plus informal subcultures, such as the "jocks" and the "grinds." Employees in every organization have "group meetings" constantly—if not structured meetings, then unstructured get-togethers over coffee or after work, usually without a supervisor present and with little follow-through of ideas. People usually resist recognizing the power of the informal groups without official status, but they have a major effect on what the organization can accomplish. Therefore, it is more productive to acknowledge them and enlist their aid in the change process. This is not hard to do, provided their special norms are taken into account.

A formalized group development program is part of the implementation phase of a Normative Systems change effort. Where work teams do not exist, they are established. For people who are already on work teams, the program provides an opportunity to develop and sustain a constructive group culture and a means of keeping individual and organizational goals congruent with one another. Work groups that meet regularly to deal with problems and issues affecting them, to set team goals, and to measure progress toward their achievement develop positive norms and contribute importantly to organizational progress.

The influence members of the immediate group have upon one another must be taken into account. If normative changes from "out there" conflict with the norms of the peer group, the latter usually prevail. The power of the "inner circle" is substantial—whether it be a street gang or a work team. The questions to which these groups address themselves encompass all the important norm influence areas that have been targeted, but the main overall question is, "How is our group doing in meeting its goals?" There are countless ramifications of this, of course, depending on the culture under scrutiny. ("How are we, as a group, doing in providing orientation for new students?" "How are we, as an agency, doing in promoting effective two-way communications?")

Most normative systems programs encourage regularly scheduled meetings which have three basic characteristics: (1) They are short—about an hour at the most; (2) they have an agenda that includes announcements, progress reports, a list of tasks and the assignment of responsibility for each, and a schedule of subsequent meetings and progress reports; and (3) very little work is done in the meeting itself; most of the activity involves reporting and checking on work done outside the meeting.

Short meetings that concentrate on reporting results produce more results, for they leave time for work to be done between meetings, while, in contrast, long, drawn-out interchanges tend to waste people's time, and substantive work gets neglected. The planned agenda disciplines the meeting so that time is spent on problems and issues in general proportion to their relative importance to the group, and so that all points are covered before the meeting adjourns. The announcement period provides an opportunity for people to have their say. People do not always say what they have on their minds; but if the environment is right, they will. If the environment is wrong for this kind of openness and trust, at the very least the meeting makes people aware that it *is* wrong, and so they can go about changing it.

Listing the issues and concerns puts all the important problems in front of the group, and so it is easier to set priorities. When new issues or new opportunities are listed, they are accompanied by the names of the persons responsible for following up. A specific time for reporting on progress on the issue is also established, so that there are no ambiguities about who is to do what by when. The time set aside for the new concepts keeps the agenda flexible and responsive to new needs as they are identified. Finally, scheduling the next meeting lets all the participants know the date by which the pertinent assigned work must be completed. Again, the actual work toward changing things is done between meetings.

Working with groups in this manner funnels both individual and group energies into constructive and effective channels. This is clearly much more productive in the long run than those unofficial gripe sessions in the car pool or over the bar, which too often produce only feelings of frustration and helplessness.

LEADERSHIP DEVELOPMENT

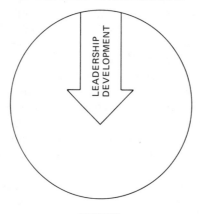

PHASE III

As we have seen, the leaders in any culture exert a tremendous modeling effect on members of the group. Obviously, successful and prominent people have a disproportionate influence on others. Consequently, the development of positive change norms by the leadership group will accelerate the change process in the whole organization. Conversely, if leaders do *not* demonstrate and support positive changes, they can subtly undermine the group's program to change things. The inner psychology of the "boss" carries a tremendous weight in our culture. How he handles himself in public, what he does, how he changes (visibly), what kind of relationships he has with others, all are closely watched and have great impact.

It is also important to recognize and marshall the influence of the group's informal leaders, each of whom models behavior that others notice and tend to emulate.

Finally, it is important to realize that any culture is influenced by the leaders' behavior, not necessarily as it *is,* but as it is perceived. What appears to be getting his or her attention and priority? This visible modeling exerts powerful force and should be given special attention in this third phase of the change program. Concomitant with norms of modeling are norms of commitment and support. As we have seen, commitment is evident in the resources leaders allocate for carrying out proposed changes. Typically, a high school football team gets this commitment, but the debate team does not. On paper and in speeches, the leaders say debating is important, but what happens? The president of the school board is always seen at football games, seldom at a debate. The football coach is well paid for his extracurricular activities; the debate coach is poorly paid, if at all. The football team gets the support of cheerleaders; there is time off from school for rallies; results are reported in detail, with pictures; the football star receives many scholarships. And the debaters? Can we seriously wonder why youngsters are more often enthusiastic about sports than about intellectual matters?

Because of the importance they play in any change process, the leadership is singled out by Normative Systems practitioners for special attention. Early in the program, the leaders start through the four phases of the change process. In the analysis phase, they examine their own norms, and learn to see themselves in relation to key influence areas. They may take part in the preliminary goal setting, or they may embellish and add commitment to the findings of other groups within the organization. A good deal of this is accomplished as part of the Phase II workshop program. In the third phase they start to put new positive norms into practice and to find ways to strengthen already existing positive norms.

A survey instrument, the leadership norm indicator, can be used in all four phases of the program, and is helpful in the initial understanding of norms and current leadership patterns. It consists of a series of statements describing possible leadership norms or expected behavior patterns. People are asked whether they agree or disagree that a particular behavior is a norm within the organization. Responses indicate strengths and weaknesses in particular areas and are used to create a norm profile of the leadership.

Not only is the leadership norm indicator an important diagnostic tool, but it can be readministered as a follow-up instrument in the evaluation and results-monitoring phase. Bear in mind that the leadership norm indicator reflects only the way people *perceive* things, and so it should not be used to place blame or to make judgments. There is no passing score, because goals differ from group to group and may also vary between various influence areas.

This sampling of some of the statements from the leadership norm indicator shows the kind of behavior that is covered and at the same time focuses on some of the norms of a good leader:

Around here, it is the norm for leaders . . .	I strongly agree	I agree	I don't know	I disagree	I strongly disagree
to demonstrate their own commitment to what the organization is trying to accomplish	—	—	—	—	—
to implement an effective system for planning and reviewing the performance of each person they supervise	—	—	—	—	—
to get together regularly with their work teams to set goals and review progress toward achievement	—	—	—	—	—
to treat those that they supervise as people and not as just "hired hands"	—	—	—	—	—
to seek out the opinions of those they supervise	—	—	—	—	—
to be constructive and helpful when they confront errors and mistakes	—	—	—	—	—
to involve people directly in the development of changes affecting them	—	—	—	—	—
to ensure that people get the training they need	—	—	—	—	—
to help people define goals and tasks clearly	—	—	—	—	—
to have a clear, consistent way to measure results	—	—	—	—	—

About a hundred of these norms, cutting across all the crucial influence areas, are scored. The indicator is used both by the leader as a self-rating instrument and by others in the organization as a feedback instrument.

FORMAL POLICIES, PROCEDURES, AND PROGRAMS

The fourth element requiring special attention during the installation and implementation phase is the structure of the organization, that is, its programs, policies, and procedures. An intense review of how the organizational setup affects norm goals is conducted at all levels. Too often, these factors interfere with the success of a change effort. For example, cooper-

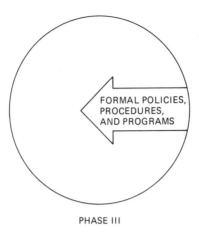

PHASE III

ation may be a group goal, but the reward system may thwart progress toward it. We found agents in one real estate office actively trying to hold down sales in the other regions, preferring to have a competitor close a sale rather than see an agent from another region of their own company succeed and thereby earn a portion of the company bonuses that might otherwise flow to them.

The formal and conspicuous aspects of a culture—rules, regulations, manuals, schedules, policies—can all become sources of continual frustration when they are outdated, unrealistic, or ineffective. During Phase III, specific programs are developed to examine the written directives of the culture and their relationship to organizational goals. Task forces are formed to deal with specific areas, recommend necessary changes in policies and procedures, and monitor the effectiveness of those changes.

Task forces formed in a large corporation recently included development of a formal communications network, health and safety regulations, and policies for bonuses, among others. Each group met on a regular basis until its task was complete, reported its plans and actions, and evaluated its progress. In a family, the rules for curfew, chore sharing, and family policy on allowances might be examined. The important thing is that the pertinent formal practives are reconsidered and dealt with as necessary, and that the organization receives feedback on what is being accomplished.

NORMATIVE PRINCIPLES THROUGHOUT

In dealing with all four elements, we encounter and utilize many of the same basic ingredients. No matter what the focus, the normative principles of change are constantly being reiterated and reinforced, the process of understanding and identifying norms takes place, key pressure points are identified, and achievable goals and objectives are agreed upon and pursued.

When we feel we have done all this, it is time—before going on to Phase IV—to ask ourselves four basic questions:

> Are we, as individual members of the organization, supporting the goals we have established?
>
> Are the various subgroups contributing to the achievement of the goals?
>
> Are the leaders modeling and demonstrating commitment to what we are trying to accomplish?
>
> Are the organizational structures, policies, and procedures supporting achievement of our goals?

If we can answer these questions affirmatively, chances are we are also beginning to taste the exhilaration of realizing our ability to create meaningful change, and to be masters rather than victims of our life situations.

Chapter 16

Keeping
It Going

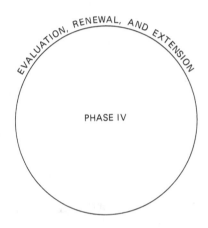

PHASE IV

EVALUATION, RENEWAL, AND EXTENSION

At the end of Phase III, there is often an exciting sense of victory. The housing is complete and former migrant workers are now homeowners; the store's pilferage rate is down; the plant's productivity is up; the warehouse workers are trading jokes with corporate executives; the ghetto resident and police are congratulating each other. True, these are heady moments—but the process is not complete.

No matter how effective a change effort has been, the culture will need continual reassessment and renewal. History is full of examples of changes, helpful when introduced, that later became obstacles to progress. The mental hospitals Dorothea Dix created in response to past inhumanities gradually developed inhumanities of their own. The dynamism of a new university course disappears in a few years, and the course takes on the boredom and inefficiency of its predecessors. Many a government agency or program begins with great expectations and soon shows great impotence.

It is easy to see that programs with poor results should be reevaluated, but it is sometimes hard to accept the fact that successful programs, too, need to be reviewed and recharged on a regular basis. The question

175

"What's happening?" applies to *all* efforts, and the answers can be used to reshape a project that is going well in much the same way that they can be used to recharge one that is doing poorly.

Phase IV provides an opportunity for:

Recognizing achievement and relishing successes

Identifying where we have fallen short of our goals and planning ways to rectify matters

Evaluating and refining existing programs and considering new ones

Reviving the excitement and enthusiasm of new beginnings

Strengthening and assimilating new skills

Keeping the organization or group focused on results

Integrating new people into the process and reinvolving old-timers

Keeping the system open and responsive

Extending the change process to other areas

This fourth, evaluation, phase of the cultural-change process supplies the vital element of assessment. People step back to look at what they have and have not accomplished, and this leads naturally into the renewal and revitalizing efforts. Extending the evaluation to other groups, other areas of the organization, or other aspects of an individual life has the added virtue of strengthening and sustaining the original application.

Effective evaluation relies on a study of results and on planning for adjustments. Those concerned with the program determine whether or not they in fact are doing what they are supposed to be doing, and decide what else needs to be done. Application of these results to subsequent planning makes it possible to evolve an effective, ongoing program.

Proper evaluation presupposes information and statistics about factors having an impact on the progress of the projects that are under way. The information base established in Phase I as a point of reference can be compared with current findings to measure progress.

In gathering Phase IV information, we again deal with the three categories of data discussed in Phase I: quantifiable data, action-tracking data, and data on cultural perceptions. New information collected in these three areas enables us to measure progress, recognize achievements, and identify problems needing additional attention.

To be useful, evaluation and renewal depend on an organizationwide communication of progress, results, and perceptions between associates and work teams on all levels. A variety of techniques and instruments may be used, most of which have been reviewed in other sections. They range from simple one-to-one interviews to comprehensive questionnaires. For instance, the same cultural norm indicators that were helpful in the first two phases can be readministered to determine how well (or poorly) the positive culture is maintaining itself.

EVALUATING HOW WE EVALUATE

While it may seem strange to think in terms of evaluating how we evaluate, part of this process is just that—determining the effectiveness of the instruments and techniques we are using to conduct our evaluation. To appraise an evaluation process, efforts are reviewed in the light of such questions as:

Is the evaluation process contributing to the ongoing improvement of the program?

Is the evaluation process developing the information needed?

Are the data useful? Are they being used?

Are our associates responding well to the forms of evaluation employed?

Can the instruments we are using be improved?

Is the generated information communicated effectively throughout the organization?

RENEWAL

Renewal meetings are scheduled from the outset, often as part of the initial planning, but can be announced (or reannounced) during the introduction or implementation phases. It tends to have a powerful impact when an organizational leader reminds the group at the introductory workshop: "One year from now we'll be standing right here looking at this list of objectives that we've just prepared; and we are going to feel great if we have reached them, and just terrible if they remain just a lot of words on a piece of paper."

While there is no mandatory pattern, most change programs are planned in such a way that they enter the fourth phase approximately one year after the program is introduced. The exact timing depends on the scope of the analysis effort, the extent and complexity of the program, and so on.

The renewal meeting is usually the opening event of the fourth phase. It gives people an opportunity to evaluate progress, receive commendation for their accomplishments, review the skills they have developed, and decide on what remains to be done.

The renewal meeting often takes the form of a weekend workshop, during which the data collected from the various evaluative efforts are disseminated and analyzed. Suggestions for adjustments to the program are solicited, and plans are made to meet the remaining needs that emerge from the evaluation. Out of such a workshop should come not only specific plans and rededication, but also a target date for the next evaluation and renewal meeting.

To many people, the systematic, humanistic approach implicit in Normative Systems work is a brand-new way of dealing with problems. Since it reverses many long-standing negative norms, it needs repetition, reinforcement, and feedback in order for it to become a "natural" way of doing things. Furthermore, the enthusiasm of new beginnings—the sheer fun of starting up—can be captured again and again during the years that follow the introduction of a culture-based program. All that is required is an occasional evaluation and renewal meeting. Finally, such meetings introduce new people to the change process, and win their commitment to continuing it. People are very interested in what they themselves have created, and the evaluation and renewal meetings permit newcomers to the organization to share in the "ownership" of the program and to participate actively.

KEEPING THE SYSTEM OPEN

An effective evaluation and renewal process helps to keep the system open, in line with the principle of democratic control. It reduces the fear that the program will be taken over by the experts or by a small clique or inside group. It also prevents the stagnation that occurs when a system is closed to new ideas and new approaches.

Systems that are not kept open tend to focus on activities rather than results. A commune may disintegrate because while the members express themselves lovingly and openly, no one does the dishes or takes out the garbage. It may also disintegrate because the necessary dishwashing and garbage removal are well structured, but no time is allotted for gatherings at which people have a chance to share their feelings and build positive relationships with one another.

EXTENDING THE PROGRAM TO OTHER PROBLEM AREAS

The renewal phase also provides an opportunity for extending the change program into other influence areas and other organizational units. Once the necessary skills have been mastered, the techniques can be applied to new problems and obstacles wherever they may arise.

The Normative Systems change process is a flexible tool. It does not attempt to impose predetermined solutions, and so it can be adapted to changing situations and to many different kinds of settings. As the process is used and becomes familiar, it can itself become a norm—the routine way in which difficulties are isolated and resolved. To help this occur, we have developed a conceptual model of the process, which is presented in the next chapter. However, it should be emphasized that no particular model and no process should become dogmatic. Concepts are necessary and helpful but need not be so rigidly superimposed on life that people get locked into their own designations and cannot flow with their experiences.

Chapter 17

The Normative Systems Model

Nothing is as practical as a good theory.
KURT LEWIN

People often think of their cultures as amorphous, like mashed potatoes, without discernible elements. Viewed in this way it is often difficult to deal with a problem; and even when there is a change, people may not know how it occurred. So faced with a problem, they resort to tossing off a memo or spanking a child—the simplistic responses we reviewed earlier. The Normative Systems model has been developed to give people a clear concept of the total change process. The four circles constitute a frame of reference—like a built-in "crib" sheet—that can be incorporated into anyone's thinking and used whenever problems arise.

Parts of the model originated with other people some time ago and will be quite familiar. Normative Systems simply assembles the parts, old and new, in a coherent and systematic way. The natural sciences learned long ago that if one gets a few concepts in mind (evolution or gravitation, for example), a lot of once-puzzling data falls into place. The social sciences are now moving in this direction, finding that a flexible, realistic, and credible frame of reference can be used with problems of any size in any setting.

The four-phased model pictured on page 182 and described in preceding chapters is generic. Any culture, of any type or size, can use it, and it can be useful to anyone working on a change program. The process is presented in chart form so that it can easily become a part of anyone's conceptual inventory. The chart depicts a systematic process through which solutions, based on the group's or culture's own experience, will evolve.

Although the basic model is the same for any individual or culture that is working on a change process, everyone and every group in an organization will not be in the same phase at the same time, nor can a given phase be expected to take place simultaneously in all parts of the culture. For example, analysis and objectives setting may be taking place not only in

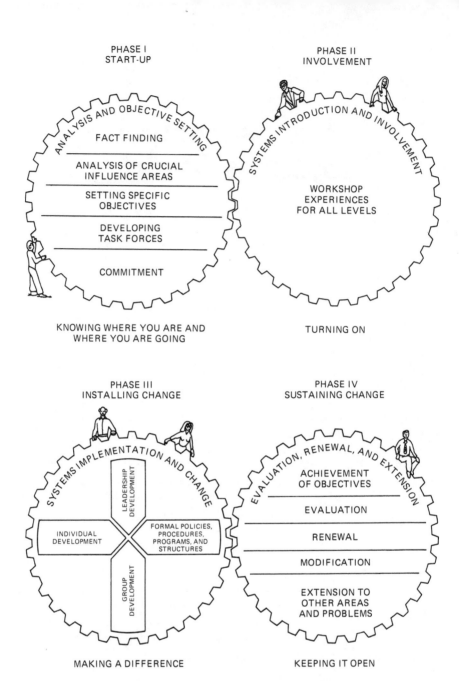

FIGURE 17-1 The Normative Systems change process: a generic model. Normative principles of change used throughout involve, from the beginning, those most directly affected; operate from a sound data base; apply systematic strategies and approaches; are clear about objectives, plans, and tasks; seek win/win, non-blame-placing solutions; are oriented toward results; and build in culture-based, sustained commitment and follow-through.

Phase I, when the preliminary work is being done, but also during Phases II, III, and IV. Nevertheless it is useful to separate the phases for purposes of the conceptual model.

The size of an organization is important not only to the sequence and overlapping of events, but also to the amount of time required. In a large organization the four phases might extend over several years, while in a family they might be accomplished in three to six months. The important thing is that flexibility is maintained and that the impact on each group is sufficiently concentrated to ensure significant change in a reasonable time. Most basic programs take approximately one year from the time of their introduction.

While we may think of the model as a map of the change program, it is important to remember that it is only a graphic representation of the sequence in which we tackle the real world of interrelationships. It was developed in field work, and will be refined continually through the same practical day-to-day experiences that created it.

Part Five

THEY DID IT: FOUR SUCCESSFUL CASE HISTORIES —AND A FAILURE

When I first came to Collegefields I thought this place was crazy, but after I was here a while I began to realize that what I was doing before was crazy, and this really gave me a chance to get free.

"JOHNNY"
From a tape recording taken
during a meeting of the Collegefields
project

It's like being born again. I'd been in houses like this, but I was always a visitor. I never thought I'd own one.

WILLIE REYNOLDS
Fruit picker

Look what the people in our city have done.

Slogan used by the media
to describe a community
litter reduction program

I never thought it could happen. It's actually fun to come to work now—and we are making money, too!

President of a large
manufacturing company

Chapter 18

From Delinquency to Freedom

Collegefields was designed to help youngsters escape the rigid and narrow world of the delinquent social system and to become free agents. The freedom potential in the change process of Collegefields now appears to be more far reaching than originally anticipated.

From a report of the Collegefields Project[1]

Johnny was 14 years old and a seventh grader in the Newark public schools in the late 1950s when a juvenile court judge assigned him to the Collegefields program. He had been on probation, first for glue sniffing, then for riding in a stolen car, and finally for being at the scene of a robbery. Ordinarily, he would have gone to an institution, to be separated from the street culture that was so deeply ingrained in him. Instead, he was bused every day to the Newark State College campus (now Kean College of New Jersey). He was free to spend his evenings at home.

Johnny disliked school, felt "work was for suckers," and had been able to come by enough money for the "necessities" of life—pills, dope, and cheap wine. Girls (yes, at 14) were free. His was the culture of the street, and no fancy program was going to change him! So when the judge assigned him to Collegefields, it sounded to Johnny as though he had "beaten the rap."

Seven months later, Johnny realized that he had indeed beaten the rap, but in a way he had never dreamed of. He graduated from the Collegefields program, went back to school—but on the *ninth* grade level—and was free, both from the negative influences of the street gangs and from his own delinquent ways. With other boys in the Collegefields program, he had helped to create a new culture with positive norms, which supported his becoming independent and self-respecting. At the same time, he and his friends had helped to develop a change process that later evolved into Normative Systems.

[1] Robert F. Allen, Harry N. Dubin, Saul Pilnick, and Adella C. Youtz, *From Delinquency to Freedom* (Washington: U.S., Office of Education, 1966).

The Collegefields Delinquency Rehabilitation Program was a non-residential, two-year program for delinquent 14- and 15-year-old boys from Newark. Funded by the Department of Health, Education, and Welfare, it demonstrated that peer-group power can be used by youngsters to redirect their own lives and their perceptions of themselves. The boys were able to change the negative norms of their street culture and develop positive norms of nondelinquency. What is more important, the positive norms were maintained.

Here in more detail is what happened.

Observations and studies of delinquent youngsters in the ghettos of Eastern cities revealed a troubling phenomenon: young people who had recently left their homes in the rural South, with no record of delinquency, were appearing in the courts of Newark, New York, and Philadelphia as little as six months later, full-fledged delinquents with all the attitudes, skills, language patterns, and perceptions that characterize long-term delinquents. Life in the Northern ghettos presented a "training program" of remarkable effectiveness.

Moreover, the youngsters who were picked up by the law and assigned to typical rehabilitation programs were further confirmed in their negative behavior by their identification as delinquents and their development of additional associations and relationships with delinquents. Even the youngsters who behaved well in institutions were often back in court shortly after they were back in circulation. The major lesson they had learned was "to get along, go along," and this was applied as strongly in the street culture they returned to as it had been in the juvenile institution.

ANALYZING THE STREET CULTURE

Analysis of the delinquent subculture showed that *reward systems* were highly developed to support the negative norms of the delinquent culture. Group members who supported the norms were rewarded by acceptance and recognition within the group, while those who confronted them risked isolation, rejection, or outright punishment.

Modeling behavior was also a strong factor in the ghetto. The admonitions of parents and teachers to stay in school, get a job, and so on were undercut by the sight of the "cool" dropout with fancy clothes, girls, and a shiny car, who "earned" his living by drugs or the rackets. Moreover, *orientation* and *training* in the ways of the street culture were effective and fast. Although new youngsters often initially rejected some of the most negative behavior of the group, as soon as they understood how important the behavior was to the others, they at least pretended acceptance. Thus there was often a period during which a newcomer "faked it."

This phase tended to end in a crisis, when the new member was required to demonstrate his commitment through some specific act, like stealing a car or robbing a store. Once he had taken part in the delinquent act, he found it was not so difficult as he had thought. He was accepted and perhaps even praised by the group, and his status in the subculture was assured. Even his arrival in court was supportive. To be identified as a delinquent by the courts helped him create an image of himself that shaped his behavior and the behavior of those around him.

In examining this process, we found that the delinquent subculture had not only its own very special training program, but also its own, carefully interrelated normative curriculum. This consisted of the norms of the delinquent culture shown below, with the statements that reflected them.

NORMS OF THE DELINQUENT CULTURE

Norm Areas	Reflective Statements
Antiwork	"Work is for suckers."
Antischool	"School is a waste of time."
Anti-delayed-need gratification	"Get it now; don't wait; what you wait for is not likely to ever happen."
Antilaw	"Laws are made to be broken and the big question is how to avoid being caught."
Anti-introspection	"Be cool, man. Don't look at yourself or at your problems. That's a sign of weakness."
Antitrust	"People are not to be trusted. Their main purpose is to do you in and to get what they want for themselves."
Anti-show of weakness	"Don't show weaknesses; if you have doubts about yourself, keep them to yourself. They will be used against you."
Anti-authority	"Who the hell do they think they are?" Authority figures (other than those in the delinquent group) are to be distrusted, resisted, and opposed, regardless of their behavior.
Pro-exploitation	"Get what you can from whom you can and don't get hung up about the effect of your behavior on others." This stricture sometimes, but not always, exempts the members of one's own delinquent group.

Pro-tough-guy	"To be a tough guy is one of the most important things." Toughness is best expressed by the successful use of physical force.
Pro-stealing	"If you want something, take it."
Pro-drugs and -alcohol	"Get your kicks, and don't worry about the consequences."[2]

Clearly, to be effective, any change program would have to make use of the same powerful cultural forces, but in a new and different direction, emphasizing the freedom of the individual to choose and create his or her own environment. If this could be accomplished, there might be a chance for youngsters to escape the culture trap of the ghetto street gang. Pilot programs were set up with these objectives:

To foster freedom by helping the youngsters achieve strength and support so that they could withstand the oppressive norms of the delinquent culture

To help youngsters who wanted to install new norms that were pro-work, pro-education, and pro-law, and which fostered openness, trust, introspection, and respect for authority

To help the boys who were potential school dropouts to change their attitudes and further their educational skills

To integrate community, public school, and university services to help the youngsters achieve this freedom

As a result of the analysis, a program was designed that sought to apply the power of the peer culture to the development of nondelinquent norms and to the achievement of greater levels of freedom for the boys assigned to the program.

INTRODUCTION AND INVOLVEMENT

The change system was initially introduced by three carefully selected staff members to a group of five delinquent youngsters from the street culture. After many meetings and discussions and much joint decision making by this original group during the first few weeks, new boys were added, one or two at a time.

From the beginning the positive norms of help, openness, and care were stressed—norms alien to the delinquent culture. The boys began to experience a culture in which they were listened to, and given power to make choices. Their advice was sought, and they were trusted. As a

[2] Robert F. Allen, Saul Pilnick, and Stanley Silverzeveig, *The Influence of the Peer Culture on Delinquency and Delinquency Rehabilitation* (Morristown, N.J.: SRI Scientific Resources Inc., 1966)

result, they began to feel a sense of ownership of the program—it was theirs, and it was up to them to make it work.

Guided group interaction sessions were held daily. In these discussions the human relations specialists played down their roles and encouraged the boys to help each other. In fact, the key word was "help." A boy who had made it, who had freed himself of his prior conformity to delinquent norms, was known as a "helped boy."

The boys attended classes daily and went home at night. This gave them daily experience in trying out the new norms under all the pressures of the outside world. By the time they graduated, they already knew they had a good chance of holding their own in the culture of the streets.

New boys coming into the program were introduced to the system, not by the staff, but by the other boys. If they violated rules, the boys themselves confronted them, and new boys quickly learned that deviation from established norms would mark them for immediate censure by the group.

MAKING A DIFFERENCE

Implementation took place on four levels: group, individual, leadership, and organization, but the group process was emphasized. The boys were together throughout the program, meeting informally every day for an hour and a quarter, discussing the problems of the group members and what the group could do to be helpful. The sessions were considered one of the most important elements of the project, both by the staff members and by the boys themselves.

The emphasis in group meetings was on decision making and the boys learned to make decisions on a multitude of issues, ranging from moving the meeting time, to whether or not a boy was ready to be released from the program.

The structuring of group membership was also important. There never was a graduating class as such. Boys graduated as they were ready to leave the program, and new boys came in periodically. Since there never was a mass turnover, the norms that were established were always passed on to new boys.

In addition to the group-related elements of the program, each boy was given a great deal of individual attention. For instance, each group meeting provided an opportunity for a different boy to review his individual progress and concerns with the other group members. This process was called "getting the meeting" or "getting help," and it was an honor that was widely sought, much to the amazement of new boys, who were unaccustomed to the sight of streetwise delinquents discussing their problems openly and asking for help from their peers. This process helped each youngster focus on his own behavior and his personal potential for change.

Leadership was also emphasized within the program. The boys themselves were the leaders, and each one was given a chance at the leadership role. The consultants saw themselves as facilitators, rather than as leaders, and during the orientation process they helped to install crucial leadership norms by which the boys were supported for taking charge.

Organizational structures and procedures were given much attention. Again, the boys themselves, who came into the program without strength, were given the power to shape and design the program and its policies. In this way they learned to use power judiciously, and the program itself was continuously improved.

To see how the system was implemented in terms of the individual, let us return to Johnny and see, through his experience, how the new culture influenced and shaped the life of one of its members.

JOHNNY

Johnny arrived at Collegefields with high hopes. He was sorry he had been caught by the police, but he was pretty sure he could get by at Collegefields without much trouble. The boys he hung around with on the street looked up to him as someone who could take care of himself, and he was beginning to believe them. The morning of his first day was quite a surprise, however. He had expected the usual orientation lectures from the staff about what he should and should not do, but instead he got only a handshake from one of the counselors. "Welcome aboard—the guys will let you know what's going on around here."

In truth, Johnny had always expected that he would find that out from the "guys", no matter what the orientation program said, but he did not expect that the staff members knew and accepted that.

Johnny found himself part of a group meeting that was in progress. Three boys were arguing over who should get the meeting that particular day. Joe, a boy he had known before on the streets as a real tough guy, seemed to have the upper hand. He was explaining how he had been helped by the program and how he wanted to let the others know just how much progress he had made. The other boys were questioning him about why he had made such progress. Gradually it emerged that conformity, not individual choice, was the motivator. The dialogue sounded like this:[3]

> STEVE: Sure you've stopped doing a lot of that stuff [fighting, and so on], but *why* did you stop? That's what we are asking you.
>
> JOE: I did it, that's why!
>
> STEVE: That isn't enough. Why did you do it?

[3] Robert Allen, Harry N. Dubin, Saul Pilnick, and Adella C. Youtz, *Collegefields* (Seattle: Special Child Publications, 1970) pp. 80–81.

JOE: Because that's what a helped boy is supposed to do—isn't that right?

STEVE: No, it's not right. A helped boy doesn't do it because he is supposed to, but because he chooses to. Joe, you know what's wrong with you? You've got an easily influenced problem, and that's the worst kind of all.

Johnny couldn't believe his eyes or ears. Did a person not only have to behave right but have to choose his own behavior as well? This indeed was a new angle that he had never thought of. He had expected lectures from the staff at Collegefields, not directives from the boys themselves. But the staff believed the utilization of the group was probably the most significant therapeutic mechanism. "The boys know you're goofing off; they come up and start screaming and whistling in your ears and calling you all different names and everything. You get to learn they want to take out your aggravation, to find out how much you can take before you blow your stack. . . . Sometimes it's hard for new boys to understand that when the boys try to get new boys aggravated they're trying to help you."

Although Johnny did not realize it, the new culture had been built up carefully, starting with only five boys several months before he came, and adding a few at a time. By the time Johnny joined the program, the original group members were all in the helped-boy phase, ready to take on the responsibility of aiding a newcomer. During Johnny's orientation they saw to it that he "got the word." Here is an excerpt from a conversation that took place during his first month as he learned the "program" through his peers:

STEVE: What are the three main requirements of Collegefields?

JOHNNY: Be yourself, tell the truth, and don't fight.

STEVE: What's an undesirable?

JOHNNY: Anyone who can get you arrested.

STEVE: What's help?

JOHNNY: A better understanding of yourself and your problems.

STEVE: What's recommendations?

JOHNNY: If you break a requirement or defy the boys or staff, you have to recommend yourself to go to jail.

The boys met in Newark every day at 7:30 A.M. (an early hour they themselves decided on in order to have more discussion time). After an hour's discussion, they rode a bus to the campus in Union, New Jersey. During the morning, formal education was provided—large group classes supplemented by small group and individual tutoring. Often the boys tutored each other. The boys used lunchtime in the college cafeteria for "spotting" behavior they felt was indicative of what was happening. Behavior that was not positive or seemed to indicate that a boy was not sincerely trying to change would be brought up in subsequent meetings. Daily afternoon meetings helped to formalize the subculture, the language, and the normative system of the peer group. But the internalization of the new norms and the development of loyalty to the new subculture actually took place outside the group meetings, in interrogations like the one above.

Johnny saw himself as a "tough guy." His early attitude was that he himself could easily take over the program and have the boys doing his bidding in a short time, and so he went along with the routine. He played a role, essentially trying to manipulate the program to his own ends. As he moved into the second phase, he held onto this attitude, not really trying to change himself. During all this time he continued to see members of his old peer group in the streets, although he did observe the 10 P.M. curfew. Even though he was still refusing to help himself, he was earning a measure of status among the Collegefields boys because of his efforts to help some of them. He was beginning to divide his loyalty between his old group and the Collegefields peer group.

In Johnny's seventh week, his crisis occurred, and the boys deliberately confronted him. This is an actual excerpt from the exchange. Johnny has "slipped," having been seen and overheard in conversation with two delinquent associates. Now he is the focus of an afternoon group meeting:

ANDREW: Why were you talking to undesirables?

JOHNNY: The two boys were walking down the street, and they said hello to me and I shook my head. They asked me if I was playing hooky.

BOYS: You're lying! [Loudly] They undesirables, why you talk to them?

JOHNNY: They asked me a question.

ROBERT: Why didn't you put them into situations? [Note: "Situations" was a Collegefields term for role playing to see reactions.]

JOHNNY: I put them in some situations!

EDDIE: Oh, you put them in some, but not the rest.

ROBERT: Explain, Mr. "Helped Boy."

JOHNNY: The situation was two boys were walking down the street. I was standing across the street leaning on the pole, down the street from Collegefields. I shook my head.

LUTHER: You just said that they asked you if you was playing hooky and you said, "No."

ANDREW: Then when he crossed the street; these boys came by. Then he talked to them, and that's when everybody ran to the bus.

EDDIE: The one boy asked you, "Did you play hooky today?" I think his name was—

JOHNNY: I don't know the boy's name.

EDDIE: No?

JOHNNY: No!

EDDIE: So then he said, "Did you play hooky today?" and he said, "No." So I think Bob turned around and started walking towards him, so he starts leaning against the pole and shook his head.

ROBERT: And I asked you why you didn't put them in situations . . . I said, "Why don't you put them in situations now?" But then Pete and I walked over, and we started to put the boys into situations. Why didn't you put them in situations, Johnny? You care about this program at all, or do you feel it's a bunch of bull?

JOHNNY: I care about the program.

ROBERT: You do? You don't show it.

EDDIE: If you care about this program, why don't you show a little care? All you do is go out and clique and come back in the morning. ["Clique:" getting in trouble outside.]

(This continues as the boys keep trying to get Johnny to demonstrate his willingness to be helped. Robert reminds him of his choices.)

ROBERT: You don't care if you go to jail, boy? You got nothing to say for yourself? You'd rather go to jail than talk? You got a big choice there, boy. You talking for your life. . . . You got the impression that nobody but staff can send you to jail. You got that impression, boy? Yes or no?

JOHNNY: Yeah.

STAFF: What's your impression of Johnny?

ROBERT: I got the impression that Johnny has been messing up ever since he came to the program, and he doesn't give one good damn about the program or himself. The only thing he cares about is not going to jail. He doesn't want the help, and he's gonna keep messing up and messing up.

STAFF: You'd better start talking.

ROBERT: Yeah, bust your role and your clique, boy.

LUTHER: So why was you talking to undesirables? You have two
            minutes to decide to talk for your life.

JOHNNY: [After a long pause] They undesirables I mess around with.

ANDREW: You had the meeting twice before. How come you never tell
            us that stuff?

JOHNNY: [Pause] Nobody, the probation officer, my mother, the
            teachers, nobody ever care what happened to me. So I
            didn't care.

BOYS: No, man, the boys care . . . and you've got to care,
            too. . . . Tell it, man . . . we giving out help. . . .

Finally, Johnny accepts the help and tells it straight:

JOHNNY: I been messing around with these jokers since before I was
            busted and came to Collegefields.

Johnny continued telling about all the negative behavior he had been
involved in since coming to Collegefields and confessed the only times he
had been his true self around the other boys were the occasions when he
had exhibited negative behavior in the classroom. As the meeting continued, he became more and more honest, with himself and with the
others. Johnny realized that, rather than recommending his return to the
court and punishment, the boys were encouraging him to be frank, and
giving him status for it. From "boy" or "Mr. Helped Boy" they had,
unconsciously it appears, switched to "man" as soon as he was honest
with them.

Johnny had come a long way at this point. He had expected Collegefields to present two worlds—the staff and the boys, which included
himself. Instead, he found his two worlds were the street culture and the
whole Collegefields culture—the staff, the other boys, and himself. This
culture had joined together in a unique system of beliefs and values that
were in direct opposition to the values of the street culture.

After Johnny finally accepted the boys' help and honestly admitted his
shortcomings, he became painfully aware that cynically using Collegefields for his own ends would no longer be possible. He realized he
could decide to give his allegiance to the street and face sanctions from his
new peer group, or he could decide to give his allegiance to Collegefields
and lose the investment of years spent gaining status on the street. He had
to choose. Leadership on the street meant arrest and jail. At Collegefields,
leadership carried only rewards. He decided for Collegefields.

A major factor that helped promote this change in Johnny was the
authority that the boys shared with the adult system. The very real power
that Collegefields afforded to otherwise powerless youngsters helped

them succeed in the program. Perhaps for the first time in his life Johnny perceived himself and his peers as actively involved in making decisions and setting policy in matters of importance.

HANGING ON TO CHANGE

After seven months in the program, Johnny graduated, a permanently "helped boy," and went back to his old school two levels ahead of where he left it. He could hardly avoid contact with his former associates in the street gang, but Johnny stayed "clean." Since he graduated from Collegefields he has had no negative contact with the law, has gone on further in school, and has started his own family. Finally, he has helped a number of youngsters who were in difficulty.

The Collegefields experience resulted in favorable changes not only for Johnny but for the whole group. Accomplishments included academic advancement of as much as three years, a significant improvement in IQ, much more favorable attitudes toward teachers, improved prospects and interest in further schooling, increased vocational orientation with ambition less focused on fantasy choices, improved favorable attitudes toward self, and increased integrity.

The most striking feature of this rehabilitation program was its successful use of the dynamics of the peer-group culture to set and achieve more humanistic goals and greater freedom of choice for the participants. From Collegefields also emerged the hope that groups ordinarily in conflict can work together for mutual benefit.

Chapter 19

Migrancy Defeated

The minute you say, "I am in a position to make my life what I want it to be, I got it in me and my people got it in them, even if we was born migrants, to be other things if we want. . . ." Well, it was like you are born again. Your whole life changes and you know you are as good as everybody else.

EMANUELA
A former migrant worker

One of the worst problems of contemporary society is the plight of some 200,000 migrant workers. They have half the life expectancy of the population at large, their incomes are pitifully low, they live in substandard housing, they lack rudimentary sanitation facilities, and they have almost no job security. Severe conditions in the fields are matched by negligible health care, education, and social services in the community. Small wonder that absenteeism and turnover rates are high, and that good relationships between workers and the companies that employ them are virtually nonexistent.

These conditions were well entrenched in the system in the citrus groves of central Florida in 1970, when an opportunity arose to apply the Normative Systems approach to change. The challenge was tremendous, for the problem was not one of isolated negative conditions, but of a deeply entrenched racist, feudal system. Yet through their own involvement, these groves workers managed to change their culture in a significant way, achieving in five years what was originally expected to require ten.

A phone call from J. Lucian (Luke) Smith, then president of the Foods Division of Coca-Cola Company (and now president of Coca-Cola's worldwide operations), introduced us to the subculture of migrant workers. He wasn't sure just how bad the situation was, but a recent visit to the migrant camps had made him realize that it was far from good. Would we be interested in doing a study of their Minute Maid agricultural operations to see just what steps, if any, should be taken to improve them? We would indeed. Unfortunately, our time and cost estimates were almost double those of a market research group with which the company had had previous dealings, and so the company decided to use that group again.

Some months later, an opportunity arose to review the market research findings. Not unexpectedly, they revealed more about the research approach than they did about the life and concerns of the migrants. The long survival experience of blacks in white-dominated cultures had prepared them well for providing "correct," as opposed to accurate, answers. The research report suggested that things were not nearly so bad as the company had feared ("Mr. Charley is doing just fine!"), and that a few relatively superficial changes would be sufficient to correct the situation.

A company task force, making use of these findings, plus its own, less optimistic, observations, prepared a generous plan that called for spending a great deal of money on a series of welfare-type programs. We were asked to review the plan before it was put into operation. Our reaction to both the research findings and the task force proposal was polite but incredulous. It seemed certain that the program being considered, well-intentioned as it was, would provide little more than cosmetic changes, and that the long-range effects would be negligible at best. There had been no attempt to involve people in the solution of their own problems, and the underlying culture would remain untouched. We felt that whatever improvements were made would probably be short-lived. As a result of this reaction, Coca-Cola decided to have another look at the situation from a cultural prospective, and a culture-based, systematic analysis began.

LOOKING AT THE PROBLEM

The first step was to involve the people in the analysis of their own problems. An HRI team moved to Florida, some to meet with the local managers and supervisors, but most to become deeply immersed in the lives of the migrant workers themselves. Three HRI staff members moved into Minute Maid's migrant camps for single male workers and applied for jobs as citrus pickers. Another moved into the company's family housing with his wife and two small children. Staff also visited the bars and churches frequented by the migrants, and became familiar with their problems on a firsthand basis.

As the staff began to meet people on their own terms, the workers' initial hesitancy and anxiety began to dissipate. Soon a group of migrants and local people emerged who wanted to do something about the situation. Several were employed as community aides so that they could devote full time to the research effort. Meetings between workers and top corporate management were held, often in the homes of the workers, so the executives could see firsthand the conditions that existed.

Meetings with the local managers also were helpful. They were not happy with what was happening either. They felt pretty much neglected since Coca-Cola's acquisition of the Minute Maid Company some ten years earlier. At the time of the acquisition they had had bright hopes that Coke would improve the situation, but this had never occurred. For its part, Coke thought the local managers wanted to be left alone.

There was a great deal of suspicion on all sides. As one worker later told us, "I didn't trust you folks when you first came here. I thought that you was just trying to get what you could, from us and the company too." Managers were even more suspicious than workers. Some recalled the old days, "when New York Jews and 'nigras' knew their place"—and it wasn't with "decent white folks."

Gradually, the total picture began to emerge. Coca-Cola had paid little attention to its 30,000 acres of citrus groves since their acquisition. The operation was making a profit, and so had been left in the hands of the original supervisors. Living and working conditions were deplorable. Sara Harris, whose husband Arnold was on the consultant team, called it "a world of total despair":

> I remember with painful clarity . . . the company housing area known as Maxcy Quarters, where Saint Emanuela and other workers out of the groves lived . . . no trees, no flowers, no grass, no playground facilities for the children . . . just twenty-six institutional green, small row shacks on a sand road littered with the kitchen carrion of poverty: chicken bones, watermelon rinds, decomposing animal and human offal.[1]

> [One resident] and her nine children and grandchildren live in a typical two-room shack with no sink or refrigeration, no indoor toilet, only an uninsulated, boxlike bedroom, and a so-called kitchen with a wood stove.[2]

Needless to say, the market research report that "everybody loves it here" was quickly rejected for what it was—an attempt to tell the boss what he wanted to hear. When Sara Harris asked a supervisor about toilets for the workers in the fields, he laughed and bet the workers themselves would say they did not want toilets. A woman nearing 60 told us that the company was "the kindest, best, and nicest people I ever work for in all my time of traveling up road and down,"[3] and said her people wouldn't want toilet facilities in the groves because the responsibility of keeping them clean would be too great.

It was clearly impossible to rely on the surface responses of people who

---

[1] Sara Harris and Robert F. Allen, *The Quiet Revolution* (New York: Rawson 1978), p. 14.

[2] Ibid., p. 15.

[3] Ibid., p. 11.

had no reason to trust either us or our purposes. A comprehensive analysis had to be carried out by the workers themselves. As people were selected and trained for this purpose, observation of the situation continued to challenge the pleasant words. The actual data showed the culture to be essentially feudal, with racist norms firmly embedded in an outdated agricultural system. For example:

> The annual income, though somewhat better than in most other companies, was roughly comparable to the $2,200 income for pickers statewide.

> Most of the pickers worked on a seasonal basis—six to seven months—then took off for the North to pick apples and cherries. Only about 200 of the 1200 workers were year-round, "care-taking" employees, paid on an hourly basis.

> Seasonal workers were paid by the number of boxes picked, and productivity standards were low. A company official said: "It didn't make much difference how many workers you had because they were all paid on a piecework basis. A hundred workers [each] picking three boxes a day was the same to the company as three workers picking 100 boxes a day."[4]

> Because of the piecework pay systems, bus or equipment breakdowns were of little significance to management. As a result, many crews spent long hours of unproductive time sitting by the roadside waiting for repairs.

> Children of all ages were allowed in the fields, and child labor laws were unenforced.

> There were no toilet facilities in the fields.

> There was no unemployment compensation; migrants are exempt from federal law.

> Turnover was extremely high—400 percent per year.

> Absenteeism was extremely high, averaging two days a week.

> Foremen were making loans to workers at usurious rates (520 percent per year).

> A worker paid 35 cents a week to his foreman for ice to put in the drinking water.

> Positive relationships between company and workers were virtually nonexistent, and there was little chance for a worker to have a career within the company. Racism was rampant.

> Company housing, unacceptable by any reasonable standards, was pro-

[4] Phil Garner, "A New Life for Migrant Workers," *Atlanta Journal and Constitution Magazine,* Jan. 23, 1972, p. 8.

vided for only 20 percent of workers. Some of the houses had been declared unfit for human use in the 1920s.

Displeased with company housing, a large percentage of workers was eager to purchase or rent their own homes. They were unable to do so, however, because they lacked year-round employment.

Accident rates were double those of other industrial operations.

Children were infested with parasitic worms and lice.

There were severe, chronic health problems.

Child care facilities were almost nonexistent.

Paternalistic approaches characterized even the most positive ways of relating to black workers.

A supportive culture was needed, particularly for the supervisors since they would be in serious trouble with neighbors and fellow employees for violating current feudal, racist norms.

When asked how the workers, especially the women and children, lived through the long hours in the hot sun, moving heavy ladders and carrying canvas sacks bursting with oranges, a supervisor answered:

Women and kids of this class and type, or men either for that matter, things just don't get to them like they do the rest of us.[5]

Local doctors tended to avoid having agricultural workers as patients, and as to hospitals, the same supervisor noted that:

I can't rightly remember the last time one of mine was in a hospital. Seem like they got a way of curing themself, sort of curling up and living through the thing till they get over it, more like a dog or cat.[6]

None of the supervisors had had first-aid training, and there was no communication facility for calling in medical help.

The project's basic guiding principles included:

1. *Involvement of people*—the project would encourage and build upon the involvement of the people most directly affected, including as many of the seasonal workers, supervisors, and their families as feasible.

2. *Emphasis on self-help*—Instead of flirting with welfare programs, the project would implement approaches within which people could help themselves.

[5] Harris and Allen, *The Quiet Revolution,* p. 4.

[6] Ibid., p. 4.

3. Total systems approach—Since interrelated problems required interrelated change efforts, the project would address a number of different problem areas simultaneously, including:

(a) Employment and income
(b) Housing
(c) Health, education, and social services
(d) Organizational support
(e) Community relations

4. *Emphasis upon long-term results on a broad scale*—The project would openly encourage people to evaluate it on its sustained results. It would have value and impact beyond the immediate situation.

5. *Assurance of economic viability*—Initially, the project would be "seeded" and sustained by the Coca-Cola Company, but ultimately it would become fiscally independent and self-generating.

Along with these principles there were specific objectives, such as:

Absenteeism to be reduced by at least 50 percent

Productivity and income at least to double within eighteen months

No employee to live in substandard housing

Accredited and/or licensed community facilities in child development, social services, and library services to open within two years

While these objectives were being settled upon, action began on some immediate steps to alleviate the deplorable conditions.

INTRODUCING A NEW CULTURE

Soon after the analysis was completed, introductory workshops were held. In this case it was decided to include aides. The four community aides (chosen from the indigenous leadership of the migrants), twenty top managers and supervisors, and six consultants from HRI met for four days in a hotel. At this kickoff workshop, Luke Smith made it clear how top management and he, as an individual, felt about some negative human relations norms:

. . . As managers and supervisors, it is your responsibility to make it very clear to all the people in your crews that words like *nigger* cannot any longer be spoken around here. Those words have got to come out of the vocabularies of anybody who wants to go on working for this company.[7]

---

[7] Ibid., p. 68.

He also warned against jokes reflecting on people's dignity.

Besides confronting negative norms and making management's commitment clear, the workshop started to build more open, trusting personal relationships. Through sharing childhood experiences, this unlikely assortment of people—educated and uneducated, country and city fold, executive and hired hand, wealthy and poverty-stricken, Northern liberal and Southern racist—found they had a great deal in common and began to sense the possibilities of working together for a shared purpose.

As Luke Smith observed:

> If we know you as people, as human beings, and if you know us that way,
> . . . if we can sit down and talk together . . . you can't ever again be
> bogeymen to us . . . I want to tell you first, speaking for all of us in the
> company, how truly sorry we are because it took us much too long to
> come here to sit down with you and learn for ourselves what you are up
> against . . . we took the easy way out. . . . I'm here to pledge our complete cooperation to you for the future. . . . We'll stand behind you in
> all of your efforts to change things here.[8]

Thus the tone was set—the project would forgo placing blame and spend its energy on getting results. In this manner the workshops continued down the organization until all management and supervisory personnel had been initiated.

NORMS IN ACTION

The system's implementation began even before the workshops were under way. Here again, helping people change the deeply entrenched negative norms of their culture involved a complex of norm influence areas on all four levels (the individual worker, the work team and task forces, the Coca-Cola leadership and groves supervisors, and the policies and structures of the total organization). These had to be dealt with through systematic strategies, with all the normative principles of change brought into play. It is possible here to highlight only a few of the most important of these elements as they were applied to the most pressing needs of the people.

The Need for Improved Conditions of Employment

As a first step, two pilot crews were established, with year-round jobs. In the beginning, much to our amazement, people doubted whether this would even be possible, since "everyone knew" that orange pickers would never pick lemons, and vice versa. But the company owned groves

[8] Ibid., p. 60.

of both types, and lemons were harvested in summer and oranges in winter. This provided an excellent chance to stabilize employment.

Once the underlying cultural norms were examined and dealt with, the old blocks began to dissipate, and the same pickers were harvesting both lemons and oranges as if it had always been that way.

Three hundred groves workers were quickly given an opportunity for year-round jobs with guaranteed weekly income, and by December 1971, this group had been expanded to 625. This did away with migrancy for about half the workers. But there were additional problems beyond the paycheck. Everyone also "knew" that migrants would not work a five-day week even if they had the opportunity, and that it would be impossible to do much to increase individual worker productivity. These beliefs likewise turned out to be untrue. Most pickers were willing—in fact, eager—to work a five-day week, and the new pilot crews soon nearly tripled the productivity of the crews that were still working within the older established pattern.

All these things were not accomplished without complications. At the end of the first week, as one of the new crews was reviewing its progress with management, one worker said that he liked the new idea and that he thought he would keep it up until Christmas. Since this was November 15, the prospect did not seem very encouraging to those of us who were building for the centuries. When asked why he thought the experiment would be so short-lived, he replied that he and his co-workers didn't like always having to be in the groves at 7:30 A.M. when anyone knew that after a rain the trees wouldn't be ready for picking until 9:30. He felt he could use his time a lot more profitably fixing his car or sleeping later, rather than sitting in a wet orange grove.

When this criticism was recognized, management immediately agreed that the workday would begin not when the clock and the consultants' norms said it should, but when the groves were dry enough for harvesting. This was a case where the norms of the managers and consultants had been superimposed upon a new work situation. The fact that this man felt free to speak up about them was duly recognized as a breakthrough in the communications process.

The worker-management meetings were a key to the solution of this and hundreds of other problems. Gradually what had been done only by a few pilot crews became the main method of harvesting. The workers' increased income was accompanied by increased productivity and the need for less mechanical equipment than had been required earlier.

The increased worker productivity decreased the number of people needed, and eventually the same number of boxes were being picked by 25 percent fewer people. However, careful planning made it possible to handle the reductions through attrition and increased job opportunities in other aspects of company employment. Training opportunities were provided even for those who decided they did not want to continue as agricultural workers.

Housing

Work on housing had to begin almost at once. With company approval, lighting and plumbing improvements, rat control, and repairs were started. Again, employees were involved in the process; those not needed in the groves were hired to assist with the improvements. Within days, work was under way, painting, cleaning up, sanitizing, providing hot water, and building playgrounds.

The task forces came up with the idea that the long-range answer to housing did not lie in improved company-owned housing, but in private housing owned by the people themselves. It is hard for a person to feel free if he stands to lose his house as well as his job if he has trouble with the company. Cooperative relationships were built not only into the planning process, but into the ownership process as well.

All regular employees were provided with medical and life insurance; retirement, thrift, and savings plans; and paid vacations, holidays, and sick leave. This was the first time these benefits had been offered in the history of the industry. Seasonal employees also were given medical and life insurance benefits, which covered them both in the groves and away. In addition, they were given the option of putting 5 percent of their pay into a seasonal savings plan, which could be drawn on whenever they wished. If a worker left the money in for the duration of the harvesting season, it was matched by the company, dollar for dollar.

Moreover, three representatives of the workers were sent North in April to check the treatment of migrant workers in the apple and cherry regions of New York State. They came back with information on the best jobs and most decent working conditions, so that workers who wished to find jobs during the Florida off-season would know the best places to go.

Health, Welfare, and Social Services

As the task forces continued their work, it became clear that medical, educational, and social services were almost nonexistent and that the surrounding community was unlikely to provide them, because of long-standing prejudice and discrimination. If there were to be such services, the people would have to develop them themselves.

"Everyone knew" that migrants could never undertake a project like this for themselves, but they did. With company assistance and federal funding, they built their own community medical center, dental clinic, library, and child development centers. These were not company-owned and -operated facilities. They were organized by community boards of workers set up for the purpose. The people discussed their needs, made decisions, and carried them out.

The problem of child labor yielded to the new child development centers and to strongly enforced company policies which banned children under 16 from the groves. The children's former income was compensated for by the better employment opportunities.

The problem of supervisor loans at usurious rates was solved by setting up an interest-free loan fund and by making the loaning of money for interest a matter for instant dismissal. Instead, supervisors were empowered to write checks for short-term interest-free loans of up to $100, which could be repaid through payroll deductions. Longer-term low-interest loans were made available through an employee credit union.

Sanitation in the fields was provided by outfitting buses with toilet and washing facilities, and ice water was provided by the company. Special art programs were developed for the children, and youth groups carried on their own educational services.

Organizational and Community Relationships

Supervisor and management development programs were instituted, and for the first time black employees were considered for supervisory positions and training.

Liaison with the local community was improved, and a voter registration campaign helped workers gain greater power within their communities. Special preschool and tutorial programs were developed in consultation with local school districts.

Other growers were contacted and briefed on the goals and purposes of the project to enlist, if not their support, at least their understanding of what was beginning to occur.

Normative Principles Followed

All these actions were taken in terms of the normative principles of change discussed earlier. The emphasis on self-help began with the hiring of the four community aides, who then began to involve more people in the change process. The aides served as an initial link between the consultants and the workers. Involvement of people in task forces further expanded this process. In all meetings, the emphasis was on listening to the people, involving them in decisions, and helping them to carry out the plans they had developed.

Leadership commitment, another important principle, showed in a number of ways. One highly visible evidence of top management's commitment was the appointment of a leading company vice president (William Kelly) to serve as on-site director of the project. In addition, a multimillion dollar budget was set aside for the effort. Executives at corporate headquarters spent a great deal of time in the groves, working with people to plan the program and to evaluate progress. They attended every function considered critical to the success of the program, and continually modeled their commitment to what was occurring.

The president of the worldwide corporation (Paul Austin) expressed his total commitment in a public statement before the Mondale Senate committee on migrancy: "We must establish a program to correct these conditions and commit whatever funds and talents are necessary to do the job."[9]

Earlier, meeting with company managers, both Austin and Luke Smith had made it clear that any executive or manager who would not support the effort should resign immediately or face termination.

Win/win solutions, beneficial to both workers and company, were constantly sought. One of the most difficult problems was the sense of paternalism that had developed, with managers generally preferring to give things away rather than let people have a chance to earn them. The company made important moves to change this. While it generously committed funds, it did not do so as welfare but as a responsible partner in a participatory effort. And it did it for its own economic sake as well as for the workers' benefit.

Perhaps the most important element in the whole program was that people understood the change process they were part of and were aware of their roles in it. Therefore, they were able to continue to apply it to new problems and new situations as they appeared.

A CAUSE FOR PRIDE

The evaluation methods were built into the initial analysis. Specific short-range and long-range goals were established in each of the project areas, and progress toward these goals was tracked by both worker and management committees. At the beginning of the project, weekly reporting procedures were set up to provide a constant and highly visible flow of information on worker income and productivity. This helped to direct the attention of the total organization to the project's progress, or lack of it.

Workers themselves were involved in these evaluations in their weekly work team meetings. Results were presented and discussed, and any slip-

[9] Timothy Larkin, "Adios to Migrancy," *Manpower* (Washington: U.S. Department of Labor, Manpower Administration, August 1974), p. 15.

page of either production or income was immediately noted and analyzed for corrective action.

Each step of the overall plan was assigned a completion date, and records were kept of whether or not these dates were met. Thus the introduction of the housing program was carefully scheduled, from initial recommendations and worker selection of the architect to the completion of the building program.

In evaluating program progress the level of participation was also carefully monitored. The voter registration program, for example, was evaluated not only in terms of the number of meetings but more importantly in terms of the number of voters registered. Cultural change was also monitored by use of normative surveys and field instruments. Refinements of these evaluation steps continue to the present time.

Although Coca-Cola has thus far put over $7 million into the project, its annual input dropped proportionately as surrounding communities and government agencies began to participate. Today it supports the project with $375,000 a year, and also by providing some consulting assistance, one full-time liaison person, and some vehicles and buildings, while state- and county-administered federal funding amounts to over $1,400,000. Well over 100 community and state agencies and organizations have entered into cooperative arrangements with the project.

Achievements Sustained

Not only was the increased income and job security an immediate achievement, but it has been sustained. By the time the project was five years old, annual worker income had quadrupled. The following year's report stated that the turnover rate had been reduced drastically.

The housing achievements are also dramatic. First, the company is out of the housing business—there are no migrant camps. Instead, an eighty-five-home model community has been developed, there is an effective homeowners' association, and several housing counselors provide outreach services.

Community services continue to be run primarily by the workers themselves, with thirteen counties receiving the total supportive services (medical, health, emergency, and relocation). Advisory councils in each of four regions are represented on a central governing board. There are three child development centers and three head-start programs, providing a well-rounded education as well as day care. The library contains one of the finest collections of black and Chicano literature in the South. Medical and dental clinics started by the project are now administered separately and serve a larger populace beyond the groves.

It is manifest in the most startling achievement of all in the groves: migrancy defeated.

Chapter 20

Changing the Litter Culture

If we can turn litterers into nonlitterers, then perhaps many of the other problems of the human environment can be reduced to manageable proportions.

ROGER POWERS
President, Keep America Beautiful

Litter is just a start. People are beginning to talk about problems they share and resources they hadn't been in touch with before.

COMMUNITY TASK FORCE MEMBER
Macon, Georgia

Nearly everyone agrees that littering is bad, and yet we continue to be a littering nation. Fines threaten us and advertising slogans scold us, but for every person who changes to neater ways, there are dozens who "keep up with the Joneses," and the Joneses are littering.

Is litter the "common cold" of the environment; the problem everyone censures but no one solves? Up to 1973, it seemed so. The most publicized effort up to that time had been Oregon's costly ban-the-bottle campaign, and it achieved only a temporary 10.6 percent reduction of all litter.

In 1973 there was a hopeful turn of events—a litter reduction program that began to show significant results. The program attacked littering as a behavioral problem, using the Normative Systems culture-based approach.

The basic problem was a widespread feeling that nothing could really be done about litter. The various approaches that had been used in cities throughout the United States were studied, and each one contained negative norms—the most prevalent being an attachment to a single-variable approach. Many cities had had one-shot campaigns that lasted a few weeks. Others had tried the ban-the-can approach. Still others had tried expensive advertising campaigns admonishing people to stop littering. But none of the approaches was multilevel or systematic—and none of them produced lasting results. It seemed a good opportunity to make use of the Normative Systems approach on a problem that was highly visible. Per-

haps people would learn from it how to work on even more crucial community problems.

The opportunity to apply the culture-based approach came through
the sponsorship of Keep America Beautiful (KAB), a national public service organization that is supported by a number of industrial and civic
groups. KAB's concern cuts across many levels of citizenry—civic
groups that want a more attractive environment, beverage companies
opposed to bottle-banning legislation, and ecological interests worried
about the future.

KAB's sponsors commissioned HRI to make use of its culture change
approach and develop an overall model that could be applied in three pilot
projects: Tampa, Florida; Charlotte, North Carolina; and Macon, Georgia. KAB provided professional and staff assistance, and county governments contributed to the eighteen-month project. At the end of that time,
the project had surpassed all expectations, and at a remarkably low cost.
Three years later, reductions in the program area were still averaging 60 to
70 percent.

EXPLODING THE LITTER MYTHS

The pilot project began with an analysis of the problem. It found that litter
has been a problem for people since early times, starting when the cave-
men threw old bones out of their caves. Here in America we have a
history of acceptance of litter. Think of the years of trash on the streets, of
the auto wrecks in open graveyards, of papers and rags trapped against
fences, and of city apartments where people "airmail" their garbage into
the streets and empty lots. When man returned from the moon, he left a
few artifacts behind, just "doing what comes naturally."

Although society has been plagued by more devastating problems, few
rank higher than litter in terms of both visibility and widespread concern.
Yet litter continues to accumulate and interfere with the quality of life.
The crux of the matter is not that people consciously choose to litter, but
that they do not give it a second thought.

The starting point of the project, therefore, was the awareness that if
something were to be done about litter, something needed to be done
about the "litter culture"—that is, the network of negative norms that
supports and reinforces littering behavior. Some of these were:

A PREVALENT FEELING OF HELPLESSNESS

"It's human nature to litter."

"Litter is a part of life."

"As long as there are people, there will be litter."

"Nothing can be done."

Reliance on Simplistic, Single Variable Solutions

"Let's raise littering penalties."

"Let's ban the can."

"Let's get the Boy Scouts to clean up."

Blame Placing and Negative Parenting

"Why can't sanitation departments take care of the problem?"

"The problem is in the ghetto."

"Slobs litter."

The analysis showed that there were a lot of misconceptions about litter. Pedestrians and motorists are popularly believed to be the chief sources of litter, but actually there are five other sources that together contribute more: uncovered trucks, loading docks, poor refuse collection, construction and demolition sites, and commercial and household garbage.

Another myth is that littering is the fault of certain individuals. Actually, it was found that people take any of four roles with respect to litter: (1) the actual litterers—people who deliberately or unconsciously litter; (2) the "gatekeepers"—people in power who make decisions that contribute to littering, such as judges and police who do not enforce laws or town officials who do not provide large enough sanitation budgets; (3) the "witnesses" who stand silently by without confronting littering behavior; and (4) the victims who have to live in a littered environment.

In a sense we are all victims, but the worst victims receive the most blame. The most frequent "fall guy" is the poor person from the ghetto area who can do little about the problem unless the "gatekeepers" of the community make it possible. Living in an area of high population with insufficient containers for refuse and insufficient collection service, and located close to major sources of litter, the ghetto resident hardly seems to deserve all the blame.

There is much confusion about what litter is. To help clear this up with some sound data, a nationally recognized expert in litter control was asked to be a project consultant. He had completed a study of litter in 105 cities in 17 states in 1971, and found it to consist of uncontainerized man-made solid waste. It was roughly 64 percent paper, 14 percent metal, 7 percent plastics, 5 percent glass, and 10 percent other items like clothing, rags, and building materials. A list of 150 such items made it evident that focusing on beverage containers ignores the bulk of the problem.

Extensive field activities verified these facts, and in addition, we proceeded to identify cultural norms related to litter, using observations, in-depth interviews, and surveys.

A general failure to see the litter problem as being culturally determined turned out to be the biggest public misconception. The basic reason that people litter is that other people do. The only way to change individual littering, then, was to change the culture. To the slogan, "Products don't litter, people do," we would add "when the system encourages them to."

Analysis showed that though littering was generally condemned, people were not involved in finding solutions. For example, nobody had asked sanitation workers, who deal with trash every day, to become involved in seeking new and more creative solutions that could make use of their experience.

The program design was an intervention model known as ARM (action research model), which called for close adherence to the principles of effective cultural change with which the reader is now familiar: involvement of all the people of the community, from the mayor and power structure to the sanitation worker and the ghetto victim of litter; fact gathering—in this case, sound information about litter and littering norms; a systematic approach to the problem; concentration on solutions in which all levels of the community would be winners; a focus on results; and positive reinforcement for a sustained effort. Overall, the plan was to build a belief that something could be done—and then do it.

In the ARM project, analysis of the problem was accompanied by the setting of both broad and specific objectives. Broad objectives were to reduce litter, to develop a model that could be used in a community of any size, to substitute a systems approach for reliance on simplistic solutions, to generate enthusiastic response on the part of the local community, and to develop a program that cities across the country could afford.

Some specific objectives were:

> To measure litter regularly and reduce it by 20 percent within twelve months
>
> To have every community member, but especially the "gatekeepers" or power structure, experience a workshop in which they learn what litter is, who is causing it, and what has to be done to reduce it
>
> To have a communitywide task force develop and implement a systematic plan for reducing litter in each of the three pilot cities.

GETTING THINGS STARTED

If it is the culture that causes littering, the big question is: What do we do about changing it? More particularly, what was actually done in the pilot program that made it possible to change such supposedly ingrained human behavior?

A vital component of the plan was tailoring the litter program to and by the community using it. As the first step, a "shared ownership" of the program was developed through a series of workshops designed to gain commitment and involvement as well as to introduce the cultural change method. Initial workshops were conducted for the community's litter "gatekeepers"—government, business, and civic leaders, including public works officials and environmental group leaders. Eventually, these workshops were conducted throughout the community.

The workshops consisted of several consciousness-raising components: what litter is, where it comes from, and what the dynamic behind it is. Through a litter-perception test people found that litter is "in the eye of the beholder." Slides of various areas were projected and people were asked to rate their litter content from 0 to 5. They found that they tended to rate an area higher if the photo was taken on a rainy day or if the neighborhood was rundown.

After a few minutes of this perception test, people got the point: Their perceptions of litter distort the facts. By examining photographs of litter within the community, they came to see that litter isn't everywhere; it's just in certain locations. It follows, of course, that those are the areas that should be targeted. No wonder generalized cleanup campaigns or billboard ads saying "Point Out Pollution" had done little good! People learned to focus on the real problem and to see that their efforts could be better spent on specific targets.

In the ARM program, all seven sources were dealt with, and all four types of people were helped to understand and change littering norms. The program was community-based because norms have to be changed right in the situations where people are involved with each other. A sign on a highway will not stop littering, but a program back home in the community can change the norm, so that even when a person is away from town he no longer litters.

Growing out of the workshops were additional studies of the litter culture, including examination of existing litter-control technology, sanitation codes, ordinances and enforcement, current programs, community structures, and organization. These studies produced a body of recommendations which was eventually refined into the "clean community system." This plan provided a blueprint for systematic modification of the cultural influences.

CHANGING TO A CLEANER CULTURE

For a closer look at what installing a new culture really means in terms of people, let's transport ourselves to one of the three cities during the early weeks of the ARM project. We see a young black man, a lawyer, sitting at a big, circular table. Across from him are a white-haired bank president and a sanitation worker. Also at the table are a high school principal, the president of the local woman's club, the assistant city manager, the vice president of a bottling company, and a behavioral scientist.

There is an air of seriousness in the room, but also a sense of achievement, relaxation, and relationship. People from diverse segments of the community are learning to know each other, to work together on common problems, and to find common solutions in which everyone is a winner. The sanitation worker finds he is listened to as attentively as the bank president.

Through committees known as task forces, this central group reaches and keeps in touch with all "gatekeepers." Government officials, businesses, and then neighborhoods all take part in a program that says, "Clean Up Your Own House."

Our group around the circular table is working on some key norm influence areas. To them, "focusing on results" has meant instituting an initial cleanup effort to remove 80 percent of the litter—most of which has been trapped for years. The group talks about changing the face of the city so that results will be quickly evident. "Nobody's going to believe we can do anything until they see it happening," says the lawyer. The group recognizes that change will be stimulated by visible signs. "Changing attitudes is bound to bring longer-lasting results than restrictive legislations," the bank president comments. The group decides to ask the city to buy three more garbage trucks—"the kind with the closed-in top and automatic feeder," says the sanitation worker. "You lose half the stuff in the street with that old open equipment."

A scene of this kind took place in each of the three cities in the pilot project. Each one established a clean city committee, much like that above. Each committee included both formal and informal leaders and met regularly to plan, evaluate progress, and provide positive support during the long months of community effort.

We realized from the outset of the ARM project that a successful change effort was going to require both technology and people. Initially, there were those who pushed for educational measures and others who saw the "equipment" approach as the panacea. All soon agreed that the best technology in the world will not work without the support of people, and that there is not much people can do without the technology that makes solutions possible.

There were no grandiose promises. Very little, in fact next to nothing, was said until actual results were in. Then, however, false modesty was not encouraged. "If you can do what you say, you're not bragging," said one of the committee members. Rather than hiding the self-interest of the participants, the idea was to make use of self-interest for the community's benefit. The recognition of success is among the most powerful reinforcements for the project.

One of the challenges of the litter project was the large number of people involved. The population of Tampa was clearly too large to be dealt with as a whole. This led the group to find and concentrate on pressure points not only in Tampa but in all three pilot cities. The critical norm influences which had direct bearing on the litter culture were identified as training and orientation (to clear up misconceptions); information and communication (accurate measurement and effective feedback); involvement of people (by both formal and informal leadership); rewards and recognition (instead of placing blame); and careful tracking and publicizing of achievements.

By the time of the meeting described above, modification of the litter culture through intervention in the critical influence areas was well under way. Field and research components were carefully coordinated and maintained throughout the project. The following are representative activities that actually went on under the auspices of the Clean Community System.

The work on clearing up misconceptions had already begun with the intensive workshops of Phase II. Through them the city council, the sanitation workers, and all other community leaders and members had gained a better understanding of the realities of the litter problem. Massive education campaigns were conducted, including normative change workshops.

The next step was to measure litter accurately but simply, on a regular (quarterly) basis, and feed the data back to the community. In each city, a baseline for measurement was established early in the project using the latest techniques.

The committees also encouraged development of up-to-date sanitation codes. Charlotte, particularly, stressed vigorous enforcement of all ordinances relating to trash. Tampa placed special emphasis on reduction of litter at the five often-neglected sources mentioned above. In Macon, the approach was to develop techniques which could be used by any community moved to initiate a clean city plan.

Because it was understood that most people might think this was "just another cleanup campaign," action and results were carefully monitored and publicized. Media coverage was excellent, and soon a belief in the change process became quite widespread.

Clean city awards were given to individuals (for example, a grocer in Macon reorganized his whole day so that incoming shipments would not leave a trail of litter), and public service newspaper advertisements cited the heroes and heroines of the effort.

The emphasis on immediate results meant a lot of action. There was the purchase of new equipment and better facilities, better service, and the cleanup of sore spots. A sampling:

Tampa—Twenty new trash receptacles were ordered for the new downtown mall; eight other styles of containers were ordered to determine those most suitable for various locations. Low-cost government housing neighborhoods were cleaned up every thirty days by the sanitation department; the largest dump in the city was eliminated through city and industry cooperative effort; the program was discussed with bar managers on 22nd Street, and they agreed to properly containerize their refuse.

Charlotte—Five hundred public works department managers, supervisors, enforcement, and sanitation employees and forty-nine beverage and packing industry representatives attended litter reduction workshops; the street-cleaning program was changed from a need to a scheduled basis, so that the entire community's streets are cleaned every twenty-one days.

Macon—The city-county government committed a $30,000 budget to the ARM effort; an executive coordinator was employed.

A CLEANUP THAT IS LONG-LASTING

The achievement in litter reduction far surpassed the original objective of 20 percent in one year, and the percentages kept on climbing. The latest available figures from KAB show the following reductions:

Tampa	69 percent	(December 1978)
Charlotte	71 percent	(September 1979)
Macon	76 percent	(August 1979)

Periodic measurements and evaluations of both litter and littering norms are an integral part of the program. All cities conduct quarterly follow-up photographic measurements and take community attitude surveys every six to nine months. These surveys determine the continuing effectiveness of the local committees' efforts and also provide insight into the prevailing negative norms that may require a special change strategy. Monthly report forms sent to KAB are another tool for evaluating local programs and helping to point out potential problems.

THE CULTURAL APPROACH SPREADS

The ARM model—now called the Clean Community System—is in use in 175 cities and counties. Participating municipalities are well distributed throughout the country and range in size from Houston, Texas (1.5 million), to Holly Ridge, North Carolina (415). Pilot programs exist on four military bases, and six other countries (Australia, England, Canada, Bermuda, New Zealand, and South Africa) use the program.

Chapter 21

Trouble
in Paradise

"We give them everything and the morale is terrible,"
the managers complained. "What's wrong?"

Excerpt from a report on a
Normative Systems change program

The corporation was large and prestigious. It manufactured high-quality, pharmaceutical and personal care products which found a ready market. Sales were high, and profits were the best in the company's twenty-year history. The buildings were beautiful and contained the latest equipment. There was a generous benefits program; nobody was ever fired or laid off, and there seemed to be unlimited money for bonuses and training programs. The 4,000 or so employees did not have to work very hard, as many departments were overstaffed, and no one seemed to worry about efficiency. The employees never bothered the company, and the company never bothered the employees. In short, it was what some would call an "industrial paradise."

But there was trouble in paradise. A routine survey showed that employee morale was extremely low. The company tried adding a few extra benefits, but nobody seemed happy with the surfeit of good things. A second morale survey a year later produced the same results; dissatisfaction was pervasive and persistent. This perplexed top management. Growing competition would soon jeopardize the company's favorable position, and when that happened, employee morale would be an important factor.

BEGINNING WITH AN ANALYSIS

After some preliminary meetings with management, the analysis was begun, involving people both inside and outside the organization. The picture that emerged was not an attractive one. Under the facade of a corporate paradise, some nasty surprises were lurking. Here was a company that, because of its outstanding products, was making tremendous profits. Hence, labor costs had been unimportant. A long history of paternalism had fostered a kind of informal bribery system. The company played the

219

part of an indulgent papa to its employees, giving generous compensation and demanding little in the way of productivity, efficiency, and cost-effectiveness. But like the poor little rich boy, the employee was not happy. A companywide cultural analysis, relying chiefly on interviews and observations, showed that people felt they were being bought off with benefits. The analysis also showed that communication norms were firmly established—one way, down, from the fourteenth (executive) floor.

Here are some of the things employees said (grouped by the critical norm areas that the remarks revealed):

Lack of emphasis on results	"This is a fat cat company."
	"Nobody measures performance."
	"We're losing credibility—we keep introducing programs that don't produce results."
	"When it comes to cutting costs, nobody gives a damn."
	"Guys who work their asses off and guys who goof off all get the same reward."
Satisfaction with less than excellence	"In the old days there was a feeling that we had to be the best. I don't think the new employees feel that way."
	"Nobody seems to care how well we're doing."
	"I can show you ten people goofing off right now—they don't give a damn."
Win/lose, blameplacing approaches to problem solving	"Just watch out that our group doesn't get blamed if something happens."
	"We spend more time finding out who's at fault than solving problems."
	"Around here, you'd better protect your ass."
Problem and failure orientation	"We're good at pointing out the problems. It's the solutions we're weak at."
	"You only hear from somebody when you do something wrong."
	"If I hear once more that it's only a symptom of a bigger problem and that's why we can't get it solved."
Lack of assumption of personal responsibility	"Look, I presented the program. It's up to them to implement it."

"I just do what I'm told."

"The company will take care of things."

Noninvolvement of people   "I like to feel I'm being listened to."

"Nobody ever asks us what we think."

"The manufacturing process is the boss."

Alienation and breakdown   "In place of communication, we've got a
of communication   rumor mill."

"The executive suite is a separate world."

"Information is seen as power; nobody
shares it with anybody."

In general, employees felt that the company was losing closeness as it grew. As one old-timer put it, "Things are not the same—nobody knows anybody." When employees on all levels were asked to indicate the most common norms existing in the organization, these were the most frequently mentioned and widely agreed upon:

Empire building

Mediocrity

Noncommitment

"Protect your ass"

"Not invented here"

"Can't be done"

"We tried it already"

Win/lose

Lack of concern for cost-effectiveness

Guardedness or secrecy

Dishonesty in announcements

Departmental divisiveness

Blame placing

Lack of consistency

Lack of trust

Bureaucracy

Activity for activity's sake

It was interesting to see that workers and president alike had the same perception of the situation: nobody liked what was happening in the company; there was general dissatisfaction. But this commonality dissolved when it came to assessing who was to blame for the situation. Each level thought the other was to blame. There was so much faultfinding that it was a tremendous surprise to all of them when later, in workshops, they discovered that they agreed so thoroughly about the miserable state of affairs.

During analysis, most of the information was collected through interviews and field observation. HRI field workers took positions at various levels throughout the company. While the results of observations on different levels of the company were very similar in terms of the norms that were expressed and the overwhelming majority didn't like the way things were, the particular manifestations were quite different. Thus, production workers slept on the job, while executives read newspapers and played golf.

There were, of course, a number of positives as well. The company had a collection of highly talented (although currently turned-off) people. Recognizing the threat of the coming competition in the market, some were prepared to roll up their sleeves and get to work if given a chance. Most, however, did not believe that they would actually be given such a chance.

All these sentiments were collected on tapes, which were edited to include only the attitudes that showed up over and over again. The edited tape was later used in workshops, where discussions verified the analysis and expanded or modified it in particular areas.

SETTING OBJECTIVES

During the initial program analysis and planning, ideas about measurable goals were secured from a cross-section of the organization. This took about six months, and was extremely difficult because most people did not believe that any change for the better was possible. Even the members of the executive committee expressed pessimism, feeling that changing norms would not work.

Nevertheless, the preliminary goals (later cast into the three types of objectives) were drawn up, and included the following:

Mobilization of a unified company effort that would involve all segments of the organization

Increased emphasis on profitability and cost-effectiveness

Improved communications between various levels and departments of the organization

Elimination of waste and ineffectiveness

Strengthening of organizational leadership, from the executive committee through the supervisory levels

Improvement of the work situation so that people would be able to contribute and gain satisfaction from their work

These general goals were later translated into more specific ones, which made measurement of progress possible and which would be attainable within certain time periods. For example:

Productivity—a 10 percent increase in net profit per year

A significant normative improvement in such work team factors as communication, involvement, and teamwork

A companywide cost-effectiveness program to be operational within a year

Key pressure points were identified, and materials were developed to help people understand and deal constructively with the problems.

STARTING FROM THE TOP

Normative Systems orientation workshops, ranging from one to five days in length, began at the top of the organization and continued with team units at the various levels. They helped make people aware of the powerful influence that the norms of the culture were having upon them. People talked about their work group norms, and identified those that were affecting the organization's effectiveness. Teamwork, trust, and the interrelationships necessary for reaching normative objectives began to emerge during this phase.

SOME STEPS FORWARD

As people were beginning to feel involved and appreciated during the orientation workshops, a four-part implementation effort was set in motion:

Performance planning and review: a focus on the individual's achievements and concerns

Work team cultures: employee meetings with their work teams and supervisors

Leadership development: starting with the executive board and then going on to managerial and supervisory levels

Organizational structures, policies, and procedures: action-planning groups or task forces—each one a cross-section of people, each group concerned with a particular problem and with making recommendations.

Things began to happen. "What I saw starting," one employee explained later, "was that once you gave people permission to question the norms and to talk about how they would really like things to be, behavior began to fall in line with personal preferences. 'How would you like this place to be?' people were asked. And they made things move in that direction."

Action study groups (or task forces) began work in such change strategy areas as communication, involvement and responsibility, cost-effectiveness, and recognition and reward. These groups spanned many departments and job levels. An action study group on results orientation, for example, had as members an assembly line worker from one end of the pay scale and a top manager from the other.

Many of the steps that resulted do not seem unusual—recommendations for informal get-togethers, for an area newsletter, for job analysis, for performance standards developed jointly by employees and supervisor. Taken together, though, they added up to many improvements, much participation, and visible productivity and morale-boosting results. For the first time in years, relevant work-related information was provided at all levels. Both task force and work team meetings used feedback charts showing carefully tracked results and bringing an increasing flow of information to all employees.

Individual Development

A far-reaching performance planning and review apparatus was the result of one task force's work. For the first time, every worker would sit down regularly with his or her boss and talk about plans and performance.

Group Development

Every employee was part of a work team and began to meet biweekly with his or her team and supervisor, at which time the positive experience at the normative systems workshop was supported and renewed.

Work team performance and culture charts provided every work team member with regular feedback on accomplishments.

Leadership Development

A leadership development program was designed to help company managers and supervisors increase their effectiveness. It consisted of a series of interrelated modules on such cultural influences as communications, work team meetings, and motivation. The program was directed to on-the-job issues and concerns, and each module began with an evaluation of specific behavioral objectives and continued through steps to put the new norms in practice on the job. Periodic feedback and ongoing participation in evaluation meetings were provided to help sustain achievement.

Organizational Structures, Policies, and Procedures

The analysis had revealed that organizational structures, policies, and procedures were frequently hampering people's efforts to do their jobs. These were thoroughly reviewed by task forces and the executive committee. Improved information systems were established, and decision making was spread throughout the organization. The results of these improvements were then communicated, not only by management, but by workers and supervisors who had participated in the development.

FINDING IT CAN BE DONE—AND KEPT

Twelve months after the program started, the formal evaluation and renewal began. Regular renewal meetings were held approximately one year after the introduction of the program to each group within the company. At these meetings groups had an opportunity to review progress and set goals for continued improvement. Evaluation focused on the three categories of objectives that had been established in the initial analysis. In terms of category I objectives, major gains were made in productivity and cost-effectiveness. One division alone reduced its costs by more than $1 million a year, without reducing its efficiency.

In the second category (dealing with organizational programs, policies, and procedures) marked improvements were made in orientation, training, compensation, and attendance systems. The attendance program, for example, resulted in 60 percent improvement.

In the third category, cultural norms were beginning to change. Field observations, the administration of norm indicators, and the use of survey data confirmed that shifts were taking place. The company was changing from a fragmented, dissatisfied collection of "kingdoms" into a more cohesive whole. This was evidenced in subtle ways: more listening, more questions of the sort that lead to meaningful change ("Are we involving others?" "What would be the results of this action?"), a new focus as people used the normative principles of change as a matter of course.

Within twelve months a large segment of the company was reorganized, and this resulted in a leaner, more flexible, and less bureaucratic organization. Complete organizational restructuring made the available managerial expertise properly effective. There was an integration of, and support for, personnel concerns and programs.

The major achievement, however, has been the feeling that something can be done, and that there is a known way to do it. There are still problems, but the people no longer feel helpless to do anything about them.

As only part of the company has undergone the Normative Systems process, some departments still have the old norms. However, even the old "games" that hang on are not so difficult to deal with, since many people have learned new ways and these changes tend to spread. Altogether, while paradise still seems a long way off, some earthbound solutions appear to be available for the first time. As one worker summed it up: "We're working harder, and there are still lots of problems, but this is a lot better place to be."

Chapter 22

A Program
That Failed

What we need to eliminate is not occasional mistakes,
but our fear of mistakes and the sense of failure we
attach to them. . . .

W. TIMOTHY GALLWEY
Inner Tennis

The brags of life are but a nine dayes wonder.

GEORGE HERBERT

Like the tennis player who learns from his errors, people involved in
Normative Systems have found that accurate feedback from projects is
valuable in refining the change process. Probably most of us can learn
more from our successes than from our failures, but there is much to be
gained by looking objectively at our errors. What happened in a retail
chain that undertook a cultural change program and failed typifies
some of the most common errors of change programs in general and offers
some useful lessons.

Pilgrim Retail Company (a fictional name) was a seventy-five-year-old
enterprise, operating thousands of small stores in a large metropolitan
area. At one time it had been a leader in its field, but it began to experience
trouble when large chains sprang up in the area, making the one-man store
obsolete. Since the entire city was in a decline, even the land on which the
stores were located was no longer especially valuable. A conglomerate
bought control of Pilgrim, only to find it a drain on finances. The larger
firm's stockholders had become unhappy and were demanding action. The
chain's top managers were looking for a way out—a kind of "cosmetic"
operation to restore their image—but the director of personnel and a few
others were interested in making some deeper, humanistic changes.

A BRIEF OVERVIEW

People at the upper level of management were congenial, but tended to
withhold results-oriented information from others. The consultants

did not know if this was because such information did not exist, or if there were fears of revealing it because of its impact on managers and employees. Perhaps it was because the national conglomerate overshadowed the chain, and the latter's books were tied into those of the conglomerate. In any case, top executives did not release financial information either to the consultants or to employees. Accordingly, the group's analysis failed to reveal some basic economic flaws that later would prove insurmountable.

General objectives were drawn up, but management was much more interested in objectives for employees than for itself. For example, specific goals in cost saving, productivity, and customer service were set up for store units, but no similar goals were set up for management.

Because of time pressures, the analysis and objective-setting phase was considerably shortened. Management felt there was an immediate need to demonstrate to the stockholders that something was being done, and wanted to get on with the action phases of the program.

Introductory workshops were conducted and seemed to go well. Employees began to see each other as people; supervisors and workers interacted in meaningful ways. However, several key top managers did not participate, and the leaders of the conglomerate were an unseen presence at the meetings. They were referred to often, but the employees were skeptical about any new norms affecting the seats of power.

Implementation, too, began to go well at the lower levels. Task forces were set up on such things as employee communications, compensation systems, information systems, and customer service. These task forces met for four or five months and drew up recommendations which were sent to management—where they were set aside and ignored. The implementation phase was interrupted at several points as new company acquisitions took up time and attention. This happened three times during the span of the project, for management saw acquisitions as a way out of its financial problems. Finally, after making a number of start-and-stop implementation efforts, the company dropped the program and eventually went bankrupt.

Since "the patient died," it is obvious that this Normative Systems program fell far short of its potential. In retrospect, it seems to have failed in each of the four phases.

Phase I.   *Analysis*. The primary problem was that the analysis was inadequate. Objectives were too vague.

Phase II.   *Systems introduction*. Though this went well on the lower levels, the key top managers were not involved.

Phase III.   *Implementation*. The principles of normative change were not followed, and there were many breaks in the process.

Phase IV.   *Evaluation and renewal*. There was one evaluation: results, disastrous. There never was time for a renewal.

Three major causes of the failure are evident. (1) Normative Systems consultants failed to conduct a careful analysis of the situation, (2) clear objectives were not set before the program was implemented, and (3) the four-phase change system was not adequately used. It may be true that certain characteristics of the organization itself made it untreatable, but it is equally possible that a careful analysis could have remedied this. Let us look at what happened in more detail.

ANALYSIS INADEQUATE

The organization was not sufficiently analyzed to reveal the basic economic flaws in the situation, nor the motivational flaw in the program itself. In the interest of speed and management secrecy, some key characteristics of the organization were overlooked. The small retail outlets were simply outmoded. Trying to make such an operation viable was probably futile. The company's stores were the wrong size in the wrong places, and they were competing with some of the largest and most modern retail chains in the nation. In addition, there was not enough information about the company's financial condition, for the books were closed to all but a few.

Negative norms were endemic in this situation. Poor communications norms were compounded by poor problem-solving norms that caused people to respond to their problems with spontaneous "solutions" that were doomed to failure. Despite the poor financial situation of the company (and perhaps to some extent because of it), there were no cost-effectiveness norms. The feeling seemed to be: "We're losing so much money already a few dollars won't make any difference."

The objectives were so general that they were more of a smokescreen than a guide. Top management didn't want to talk about specific results, but resorted to vague statements about keeping people happy—which really meant that people should do as they were told without complaint or question. Instead of dealing with objectives for getting results, the management dealt with objectives that had to do with the maintenance of secrecy and power.

INTRODUCTION GOES WELL, BUT . . .

Although many good things happened in the introduction phase, the absence of top management at the earlier workshops meant that the program lacked sufficient commitment. Top managers were interested in convincing the stockholders that they were doing something. They were not really interested in making substantive changes.

This introduction experience provided a clear demonstration of the potential failure of even well-designed and well-implemented training when it is not part of a viable total systems effort.

It was not clear to either the consultants or the participants at the time of the workshops that the project's chance for success was never more than a remote possibility. As a result, the program's eventual failure was even more disappointing to those who had developed an initial commitment to it.

IMPLEMENTATION THWARTED

The implementation phase lacked both purpose and achievement. Following the introductory workshops, the various task forces enthusiastically produced a number of excellent recommendations, but their work came to naught because top management did not review the suggestions. Interestingly, the task force on *increased profitability* made a number of recommendations that, in retrospect, proved prophetic. One such recommendation read: "There is a need for an immediate review of our overall business plans at every level. This review should focus on the viability of our present competitive position in the industry, and seek to revise this position as soon as possible if this should prove necessary."

Recommendations also included across-the-board cuts in compensation until the existing economic situation could be rectified. The task force members, in a show of good faith, offered to be the first in this cost-cutting venture. However, their ideas never came to fruition.

Existing organizational policies, programs, and procedures were maintained despite strong and well-thought-out recommendations for change. One such recommendation had to do with a change in the compensation system designed to increase teamwork. The existing system had been accurately seen by the task force as promoting win/lose competition between departments, and this was proving destructive to both teamwork and profitability. Again, the recommendations were never enacted.

NOTHING COMMITTED, NOTHING SUSTAINED

As for the final phase—evaluation and renewal—it never happened. There was no sustained (or even initial) commitment to the program. It was officially aborted after approximately eleven months, and ten months after that the company declared bankruptcy. Clearly, though, another and perhaps even more tragic type of bankruptcy preceded it—a bankruptcy of the human environment.

Part Six

BUILDING SUCCESS ENVIRONMENTS

A new vision is emerging of the possibilities of man and of his destiny, and its implications are many, not only for our conceptions of education, but also for science, politics, literature, economics, religion, and even our conceptions of the non-human world.

ABRAHAM MASLOW

Most men do not anticipate the future, but yield to it—often grudgingly, belatedly, and inadequately. Yet today, for the first time, we are reaching a point where we can bring the accumulation of a considerable and ever increasing body of knowledge and understanding about the process of change itself to bear on our destinies. No longer is it necessary to have change happen to us, or to let it be imposed on us from without. We can rise up from within to meet new challenges in an anticipatory fashion.

WOLF WOLFENSBERGER

It is the greatest of all mistakes to do nothing because you can do very little. Do what you can.

SYDNEY SMITH

Chapter 23

Moonshots:
Uses of
Normative Systems

What we need are moonshots for our earthbound prob-
lems: systematic countdowns that involve people
working responsively with one another toward
mutually-set objectives. Like science's moonshots, the
targets will be visible, the data will be carefully pre-
pared, communications systems will be highly
polished, goals will be shared.

ROBERT THEOBALD

Since cultures exist in every facet of our lives, and since Normative Systems is a basic process from which specific programs evolve, helping people change whatever situation needs improving, the possible applications are virtually limitless.

All of us belong to a number of different groups, organizations, and communities, each with its own patterns of norms and norm influences. Anywhere a group of people come together with common goals, tasks, and expectations, it is possible for them to apply the method these pages have been describing. Already it has been used in a wide variety of cultural settings, from the ghetto streets to the locker rooms of police departments; from the shanties of migrant laborers to the paneled offices of chief executives; from the in-baskets of accountants to the trash barrels on city sidewalks. Over the past twenty years, hundreds of groups and organizations have used the Normative Systems change process to help solve countless problems. The ten categories of uses below will, no doubt, be expanded as new people learn, apply, and modify the process.

One of the most exciting things about the process is that many applications can be carried out by people working together in their own organizations and communities. In some cases, however, external consultants can be useful. Where this is true, it is important that the consultant act as a facilitator, helping people understand themselves and their cultures, introducing them to methods that lead to long-lasting change, and then pulling out to let people continue the work themselves. When consultants stay aloof from the cultures they are studying, they become either remote authorities or dictators of solutions, only adding to the problems they have been employed to resolve. A culture-based model helps consultants avoid these pitfalls. Because the emphasis is on people's ability to sustain their own programs, consultants can use their expertise to help people free themselves from cultural traps without compromising their intrinsic capacity to create their own environments.

BUILDING A NEW CULTURE

Our highly mobile and rapidly changing society offers many opportunities to create new cultures. Unfortunately, most of these opportunities are not explored, and so the new cultures turn out to be pretty much the same as the old. Thus a new plant often takes on the negative norms that plagued the parent company, and the new classroom cultures created each September act pretty much like the old ones. This is not always the case, however, nor need it be. Some of the most exciting applications of the cultural approach have been those that helped mold new cultures.

The opportunity for building a new positive culture is great, for there are fewer entrenched norms to deal with, there is usually less blame placing, there may be a new and still neutral physical setting, and there is a tacit agreement that a fresh start is possible.

The preliminary work concentrates on what people really want the new culture to be like. "In our new store, we hope to create a situation in which people can be helpful to each other instead of getting on each other's backs," Or "In our new plant, we'd like a great deal of teamwork and an orientation to results and profitability, not fiefdoms."

Most Normative Systems work has been done in business organizations and communities, but there are tremendous opportunities in other types of cultures. For example, in the sports world, a few coaches are experimenting with the cultural approach.

SOLVING CHRONIC PROBLEMS

In our society many problems have become chronic: traffic accidents, alcoholism, obesity, smoking, theft, drug abuse, violence, absenteeism, safety, vandalism, poverty, corruption, and so on. But most problems can be solved if they can be cut off from the support of the culture. Treated systematically, in a cultural context they are solvable, or at least reducible, in a reasonably short period of time. A more minor illustration of a chronic problem is the one encountered a few years ago, in which a company could not get its construction workers to wear hard hats and safety shoes. A cultural analysis showed that the supervisors were not wearing them—i.e., they were modeling negative norms. The problem was solved by making the wearing of hard hats and safety shoes the norm around the construction site.

Another chronic problem is food waste. A study of Michigan State University cafeterias found that about four *tons* of food were being wasted every day out of the 65,000 meals served daily. How much are we throwing out nationwide? How do we reduce that? Such a problem may seem mind-boggling, but a recent analysis of plate waste from a normative viewpoint has sparked hope that something can be done. Like United States families, school food services have deeply embedded norms that support and reinforce food-wasting behavior. Until these norms are modified, no advertising campaign, educational program, presidential exhortation, or other response is going to be effective.

However, a citizens' group working on attitude changes in a large city has found that its consciousness-raising efforts *are* effective—and spreading. Junior and senior high schools are undertaking a program to help young people become aware of the problem and find ways to solve it through an understanding of its cultural base. In addition, fifteen universities have decided to work with the program, and a statewide civic organization is working with schools, institutions, communities, and restaurants to raise consciousness about food waste and to change food-serving norms.

Another chronic problem in our society is that of disease and ill health. The vast majority of us are born healthy, yet suffer disability and premature death as a result primarily of poor individual health practices which are supported by strong but destructive cultural norms. Smoking, eating, drinking, sedentary, and driving norms alone cost the nation billions of dollars a year, to say nothing of the inestimable anguish. Nationwide, 4.4 million life-years are lost annually as a result of unhealthy life-styles, which account for 53.1 percent of premature deaths below the age of 65.

A culture-based change program called "Lifegain" is now helping organizations, families, communities, groups, and individuals to improve their health practices and life expectancy. Several corporations are involving employees at all levels in a review of their health practices. Films, workshops, norm indicators, and self-help modules are being used, and support groups are helping to facilitate and sustain change.

Meanwhile, a counterpart cultural change program called the "Caring Community" is being used to address systematically another chronic problem: mental illness. The Caring Community program utilizes consciousness-raising workshops, goal setting, task force participation, and ongoing evaluation, with a heavy emphasis on practical accomplishments. The basic idea is to involve as many people as possible in the evolution of an environment where mental health can be achieved and sustained. Objectives include changing:

> Norms of isolation and loneliness (including norms that call for hiring others to do our caring for us, isolating those most in need of relationships)
>
> Norms of apathy and indifference to the mentally ill
>
> Norms that focus on illness and dependency, rather than on wellness and independence
>
> Norms that label disturbed people "schizophrenic," "manic depressive," and so on, foreclosing their (and our) economic and social possibilities (It's "mental patient" for a time, most likely too long a time, and then it's "ex-mental patient" forever.)

A culture-based change program—complete with workshops, norm indicators, action plans, a film, and background materials—is available for those who want to change the mental health norms of their communities. Some limited work has been done with it in New Jersey and in New York City.

INSTALLATION OF TRAINING SYSTEMS

The training function can be either a great help or a great source of frustration to organizational managers. The emphasis on humanistic and cultural variables often makes the difference.

Behind every trainer stands a "shadow trainer" who can either support or drastically undermine the work of the trainer. This elusive, and often unrecognized, "shadow" has tremendous power. When a training program starts well but trails off fast, when a beautifully planned, expertly executed program does not achieve results, or when a training program is considered detrimental by operations people, look for the shadow trainer quietly at work.

This hidden force is the organization itself—the store, the office, the factory, the school—or, more correctly, the groups of people who work there. A basic understanding of the teaching role of this organizational culture is probably the most important and most frequently overlooked ingredient in the development of training strategies. Many programs have been rendered ineffectual because they have come into conflict with the *real* training being done by the norms within the particular culture.

What the culture supports and what it fails to support (or even attacks) provide the real curriculum for learning, regardless of what is presented in the seminar, class, or training session. A great deal of money and time could be saved if organizations first considered whether their training programs were really being supported. Unless adequate budget, time, and energy are committed to a program, there is no point in starting it.

Moreover, the Normative Systems experience has been that unless the influential norms are considered, understood, and dealt with systematically, training programs are not likely to take hold. A key factor in making a training program work is for the trainer to see himself as a change agent dealing with a culture. This way, the trainer can help people make purposeful use of the norm influence areas, rather than letting that "shadow trainer" manipulate him and the people in the program.

DEVELOPING NEW PROGRAMS

Sometimes (as seen in the cases in Part V) change requires the installation of new programs. However, as we have seen, the installation of a program is not synonymous with its success. We are all familiar with new programs that remain superficial appendages to the existing culture. A new program's success will depend almost entirely upon development of new norms and associated ways of behaving. When a new program does not seem to be taking hold, chances are that the old norms are getting in the way.

When the development of the program involves the people who will be using it, it is more likely to be closer to their individual and group objectives. The cultural analysis and objective-setting phase emphasizes this involvement. The installation of automatic checkstands in a supermarket is a case in point. Before Normative Systems was used, the checkstands had been installed without consulting store employees or customers. The results were unfortunate. Neither cashiers nor customers had any confidence in the machines' accuracy, and, in fact, they were openly pleased when a machine made a $1 million error. They so resisted the checkstands, the management suspended their use. Later, after both customers and cashiers became involved in a norm-change program, the resistance vanished.

MAKING EXISTING PROGRAMS WORK

Many organizations have at least one program with which they are not really satisfied. They feel that the program itself is good, but it is just not working for them, and they do not see why. One of the most important programs nationally, as far as businesses are concerned, is management by objectives (MBO). Recent surveys show that one out of every two businesses has an MBO program, but half of those that have them feel the program is not working very well. An even greater proportion think the program is not attaining its full potential. Often the problem is not MBO, but lack of a systematic, culture-based approach to implementing it.

The same thing is happening with another excellent concept, zero-base budgeting. Too many people derive their budget in the same old way and then take out the zero-base budgeting forms and figure a way to fill them out so they produce the same figures. All zero-base budgeting does then is add an extra chore. A cultural analysis of these situations would probably show, as it has in others, that zero-base budgeting does not work because:

People are not trained to use it

There is no reward for using it

The leadership does not model the proper behavior

Information and communication are inadequate

The plan is imposed without adequate involvement of the people who will use it

The program does not focus on results

Clearly, these are just the opposite of the influences needed to make a program work. One organization found that by applying normative change concepts it could make zero-base budgeting work. It took two years to accomplish the change, but the results, in terms of improved morale and effectiveness, were worth the effort.

Programs designed for increased use of minority people or for any of a host of other organizational and social objectives that require the defusing of "culture shock" have also been made workable by the sensitive application of Normative Systems techniques.

PERFORMANCE IMPROVEMENT

Performance improvement is one of the most talked-about, but least acted-upon, concerns of organizational life. Quality-of-work programs have become the subject of national advertising campaigns, industrial engineers have examined and refined the physical aspects of work environments in order to improve them, and managers have been hired and fired, based on their record of improving organizational performance.

Managers tend to forget, though, that improvement in performance is, to a considerable extent, a function of the group in which people find themselves. While members of a "low-performance" crew, migratory workers picked an average of forty boxes of fruit a day. But when assigned to a "high-performance" crew, many of these same workers picked an average of ninety boxes a day. The same differences in performance are found among warehouse workers, students, route workers, secretaries, or what have you. Of course, there are always exceptions, but the exceptions are almost always exactly that: exceptions to the rule (or norm). Clearly, then, the cultural approach to performance improvement has much to offer, by involving workers in setting standards, keeping track of results, and developing rewards systems.

RESOLVING CONFLICT

Efforts at conflict resolution are also very much enhanced by a cultural approach. Too often, destructive conflict accompanies the contact of one subculture with another. The misunderstandings, differences in perceptions, and discrepancies in stated goals often create volatile situations that can erupt into confrontation or even violence, and promote polarization of the affected groups. However, when normative principles are brought to bear in such a situation, we often see an exciting, not to say heartwarming, reversal of attitudes.

Such was the case with a newly opened, unionized distribution center which management was threatening to close because of wildcat strikes and poor production. After application of the culture-based model, relations (and negotiations) are no longer conducted in a climate of belligerence—and productivity has increased from 120 pieces to 148 pieces per hour. In projects such as these, win/win solutions based on mutually beneficial results replace win/lose confrontations and accusations.

In a program in Grand Rapids, Michigan, police and ghetto residents examined the cultural norms that were affecting them and decided they wanted to bring about change. They did so with remarkable results, developing strong and meaningful relationships with one another that were instrumental not only in staving off destructive conflict, but also in solving critical community problems.

ORGANIZATIONAL AND COMMUNITY DEVELOPMENT

Probably the most effective and ideal way of the cultural approach is in total organizational improvement. In these situations, whether it concerns a business, a union, a hospital, a school, or a total community, the whole culture is involved and committed to a clear look at itself and to making necessary changes. When people view themselves as a total culture, they can be helped to modify their environment and make it more reflective of individual and group needs and aspirations. With built-in feedback and evaluation procedures, new norms are far-reaching and long-lasting. Furthermore, the organization becomes responsive to itself, its environment, and the changing needs of both, and avoids the stultifying institutionalization that so often sets in.

Because of the depth and breadth of the total program, this type of application has profoundly changed people's lives, including the quality of their work environments and their approaches to handling human relationships both at work and leisure.

Businesses

As we saw in Chapter 21, the business setting is particularly fertile ground for a systematic cultural change program. The hierarchical setup, the already established information flow and rewards system, and the constant desire for improving efficiency, productivity, and performance make it especially appropriate. The partial list of Normative Systems business projects in Appendix E will give an indication of the range of programs already undertaken.

Perhaps the key difference between this approach and other organizational development (OD) efforts is the depth to which it takes the cultural implications of the OD movement. Normative Systems hopes to undergird the already emerging trend in OD work toward the acceptance of the culture's power and usefulness, and in this way help OD programs attain a greater longevity, flexibility, and responsiveness to the changing demands of the socioeconomic environment.

Unions

Several union organizations have used the culture-based approach to modify their own organizational cultures, with positive results. They have found ways of involving people, of developing good feedback norms, of building effective work groups, and of developing leadership skills.

One group of trade union leaders, for example, met for a three-day Normative Systems leadership training seminar. It paralleled seminars that had been conducted for management officials, for these labor officials were also looking for concrete help in confronting "people problems." Some of the problems they dealt with were similar to those of other organizations: "Can we change the norms of how we deal with our younger members, with women, with older workers?" "How can we overcome the apathy of people who feel that their union organization does not really belong to them?"

The group found ways to work on the negative norms that were producing the communications gap underlying these difficulties and concluded that equal stress on task accomplishment and satisfying people's needs was both necessary and attainable.

Hospitals

We have seen in Chapter 5 how health-care institutions that were originally developed to preserve life and improve health too often destroy and dehumanize individuals. But these negative ways can be changed. The hospital ward, the nursing home, the facility for the mentally retarded, all are appropriate settings for cultural change programs based on normative principles. Currently the Caring Community program mentioned above involves both hospital and community people at all levels in reexamining just how they want to treat mental illness, and particularly how they can turn from treating people in houses of horror to creating caring communities.

Educational Settings

In a democratic society our educational process is extremely important. Americans spend from seventeen to twenty years of their lives in educational environments; yet few people seem completely satisfied with what is occurring in many of our classrooms. Discussions with teachers, students, and administrators suggest the need for improvements.

Would it be possible for students and teachers to come together to modify their classroom environments and make them nearer to what they would like them to be? If the classroom could be so modified, could not the whole school culture also be improved? Perhaps the whole educational process? There is evidence that such changes are possible.

People on many levels of the educational ladder have tried the cultural approach. One graduate school, for example, experienced a dramatic change. Instead of perpetuating old negative norms of noncommunication, power plays, and grammar-school competition, it became a group that made decisions for itself, gave individuals support to grow creatively, and changed the classroom environment into one in which sharing, trusting, and communicating were the norm.

Likewise, a high school classroom in a public school looked at itself and found that it could develop norms of creativity and freedom that were not found in the rest of the school. The students used their English class to strengthen these norms and provide a base for holding onto positive values. For most of them it was an eye-opening experience to find that education could consist of self-education rather than feeding back to the teacher what he expected. It was also a new experience in decision making that they hoped to be able to apply to other situations.

Another example: Several years ago a Southern college that was open-ing a new campus was concerned that it might become a playboy, country-club sort of place. Out of five dormitories, one was selected for a program of conscious cultural planning. Students were invited to come before the semester opened to work for a couple of weeks on the basic question: "What kind of dormitory do you want this to be?"

The students talked about their desire not to become a mere "social club". They didn't want to feel embarrassed if they felt like talking about books or working on their studies. They also wanted to feel they could help each other with research papers without getting into problems of cheating. They worked out ways to help each other without exchanging papers.

The students had additional concerns; one was racism—they wanted very positive integration. Another was privacy—it was important to them to have a chance to be alone when they wished to. Fifteen such objectives were identified, and as new people joined the dormitory, these ideas were shared with them in exchange for theirs.

Four years later, without the continued help of outside professionals, the positive norms of a helping, open, trusting, nonracist culture were still in operation. The other dorms had become the "drinking dorm," the "party dorm," and so on, but the dorm that had taken the cultural ap-proach was able to follow and renew the positive norms that it had built in from the beginning.

Communities

The migrancy project in central Florida and the litter projects in Tampa, Charlotte, and Macon were wide-scale community projects demonstrating ways people of all levels can come together to work for planned change. The migrancy project demonstrates a total community change, while the litter projects focus on one aspect of community life. These are continuing efforts, and the experience has the possibility of making vast changes in people's ways of working together.

KEEPING SOMETHING OF VALUE

In all the preceding illustrations, the emphasis has been primarily on change. This has been intentional, since there is a great deal that needs changing in our organizations and communities. There are, however, some things that should be maintained. Holding on to what is valuable is also an important use of the Normative Systems process.

Many families want to hold on to the values that are important to them, but they face pressures from the surrounding culture. The so-called sexual revolution, changing attitudes toward women, the technological invasion of the home, and the mobility and fragmentation of American society are all impacting on the family's norms and values.

One family that used the cultural approach had been wondering why it was not getting the interest and cooperation of its teenage elder son. A review of the family as a culture revealed a number of reasons. The son got no feedback at home on things that he did well, only on things that he did wrong. His recognition and rewards came from his peers outside the home. Family resources were not allotted to doing things together just for fun. Most of the communications system involved instructions and scoldings from the parents to the boy. He had never been given an opportunity to train for a skill that would give him a sense of satisfaction. The family did not share space together or interact socially, except for one brief dinner hour each evening, and frequently the whole family was not present for this meal. With these new understandings of family norms, they were able to change them in ways that helped all members.

Another family of six, consisting of a pediatrician, her engineer husband, three sons, and a grandmother, introduced the change process at a series of family meetings on three successive Friday evenings. They found that the grandmother wanted to do more things around the house, and was capable of doing a lot more than she had been allowed to do. She felt useless being waited upon by the rest of the family.

All the family members wanted to bring friends home more often, but all felt uneasy about doing so. They decided to help each other entertain outside friends on a regular basis. Job responsibilities in the family were equalized, and many role stereotypes were broken: the boys helped with kitchen tasks; the women did some house repair and yard work. Probably the happiest switch was made when the grandmother traded jobs with the youngest boy and relieved him of the work he hated most—wheeling the garbage cans out to the curb once a week.

When a family has something good it wants to hold on to, but feels surrounded by pressing negative norms from the outer culture, it can take steps to protect what it wishes to preserve. This was the case with a family who moved to a white, racist, suburban neighborhood and feared that the humanistic values the parents had taught the children would be undermined. Indeed, the children were heavily exposed to racist thinking in the schoolyard and in neighborhood activities. But through a conscious, planned family program, in which cultural norms were explained and normative influences were put to use, the family values were kept intact.

One of the techniques that has helped many families find more meaningful experiences in the home setting is the *family cultural norm indicator*. Similar to the indicator used in organizations, it includes categories that are unique to family situations—norms of privacy, family pride, assignment of work, care of family property and resources, use of alcohol and drugs, husband-wife and parent-child relationships, family meetings, and others. (The complete family norm indicator is found in Appendix B.)

Churches, too, often find themselves struggling to hold on to their values. A group of parishioners in a small Lutheran church in central New Jersey came to see that the culture that they had created was actually interfering with their religious objectives. Far from being a community of people working together, the community they had created was one of competition and strife. Even the Sunday School pitted the children against one another in terms of "religious excellence."

When church members looked at their practices, they decided that they needed to spend a great deal more time in "fellowship activities" and less time in listening to more abstract presentations about fellowship. They elected to spend more time being genuinely helpful to one another (baby-sitting, providing food during times of family illness, and giving support during times of stress) and less time on talking about good works. They found also that poor people who attended their church often dropped out after a few meetings. It was clear that the Christian spirit they were espousing had not permeated their relationships, and they set about changing that.

A program to hold on to something of value has appeal to business people, too. Many business leaders fear that company expansion will mean loss of a friendly work atmosphere, personal contacts with employees, and esprit de corps. Experience shows, though, that with an effective norm change program a company can become big and multileveled and still hang on to the good things it had when smaller.

Companies opening up new plants or divisions have a similar problem. They ask, "How can we keep the good values of the parent company, even while changing some of the things we didn't like?" A systematic cultural approach can make that possible.

Speaking more generally, it might be helpful if, at this point in our society's development, we could spend more time and energy in deciding which parts of our present culture we would like to preserve, and then take the systematic steps necessary to ensure that preservation. We need only remind ourselves of the positive aspects of fifty years ago that we might have been able to maintain if we had chosen to do so.

Looking to the future, as the "new visions of the possibilities of man and his destiny" that Maslow predicted emerge, there will be many more uses for a humanistic, results-oriented, democratic approach to change. It only remains for the imagination of individuals, working within supportive environments, to bring about meaningful change.

Chapter 24

Walking Ahead in the Sun

If we've moved up at all out of darkness, it's because a few have dared to walk ahead in the sun.

GEORGE SAND

In paying respect to those who "walk ahead in the sun," George Sand reminds us that in the continuing enlightenment of the human race, the impact of the individual is pivotal. So far, though, this book has concentrated almost exclusively on fostering cultural change by and through groups. Effective groups are certainly more than collections of individuals, but in groups, too, the impact of each individual is (or can be) pivotal. In this chapter we consider the application of normative principles by individuals. Properly used, a cultural approach can enable an individual to bring about meaningful and lasting change both for himself and for others.

If we want to lead change, we need to reflect that change within ourselves. As Malcolm X once said, "Only those who have already experienced a revolution within themselves can reach out effectively to help others."[1] This revolution within does not mean a narcissistic isolation of self from others, but a realistic view of oneself as part of one's culture, influenced by cultural norms and responsive to the social environment. It means that the leader must be involved in the struggle, not as an observer or adviser, but as a participant. If you really want to change the health practices of your organization, for example, you need to do more than work for others; you need to start to improve your own health practices.

This chapter will show how we can apply some of the lessons learned in working with groups to individual change and make ourselves more effective in leading others. As a bonus, the changes can lead to greater personal satisfaction and fulfillment. It is not necessary for leaders to *accomplish* these changes in themselves before they can help others, or the group as a whole. But they need to be involved in the struggle. Perfection is hardly called for, but there must be a willingness to look within and work on oneself.

[1] Malcolm Little (Malcolm X) from a poster used in the antipoverty program.

In developing our primary thesis, we emphasized that by transforming our environments we are recreating ourselves, giving ourselves more choices and, therefore, greater freedom. As we focus on individual change, we will see that the reverse is also true: by recreating ourselves we are transforming our environments and bringing about greater freedom for others as well as for ourselves.

YOUR ACTION SPACE

To understand the area of interaction in which the individual can operate most effectively, it is helpful to consider the viewpoint of the human predicament first developed by Kurt Lewin and later amplified by Gardner Murphy and others. In his highly illuminating "field theory," Lewin offered a new conception of the relative inseparability of person and world. The skin is no longer seen as the boundary, where the individual ends and the world "out there" begins. Aspects of the person extend beyond his skin and act upon the world outside. Reciprocally, aspects of the world act upon the person. Lewin calls this area of interaction, where self and environment overlap, a "life-space." He saw this field of action as crucially important in the development of a human being's potential. Self-fulfillment, he wrote, lies in developing the potential of the life-space. Murphy went further: ". . . in my experience, nothing springs from me, and nothing from my environment, but everything from the interaction, the 'life-space' in which I, as a person, navigate."[2]

The outer environment is made up of both physical and social environments. The latter—our cultures—being the most malleable and most ignored, are usually the most important arenas for a change process. But they are not, of course, to be dealt with apart from the individuals who interact with them. Social cultures are fields in which the individual acts, arenas in which action takes place. The action space of an individual is filled with cultural norms, and these are the focus of the change process.

With this view, it is evident that change will not take place if only the inner life is considered. If it is to last, change must take place within the action space where the individual and the culture interreact.

The greatest obstacles to our becoming whatever we want to become are not the inner blocks (what we think of as our natural limitations and deficiencies) and not even outside cultural barriers (the problems with "human nature," the job market, the government, the state of the world). The most important obstacles are the *misconceptions* we have about those cultural barriers and about our ability to change. If we really see cultural barriers for what they are, man-made, socially created, malleable, and if

[2] Murphy, *Human Potentialities* (New York: Basic Books, 1958), p. 303.

we really see how they fool us into thinking we cannot do anything about them, then we can lift the ceilings on our minds and make the changes we want. Each person can ask: "What negative norms in my action space are putting ceilings on my mind?"

CONFRONTING A DOUBLE NEGATIVE

The seed of the change process is often a positive approach to a double negative: (1) a beginning awareness that some things in the culture are not helping us, linked to (2) a realization that our lives are not as satisfactory and productive as they could be.

When we look at our dissatisfactions, wants, or concerns, we find most of them fall into these areas:

Human relationships	We want more authentic relationships with family, friends, loved ones, co-workers.
Health, strength, and longevity	We want better health, a longer life span, freedom from aging, more physical energy, greater skill, happier sexuality.
Career advancement and achievements	We want more money, comfort, security, prestige, career advancement.
Intellectual development	We want more knowledge and better ability to communicate, to handle ideas, and to understand.
Spiritual development	We want expanded awareness, greater consciousness, more meaning in life, and a way to cope with death.

Knowing that we will have a chance to refine and modify our general goals as we decide upon specific objectives, we begin by asking ourselves broad-gauged questions: "What is it I want?" "What is really important to me?" "Am I using my full potential?" "What do I want to do differently?" "In what ways can I expand and live more fully?"

The process for individual change makes use of the same approaches that apply to group change. As an individual you go through the four phases, now so familiar. First you discover where you are and decide where you want to be (Phase I, analysis and objective setting). Next, you work out a plan for change and try out the first steps (Phase II, introduction and involvement). That done, you put a plan into action, using the critical norm influence areas (Phase III, implementation and change). Finally, evaluate what you have done, renew your efforts, and reach out to other objectives (Phase IV, evaluation, renewal, and extension).

Familiar as this basic framework is to those who have read the previous chapters, several imperatives bear particular emphasis now that we are focusing on individual change:

Understand your own commitment.

Develop a systematic plan.

Use culture power, focusing on the same normative influence areas we saw in working in group change programs.

Reward yourself.

Find, create, or develop a support group.

Enjoy yourself.

Be open and reach out to others.

UNDERSTAND YOUR OWN COMMITMENT

Sometimes we think we want to change things (or ourselves), but we really are not committed to it. This is often hard to perceive, for our strong feelings get in the way. We spout and gripe and analyze and fume, and may indeed have ideas about what needs to be done. But then we find ourselves saying: "I don't have time." It would take too much money, or energy." "I have too many other things to do." If this happens, we need to take a good, realistic look at our commitment. Perhaps we really don't want to work on that change after all. If we want to move from the arid pastime of griping to the green pastures of *doing,* we need first to be sure that we really are committed, and then demonstrate that commitment by action.

If you want to become an effective leader and help your organization or group or institution to change, it is helpful to look into the possibilities of personal change. You may find that your dissatisfaction centers upon your interactions with others, or on how you relate to the group's goals, or on the extent to which you feel you have developed your own potential. Sometimes personal goals overlap group goals, but many personal goals are unique to the individual.

Suppose you are involved in an organizationwide effort to combat absenteeism. You may also have a personal goal of developing better rapport with the supervisors who work under (or over) you. You may have another, even more personal, goal of developing your musical talents. As long as the goals don't clash, you can work for a win/win solution for both yourself and the group. If the goals clash, then a realistic appraisal of what you really want is in order. What is your real commitment?

A visible, audible commitment to the preliminary goal is a positive step for an individual as well as for a group. Once the commitment is made in public, it adds to the impetus to get things done. Ask yourself: "Have I made a commitment to change?" "Is it visible?" "Have I announced it, or shown my written commitment to others?"

A member of Alcoholics Anonymous who gets up in front of the group and says, "I am an alcoholic. I no longer drink," is helping himself abstain. He is more likely to keep his commitment than is the alcoholic who makes a silent New Year's resolution or writes it in a private diary.

Paying in advance for a weight reduction program, an exercise group, a smoke-cessation clinic, or a series of tennis lessons is a way of saying, "I am committing myself to a certain amount of effort. I am willing to give up the other things this money could buy in order to make this change in myself."

DEVELOP A SYSTEMATIC PLAN

A plan is just as necessary for individual change as for group change. This seems elementary, but in fact we often try to get by without a plan, counting on our own desire, our wits, or our commitment to show us the way, moment by moment. We may want to have better relationships with our children, for example, but our "plan" is confined to a vague resolve to "try to be nice" or to "be more available." It doesn't occur to us that the kind of planning we need to accomplish something in our organizations is just as necessary in other areas of our lives.

In developing a plan, it is well to keep in mind the normative principles of change that were discussed in Chapter 11. They apply to individual efforts as well as group efforts. In fact, the "rain dances" (or negative ways we go about trying to change) are worth looking at from the individual's point of view. Since they are just the reverse of the change principles, they underscore the latter's importance:

"Pass the Buck"	Looking for someone to blame is wasted energy. Seek solutions rather than try to find the "cause" or punish the offender.
"The Win/Lose Waltz"	Is there someone you will come into conflict with when you try to institute this change? If so, can you find some way in

	which that person also can benefit from the change?
"Starting with the Last Step"	Simplistic solutions are tempting, but seldom successful. Changing a single habit, like smoking, requires a multilevel approach. One needs to be as systematic in individual change as one is in organizational change.
"The Patchwork Pavane"	Crash programs are short-lived, as many a dieter knows. A sustained effort is necessary in order to strengthen and maintain new positive norms.
"If You Can't Do Everything, Don't Do Anything"	This blues number has kept many people from taking that first encouraging step that starts a change process.
"The Stumble-Bum Gavotte"	Is there a skill you need to acquire in order to become a more effective change agent?
"The Grand March of the Philosopher Kings"	You may be tempted to watch from the sidelines as changes occur—or fail to occur. "If only I had more time or more money or more help." That first step, however small, will get you moving.
"The Promises Polka"	It is easy to make promises to ourselves and never fulfill them. Better than a promise is a goal, with a list of ways to achieve it.
"The Solo Hustle"	This strange dance focuses on one of the dancers, as though he were alone. He looks long and deep into his own rhythms and movements, but doesn't take anyone else's into account.

USE CULTURE POWER

Understanding the uses of the key norm influence areas (see Appendix A) is conducive to individual change. More and more people are making use of these cultural forces, either consciously or unconsciously. For example, here is a woman's description of her success in a weight reduction program—a success attained only after numerous attempts at dieting and exercising at home alone. Though she doesn't see what is happening in terms of norm influence areas, they are at work. If she *did* understand, she would be able to make use of them in other situations, and she would be more likely to sustain the weight loss.

Original Text	Translation into Normative Systems Language
I was sick and tired of being so fat, and I asked my doctor what I could do. He said, "Join a weight reduction class." So I talked it over with my husband—you know, it was going to take time and money and effort. Well, Tom had lost seventy pounds a few years ago; so he knew it was possible, and I did too—there was the evidence! He's felt so much better ever since. Well, I hesitated and had a hard time dragging myself out that first night. If I hadn't told him I would—you know it's really important to commit yourself to it. But I finally got there, and that first week, I lost five pounds and that was so encouraging! It wasn't at all hard to go back the second time, and Tom says I look better already. I can get into clothes I haven't been able to wear, and my waistline has gone down eight inches now. Part of the secret of it is you get exact instructions on what you can eat and how much. For instance, over Christmas, they said, don't try to cut out everything, but eat small amounts. Try eating just a little bit of your favorites. And cut out the alcohol. I found I was just as happy with a glass of soda or ice water in my hand. After Christmas it was fun to go back to the group and compare notes, and even those who might have lagged a little bit got going again. It's not hard when you have others around you doing the same things. I don't think I could ever do it alone.	Finding a support group Sound data base Modeling behavior Visible commitment Immediate results Recognition and reward Measurable results Skills and training Ongoing renewal

Here is a male business executive who has learned about the culture's impact upon him and has become more aware of the cultural forces that he is using to change:

Original Text	Translation into Normative Systems Language
I had always had a secret yen to paint pictures, and nobody knows how often I went into museums and gazed longingly at those Picassos, Cezannes, Braques! And I went to every movie about these heroes of mine, read	Modeling behavior

books about their lives, and envied their vigor in old age. But I didn't really do anything	Finding facts
about it until last October, when I plunked down the money and signed up for a	Commitment
beginner's painting class at the Art Center. I tried out several different mediums and found	Skills and training
I liked watercolor best, and did better in it than I did in oil. That was a surprise! After a	
month my family looked over one of my paintings and insisted it be reproduced for our	Finding support groups
Christmas card this year. I liked that. I never thought they'd really take me seriously. I	Recognition and reward
knew it was important to keep track of results, but I didn't expect much in the way of prizes	
and fame. So I kept track of how it made me	Keeping track of results

feel—kept a little diary about that—and you
know, it worked! I realized that the involvement in the process was very satisfying in
itself—and just as important to me as any end
product, perhaps more. I felt better about
myself, and now I look forward to weekends
when I have time to get out the paintbox and
paper and go at it. Even retirement has lost its
threat!

REWARD YOURSELF

No change is going to be sustained unless it is rewarding to you in terms of fun, satisfaction, status, or material rewards. If rewards don't come naturally or quickly enough, invent them.

From the very beginning, as soon as you make that first step toward change, see that you get a reward. Give yourself a present. It may be a gift of time, say, rather than a material gift, but say to yourself, "I deserve a reward for taking that step."

> A person who was trying to stop smoking used the money saved the first week by cutting out cigarettes to buy a long-coveted recording.
> A young man who signed up for piano lessons rewarded himself after a month of practicing by taking the evening off and going to a concert.
> A woman on a weight reduction program bought herself a new skirt every time she took two inches off her hipline.

When people reward themselves or get recognition from others, it makes them feel good, and the new norm is reinforced. Even though the reward may seem contrived, it usually has a positive effect. Being good to yourself is a motivator.

Sometimes the plan you have undertaken seems rewarding in itself, because it gives you a sense of control over your life or a feeling of achievement. At other times, there may be a lot of hard work and frustration before you experience much satisfaction. Then it is important to reward yourself just for sticking to your plan over the rough times. If your plan continues to be frustrating over a long period of time and the rewards you contrive do not seem to help, it may be necessary to reevaluate and modify the plan so that you will enjoy the process more.

FIND, CREATE, OR DEVELOP A SUPPORT GROUP

A supportive environment is necessary for every person who is trying to change. In fact, leaders need support groups as much as anyone else. We learned during the migrant project that support groups were imperative not only for workers, but for the executives backing the program and the consultants who were advising them. People tend to think of leaders as autonomous, "together" individuals who can stand alone, not realizing that what looks like "backbone" is often invisible support from a group of peers or from a reference group. Thus, a behavioral scientist working on a challenging social change project may seek the support and consultation of others in his field. Moral, intellectual, and emotional stamina is not entirely built on inner resources. We owe a great deal more to outer resources than we usually acknowledge.

The development of group support is probably the most important of all the strategies individuals use for accomplishing change.

> A vice president in charge of a companywide effort to develop a more harmonious, and at the same time profitable, organization found that workshops involving the top eight executives of the company gave him a support group that helped him be more creative and effective in leading the change program.

> A welfare mother who didn't want to give up family-oriented values that she had built up with her children found support by joining others in a welfare mother's league to work for better legislation that would enable them to stay home with their infants.

> A student who loved to draw and paint, but wasn't spending much time on art because his family did not feel he could make a living at it, joined an evening art class and found new friends who encouraged his artistic endeavors, and encouraged him to find full-time work in that field.

In current American society, the growth of so many support groups indicates our growing recognition of the importance and power of key reference groups. Treating an individual problem in a cultural setting is proving to be highly effective in changing long-standing habits. We see many examples of this group phenomenon—within companies, in psychotherapy, in both lay and professionally led human growth groups, and in task or problem-centered groups such as Parents Without Partners, Divorcees Anonymous, SmokEnders, the Fortune Society, and Alcoholics Anonymous. In all these cases, a new culture is created, the culture of the particular group. People who do not know each other initially come together, share objectives, and create new norms to suit their needs. In this connection, it is interesting to note that the usefulness of anonymity is dwindling. More and more ex-alcoholics, ex-inmates, and ex-addicts are finding it possible, within a group support system, to make a public commitment and announce their changed status. In announcing their commitment to a group, these people renew and strengthen the positive norms that help them sustain the change. Clearly, a spreading knowledge of behavioral change factors is nurturing a greater variety of human growth groups and problem-centered groups. Also emerging is a different kind of group that purposefully makes use of the culture's power. In Lifegain health groups, which teach and support the basic cultural change process itself, there is often a cross-section of people with a wide variety of concerns. Members support each other in whatever changes each has decided to make in his or her health practices. Members discuss strategies for working in their life-action spaces, and explore the cultural dynamics and inner resources they can bring to bear on particular problems.

These group cultures are highly supportive of new norms, and they recognize and reward people for their efforts in ways that help people who would never be able to change without such support. There is a tremendous need to counteract the false dichotomy between the individual and the group that has long been an obstacle in Western culture. Support groups like these play an important role in overcoming the dichotomy and helping society progress toward sharing and caring communities.

ENJOY YOURSELF

If the process is not giving you much fun, it probably will not do much good in the long run. There must be joy in the process, reward in the doing, or it will not long continue. Our gut feeling that fun is better (despite the old Puritan ethic that pleasure is a sin) is upheld by some recent scientific evidence. A long-time study of Harvard's best and brightest graduates shows that "the ability to play is a good indicator of successful adjustment . . . and is shown when a man is able to play competitive games such as tennis with friends, and take long and imaginative vacations from work."[3]

Play is not so much an activity as an attitude. Work becomes play when it is attacked with enthusiasm, an openness to what the moment brings, and

---

[3] Judy Klemesrud, "Keys to Success: The Grant Study of 95 Men," *New York Times,* Sept. 28, 1977.

when it brings enjoyment and satisfaction to the worker. This is as true for the president as for the clerk. The excitement and stimulation of work that is seen as play sustains the work. By extension, the fun of bringing about change will help sustain the change process.

BE OPEN

Finally, holding yourself open to the ideas of others is a decisive ingredient in successful and sustained change, whether you are seeing change from a group leadership position or looking at your own personal attempt to change. Nothing dampens a change program faster than a leader's self-righteousness. While you may feel you really have the answer—you *have* found the way—examine that feeling and see what it does to you. Throw in a doubt. There *may* be another way. Hold yourself open to other ideas, even while you are sure of your own. There just *might* be something more you can learn from someone else; there may be valid ways to further modify your programs.

Many opportunities arise to help others learn what we have learned concerning the tyranny of culture and how to harness cultural forces to bring about the changes we want. You can help others fulfill their potential by avoiding overcontrol, by letting each person be himself without judging him, by encouraging the sensitivity of others and giving them the freedom to develop their own sense of order and control over reality. At the same time, you can share what you have learned. The all-important attitude here is one of service. ("This is what I have done that has helped me; it may be helpful to you.")

This essential humility does not undercut effectiveness but undergirds it. It is based on involving people in the change process—even so personal a change as reducing weight or becoming a poet. It is also based on the openness that comes from seeing yourself and your ideas as part of the cultural scene, existing at a particular moment when all the influences that have converged on you have produced this phenomenon: you, acting in this way, thinking in this way, doing things this way, changing things this way.

AND REACH OUT TO OTHERS

Being open to the needs, concerns, and ideas of others is a mode of existing that can help us go beyond our nearby life-spaces and reach out to all humanity, even to the future of the human race. Treatment of the elderly, resolution of conflicts between nations and races, increasing the healthful longevity of the human race, exploring the frontiers of human consciousness—all these concerns have brought people together to engender research and creative thinking that will benefit all people. In reaching out to others with what we have learned and keeping open to what we can learn from them, we become part of this ever-ongoing ''ascent of man''—and at the same time gain great personal satisfaction.

RELATE YOURSELF TO THE PROCESS

Finding your potential and using it is a never-ending process, with increasing rewards. You will find that as you reach one goal, another presents itself—and another and another. But the rewards turn out to be more in the process than in the product of actions.

It is this attitude that carried great culture changers like Louis Pasteur, Martin Luther King, Marie Curie, and Mahatma Gandhi through years of tribulations. Each of them followed essentially the process that we have been describing. They each analyzed the problem thoroughly, looked for underlying cultural forces that were at work, set their objectives, and were open and clear about them. Each introduced others to new possibilities, then inspired them to act and helped them to believe that change was possible.

Each of them felt that the process itself was important and that the means to the end must incorporate high values and not give way to opportunism. Each was open to new ideas and new data, and each was responsive to the people they dealt with. The process they used to initiate tremendous changes in their social environments, and their attitude toward that process, can help us make less sweeping, but equally valid, reforms of our personal environments.

Chapter 25

Conclusion: Getting Free

He only earns freedom and existence who daily conquers them anew.

GOETHE

We have now come full circle—to choose the environments that create us is to choose ourselves. We are constantly creating and recreating ourselves when we are deciding what our cultural milieu is to be. Since to be human is, unavoidably, to be social, it follows that conscious, purposeful involvement in choosing our own social norms is the best hope for greater humanity, and along with it, greater individual freedom.

We can never be free of the culture (nor would we want to be), but we *can* be free of the culture's tyranny over us, and most important, its power to destroy us. This freedom permits us, and indeed compels us, to attain a greater measure of true individuality.

Recognition of the true nature and scope of cultural influences opens up more alternatives than we thought existed. It is apparent now that we need not choose between a sterile holding on to the past and the uncontrolled exigencies of the future. Instead, we can purposefully design our cultures to make them more humane, more rational, and more emotionally rewarding.

This book has set out to underscore the need for such a humanizing process and to show some very practical ways in which that process may be made part of the fabric of our lives. It has not meant to suggest that this is easy, or that the system presented here is the cure for all the world's ills. It has, however, been tested and tempered in many disparate situations. It has not provided for a straight-line progression to a particular end product, but for that open-ended spiral so characteristic of most other human growth.

Perhaps the most important thing about this process is that it works. It actually has helped people build new lives and new environments. As we see it, there are few efforts more crucial in today's world.

Additional Credits

Page 51   Erving Goffman, *Asylums* (Chicago: Aldine, 1961), p. 14.

           Terry Williams, as quoted in the *Congressional Record,* Apr. 7, 1971, and in John Kerry and Vietnam Veterans against the War, David Thorne and George Butler (eds.), *The New Soldier,* (New York: Macmillan, 1971), p. 60.

Page 63   Ken Kesey, *One Flew Over the Cuckoo's Nest* (New York: Viking, 1962), p. 40.

Page 81   John Gardner, "Educating for Renewal," *Occasional Papers,* 101 (St. Louis: American Association of Collegiate Schools of Business, 1965).

Page 199   A personal recollection from a migrant worker, tape recorded in field research for the book by Sara Harris and Robert F. Allen, *The Quiet Revolution,* (New York: Rawson, 1978).

Page 231   Abraham Maslow, *Toward a Psychology of Being* (New York: Van Nostrand, 1968), p. 189.

           Wolf Wolfensberger, *Normalization* (Toronto: National Institute on Mental Retardation, 1972), p. 123.

Page 233   Robert Theobald, *Futures Conditioned* (Indianapolis: Bobbs-Merrill, 1972), p. 213.

Norm Influence Areas to Be Considered in Analyzing a Culture*

A. Basic influence areas

   1. Rewards (support and confrontation)
   2. Modeling behavior
   3. Information and communications systems
   4. Interactions and relationships
   5. Training
   6. Orientation
   7. Commitment and resource allocation

B. Developmental influence areas

   1. Individual development
   2. Group development
   3. Leadership development
   4. Programs, policies, and procedures

C. Programmatic influence areas

   1. Task and goal clarity
   2. Planning and organizing
   3. Problem solving and decision making
   4. Success orientation
   5. Involvement and motivation
   6. Teamwork
   7. Organizational pride and excellence
   8. Results achievement
   9. Follow-through
   10. Principles of planning, implementation, and change

D. Other cultural influence areas

   1. Economic factors
   2. Significant reference groups
   3. Hierarchical and role factors
   4. Views of time and space

* See also *The Handbook for Cultural Analysis of Groups, Organizations, and Communities* (Morristown, N.J.: HRI Human Resources Institute, 1977). This handbook describes these variables, with illustrations for each one and detailed steps for making an analysis of a culture.

Appendix B

Cultural
Norm Indicator
for Families

(Note: In addition to the cultural norm indicators for families and for organizations in Appendixes B and C, cultural norm indicators for small groups, leadership, colleges and universities, elementary school classes, and health cultures are also available through HRI Human Resources Institute. There are answer sheets, scoring directions, and scoring forms for all these. HRI's *Handbook for Cultural Analysis* gives directions for constructing more specialized cultural norm indicators for use with other problem areas or other types of cultures.)

One of the most important characteristics of all groups or organizations is the pattern of norms that tend to develop within them. This survey is designed to help identify some of the key norms that may or may not exist in your family. The results of this survey can be useful in planning for improvement and change.

A norm is what is "expected" and "supported" within a group or an organization. Norms are really the "way things are," not necessarily the way we would like them to be. Often these "unwritten" rules, or norms, of the organization go against the "official" rules and policies that have been established.

We have listed a number of possible norms that may or may not exist in your family. We would like you to indicate your level of agreement or disagreement with each statement by placing an X in the appropriate box on the answer sheet. If you change your mind after you have marked a response, blacken out your old response and mark your new response with an X.

Several sample questions have been provided. In order to see if you have the hang of it, read each statement and check to see if the answer is the same as the one you would have chosen for your family:

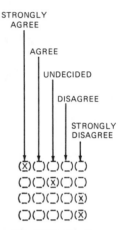

AS I SEE IT, IT IS A NORM IN OUR FAMILY:

1. For family members to shoot each other when they disagree.

2. To serve apple pie and ice cream as the main course for breakfast.

3. To regularly serve most family meals in the bedroom.

4. For one family member to walk around without clothes on when another member has guests.

Answer all questions on the answer sheet on page 268. KEEP IN MIND, ALL THAT IS NEEDED IS YOUR OWN PERSONAL OPINION. YOU ARE NOT BEING ASKED HOW YOU THINK IT SHOULD BE, BUT RATHER *HOW YOU SEE IT.*

AS I SEE IT, IT IS A NORM IN OUR FAMILY:

1. for family members to feel involved and responsible for the well-being of the family.

2. for family members to have pride in the family and in each other.

3. to assure that all family members have a clear understanding and commitment to family goals.

4. for family members to assume responsibility for their share of the work of the family.

5. for family members to be out for themselves and not to care about the other members.

6. to try very hard to create an atmosphere of warmth and understanding.

7. to be considerate of one another and of one another's feelings.

8. to really enjoy our family.

9. to make sure that each person has his or her own privacy respected.

10. to be careful in the use of family property and resources.

11. not to use force in problem solving

12. to see that all family members are involved in the decision-making process.

13. to see that everyone assumes responsibility for leadership.

14. to see that the roles and responsibilities of husband and wife and parent and child are clearly understood and agreed upon.

15. to see that family members get together regularly to discuss and plan ways in which family life can be improved.

16. to encourage people to say what is on their minds and not to hold feelings back.

17. to be on the lookout for new and better ways of doing things.

18. to view others outside the family to be just as important as family members.

19. to provide support for those behaviors that are in support of what we are trying to accomplish.

20. to view discipline as "training" and the training as appropriate for any family member.

21. to accept and to even encourage a wide range of disagreement between family members.

22. to be satisfied with low levels of individual and family commitment and participation.

23. to see that everyone has an opportunity to contribute to the setting of family goals.

24. to see that family work responsibilities are clear, agreed upon, and followed through.

25. to be ready and eager to help out other family members when they are in difficulty.

26. to pay little attention to other people's feelings.

27. to hurt another family member's feelings unnecessarily.

28. to look for ways to make our family fun and enjoyable.

29. to make sure that we do not interfere with each other's privacy.

30. to fail to care properly for family property and resources.

31. never to use force in problem solving.

32. to see that family members are involved in decisions affecting them.

33. to assume that leaders set a good example for others to follow.

34. to not have agreement on husband-wife and parent-child relationships.

35. to get together occasionally and usually only when problems arise.

36. to communicate constructively and clearly.

37. to be so stubborn in the old ways of doing things that we cannot or will not change.

38. to become so focused on the family that we forget other responsibilities outside.

39. to constructively confront negative norms and behaviors that are getting in the way of family life or the goals of individual members.

40. to view discipline as punishment.

41. to assume responsibility for the success of the family.

42. to show little pride in the family or in its accomplishments.

43. to see that individual and family goals are integrated.

44. to assure that family work assignments are equitable and fair.

45. to practice good teamwork in relationship with one another.

46. to express feelings of love and warmth to one another.

47. for family members to do anything that they want to do even if it hurts other people.

48. to see the family as kind of a responsibility.

49. to see that things that we say to each other in privacy are not repeated to others without permission.

50. to see that family property and resources are shared properly and appropriately.

51. to go about solving our problems constructively and without ill feelings.

52. for one or two people to make all the decisions for the family.

53. to see that the leader is supportive and listens to things that are of importance to other family members.

54. to openly discuss the roles and responsibilities of husband and wife.

55. not to have family meetings.

56. to agree that anything that is important to one family member is worthy of being listened to by the others.

57. to continuously check the norms of the family so that they can be improved or changed.

58. to view the family as a base from which we operate rather than as an enclave where we separate ourselves from others.

59. to be passive about behaviors that are getting in the way of family life.

60. for family members to avoid putting each other down.

61. for family members to accept responsibility for their own behavior and for the impact that their behavior has upon others.

62. to strive for excellence in family commitment and activities.

63. to help each other achieve our individual goals.

64. to see that disagreements regarding family work assignments are settled openly and constructively.

65. to disregard good teamwork in relationship with one another.

66. to openly communicate feelings of sadness, love, and joy to one another.

67. to discredit an opinion of a family member without proper consideration of the facts involved.

68. to try to see that each family member gets as much fun out of the family as possible.

69. to use things belonging to others without asking them.

70. to see that the entire family may have a say in how family resources are allocated and cared for.

71. to let problems become chronic.

72. for only the older family members to be involved in the decision-making process.

73. to see that the leader accepts the same as or more responsibilities than other family members.

74. to openly discuss the roles and responsibilities of parent and child.

75. to focus sometimes on the success of the family and not just on its problems.

76. to seek out ideas and opinions of other family members.

77. to change things so slowly that by the time the change takes place it is of little use.

78. to allow alcohol or other drugs to interfere with family life.

79. to only point out negative norms and to do so in a negative manner.

80. to have family agreement on the type of discipline.

81. to have rigid expectations for each other's behavior.

82. to plan, to look for ways, and to integrate periods when family members can unwind and relax.

83. to use the leadership role as a way of getting out of family work assignments.

84. to expect and to even encourage a wide range of difference in point of view within the family.

85. to provide time when we can do things just for the enjoyment of it.

86. to have the leader decide what is proper and important without the family's discussion.

87. to stress and encourage conformity in relationships with one another.

88. to see the leader not setting good examples for others to follow.

89. to be so busy and involved in work that there is no time for people to just enjoy themselves.

90. to impose the shoulds and should not's of one upon the other.

91. to view the freedom of each family member as an essential component of family life.

92. to investigate and find new sources of enjoyment for each individual family member so that everyone can enjoy these activities together.

93. to strive for an effective balance between individual freedom and group responsibility.

94. to see the leader indifferent or unavailable to listen to things that are important to other family members.

95. to assure that each member feels free to contribute to the ideas and suggestions.

96. to assure that each member has an option to be involved and to participate fully in the life of the family.

97. for family members to feel free to be themselves within the family.

98. to assure that individual freedom does not interfere with the freedom of others.

99. to hold back feelings unnecessarily.

100. to see that the property of others is respected.

101. to waste family resources needlessly.

102. to use drugs or alcohol in a way that hurts the family or a family member.

103. to recognize that people are a natural part of living together.

104. to work at our problems to try to find ways to solve them.

105. to overlook the use of drugs by a family member in order to keep the peace.

106. to continuously examine family procedures and ways of doing things to see that they contribute to the attainment of family goals.

ANSWER SHEET FOR CULTURAL NORM INDICATOR FOR FAMILIES.

NAME _____   DATE _____

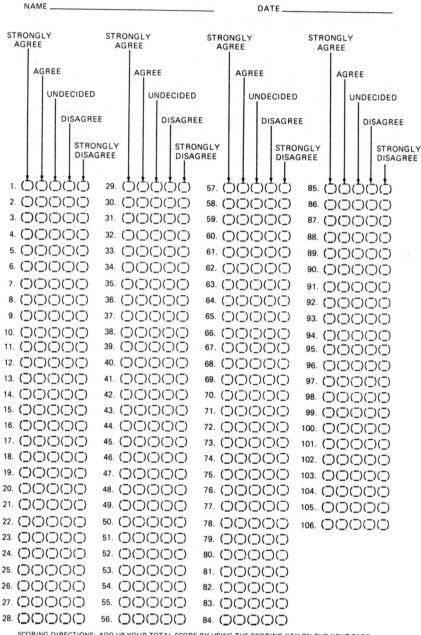

SCORING DIRECTIONS: ADD UP YOUR TOTAL SCORE BY USING THE SCORING KEY ON THE NEXT PAGE.
THE TOP SCORE POSSIBLE, INDICATING THE GREATEST NUMBER OF POSITIVE
NORMS, IS 530. THE LOWEST SCORE POSSIBLE IS 106.

COPYRIGHT SEPTEMBER, 1975, HUMAN RESOURCES INSTITUTE

SCORING KEY FOR CULTURAL NORM INDICATOR FOR FAMILIES.

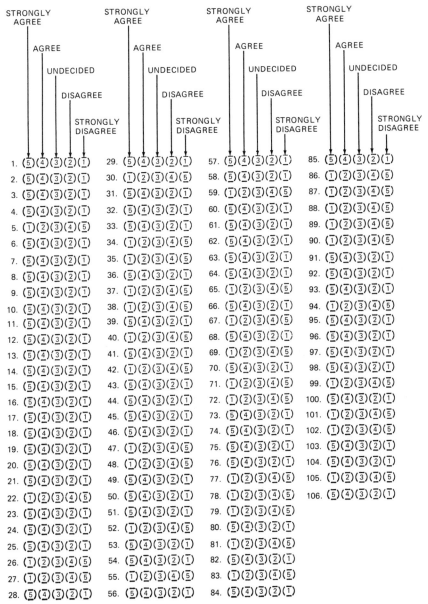

STRONGLY AGREE · AGREE · UNDECIDED · DISAGREE · STRONGLY DISAGREE

1. (5)(4)(3)(2)(1)
2. (5)(4)(3)(2)(1)
3. (5)(4)(3)(2)(1)
4. (5)(4)(3)(2)(1)
5. (1)(2)(3)(4)(5)
6. (5)(4)(3)(2)(1)
7. (5)(4)(3)(2)(1)
8. (5)(4)(3)(2)(1)
9. (5)(4)(3)(2)(1)
10. (5)(4)(3)(2)(1)
11. (5)(4)(3)(2)(1)
12. (5)(4)(3)(2)(1)
13. (5)(4)(3)(2)(1)
14. (5)(4)(3)(2)(1)
15. (5)(4)(3)(2)(1)
16. (5)(4)(3)(2)(1)
17. (5)(4)(3)(2)(1)
18. (5)(4)(3)(2)(1)
19. (5)(4)(3)(2)(1)
20. (5)(4)(3)(2)(1)
21. (5)(4)(3)(2)(1)
22. (1)(2)(3)(4)(5)
23. (5)(4)(3)(2)(1)
24. (5)(4)(3)(2)(1)
25. (5)(4)(3)(2)(1)
26. (1)(2)(3)(4)(5)
27. (1)(2)(3)(4)(5)
28. (5)(4)(3)(2)(1)

29. (5)(4)(3)(2)(1)
30. (1)(2)(3)(4)(5)
31. (5)(4)(3)(2)(1)
32. (5)(4)(3)(2)(1)
33. (5)(4)(3)(2)(1)
34. (1)(2)(3)(4)(5)
35. (1)(2)(3)(4)(5)
36. (5)(4)(3)(2)(1)
37. (1)(2)(3)(4)(5)
38. (1)(2)(3)(4)(5)
39. (5)(4)(3)(2)(1)
40. (1)(2)(3)(4)(5)
41. (5)(4)(3)(2)(1)
42. (1)(2)(3)(4)(5)
43. (5)(4)(3)(2)(1)
44. (5)(4)(3)(2)(1)
45. (5)(4)(3)(2)(1)
46. (5)(4)(3)(2)(1)
47. (1)(2)(3)(4)(5)
48. (1)(2)(3)(4)(5)
49. (5)(4)(3)(2)(1)
50. (5)(4)(3)(2)(1)
51. (5)(4)(3)(2)(1)
52. (1)(2)(3)(4)(5)
53. (5)(4)(3)(2)(1)
54. (5)(4)(3)(2)(1)
55. (1)(2)(3)(4)(5)
56. (5)(4)(3)(2)(1)

57. (5)(4)(3)(2)(1)
58. (5)(4)(3)(2)(1)
59. (1)(2)(3)(4)(5)
60. (5)(4)(3)(2)(1)
61. (5)(4)(3)(2)(1)
62. (5)(4)(3)(2)(1)
63. (5)(4)(3)(2)(1)
64. (5)(4)(3)(2)(1)
65. (1)(2)(3)(4)(5)
66. (5)(4)(3)(2)(1)
67. (1)(2)(3)(4)(5)
68. (5)(4)(3)(2)(1)
69. (1)(2)(3)(4)(5)
70. (5)(4)(3)(2)(1)
71. (1)(2)(3)(4)(5)
72. (1)(2)(3)(4)(5)
73. (5)(4)(3)(2)(1)
74. (5)(4)(3)(2)(1)
75. (5)(4)(3)(2)(1)
76. (5)(4)(3)(2)(1)
77. (1)(2)(3)(4)(5)
78. (1)(2)(3)(4)(5)
79. (1)(2)(3)(4)(5)
80. (5)(4)(3)(2)(1)
81. (1)(2)(3)(4)(5)
82. (5)(4)(3)(2)(1)
83. (1)(2)(3)(4)(5)
84. (5)(4)(3)(2)(1)

85. (5)(4)(3)(2)(1)
86. (1)(2)(3)(4)(5)
87. (1)(2)(3)(4)(5)
88. (1)(2)(3)(4)(5)
89. (1)(2)(3)(4)(5)
90. (1)(2)(3)(4)(5)
91. (5)(4)(3)(2)(1)
92. (5)(4)(3)(2)(1)
93. (5)(4)(3)(2)(1)
94. (1)(2)(3)(4)(5)
95. (5)(4)(3)(2)(1)
96. (5)(4)(3)(2)(1)
97. (5)(4)(3)(2)(1)
98. (5)(4)(3)(2)(1)
99. (1)(2)(3)(4)(5)
100. (5)(4)(3)(2)(1)
101. (1)(2)(3)(4)(5)
102. (1)(2)(3)(4)(5)
103. (5)(4)(3)(2)(1)
104. (5)(4)(3)(2)(1)
105. (1)(2)(3)(4)(5)
106. (5)(4)(3)(2)(1)

Cultural Norm Indicator for Organizations

Mark your choices on the answer sheet on page 274.

AS I SEE IT, IT IS A NORM IN OUR ORGANIZATION:

1. for people to feel "turned on" and enthusiastic about what they are doing.

2. for individual and organizational goals to be in harmony with one another.

3. for teamwork to be neglected.

4. for organizational policies and procedures to be helpful, well-understood, and up-to-date.

5. for people to communicate well with one another.

6. for people to point out errors in a way that is constructive and helpful.

7. for people to blame other people for their own mistakes.

8. for people to feel they can only succeed at the expense of other people.

9. for people to start a new job without having the information they need to do it well.

10. to organize and schedule time and resources effectively.

11. to merely fit people to the job rather than fitting the job to people.

12. for people to get whatever training is needed to help them succeed in their work.

13. for people to avoid making decisions and to allow problems to become chronic.

14. to have a clear way of measuring results.

15. to consistently maintain the progress that is made.

16. for change efforts to be based on sound information.

17. for leaders to fail to practice what they preach.

18. for people to care about and strive for excellent performance.

19. for people to approach change efforts haphazardly without taking into account all the important factors.

20. for people to be involved in setting their own work objectives and work methods.

21. for people not to have any way of measuring how well they are doing.

22. for people to try to work together effectively.

23. for organizational policies and procedures to get in the way of what people are trying to accomplish.

24. for people to actively seek out the ideas and opinions of others.

25. for people to be recognized and re-warded for excellent performance.

26. for people to feel responsible for doing their own jobs right so that the whole team succeeds.

27. for people to help each other when they are having difficulty.

28. for people to be clear on what they are trying to accomplish.

29. for needless duplication of effort to occur.

30. for selection and promotion practices to be fair and equitable.

31. to have a lot of training sessions which do not really help on the job.

32. to look for solutions to problems from which all people will benefit, rather than solutions from which some win and some lose.

33. to focus on effort or talk rather than on results.

34. for leaders to be too busy to follow up on jobs they have assigned to people.

35. for people to avoid blame placing and, instead, to look for constructive approaches to change.

36. for leaders to be concerned equally about both people and production issues.

37. for people to care about doing their best.

38. for people to approach change by dealing with the real causes of problems and not just the symptoms.

39. for people to feel "turned off" by their work in the organization.

40. for people to get feedback on how they are doing so they can develop as individuals in a planned way.

41. for each person to have an opportunity to be a member of a functioning, effective team.

42. to regularly review organizational policies and procedures and make changes when they are needed.

43. for people to practice effective two-way communications.

44. for people to constructively confront negative behavior or "norms" when they occur.

45. for each person to assume responsibility for improving his/her own performance.

46. for people to treat each other as people and not just "a pair of hands."

47. for people to define goals clearly.

48. for some people to be overworked while others have nothing to do.

49. for job assignments to be made on a "hit or miss" basis rather than through a systematic process.

50. for new people to be properly oriented to the job.

51. for decisions to be made in a haphazard way.

52. for leaders to help their work team members succeed.

53. for improvements to be only temporary.

54. for people involved in change efforts to focus on promises rather than on results.

55. for leaders to continually try to improve their leadership skills.

56. for people to take pride in their own work and the work of their organization.

57. for people to follow through on programs that they begin.

58. for people to feel really involved in the work of the organization.

59. for people to regularly plan their work goals and review progress toward their accomplishment.

60. for people who work together to meet regularly to deal with important issues and to focus on ways of improving performance.

61. for people to view policies and procedures as things to be "worked around" or avoided.

62. for people to need more information than they have in order to do a good job.

63. for leaders not to notice what people do unless they do it wrong.

64. for people to assume responsibility for what happens in the organization.

65. for people to give and receive feedback in helpful ways.

66. for people to know exactly what their job requires.

67. for a leader to make the best use of the work time available in his or her work group.

68. for selection and promotion practices to be prejudiced against women or minority groups.

69. for new people to have to "sink or swim" in learning their job.

70. when something goes wrong to blame someone rather than doing something about it.

71. for people to get regular feedback on how well their work team and organization are doing in meeting their objectives.

72. for people to start things without following through.

73. for people to understand what it really takes to improve things in an organization.

74. for leaders to demonstrate their own commitment to what the organization is trying to accomplish.

75. for people to be satisfied with less than their best performance.

76. for people to be directly involved in the development of changes affecting them.

77. for more attention to be given to failures and mistakes than to successes and correct actions.

78. for a spirit of cooperation and teamwork to be felt throughout the organization.

79. for people to focus on activities and problems rather than the results to be achieved.

80. for rivalry to exist among groups within the organization which gets in the way of achieving results.

81. for people who work together to work as positive and effective teams for getting the job done well.

82. for people to emphasize the negative rather than the positive in assessing performance.

83. for people who work together to meet only when they have gripes to share.

84. for every effort to be made to assure that people have many success experiences.

ANSWER SHEET FOR CULTURAL NORM INDICATOR FOR ORGANIZATIONS.

NAME _____   DATE _____

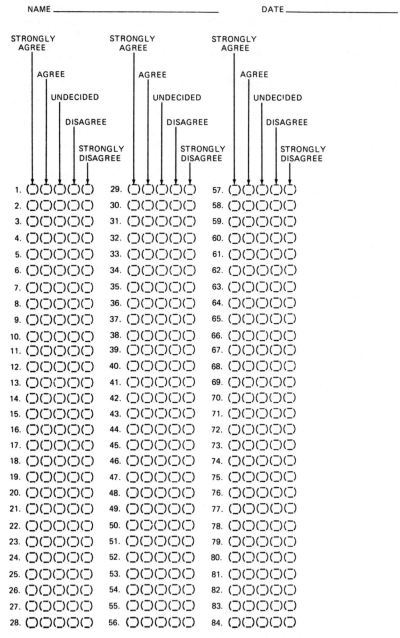

SCORING KEY FOR CULTURAL NORM INDICATOR FOR ORGANIZATIONS.

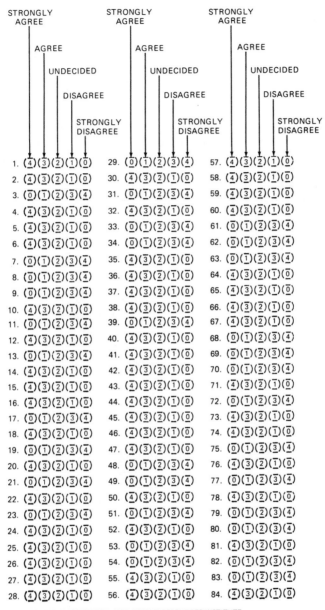

STRONGLY AGREE
AGREE
UNDECIDED
DISAGREE
STRONGLY DISAGREE

STRONGLY AGREE
AGREE
UNDECIDED
DISAGREE
STRONGLY DISAGREE

STRONGLY AGREE
AGREE
UNDECIDED
DISAGREE
STRONGLY DISAGREE

1. (4)(3)(2)(1)(0)
2. (4)(3)(2)(1)(0)
3. (0)(1)(2)(3)(4)
4. (4)(3)(2)(1)(0)
5. (4)(3)(2)(1)(0)
6. (4)(3)(2)(1)(0)
7. (0)(1)(2)(3)(4)
8. (0)(1)(2)(3)(4)
9. (0)(1)(2)(3)(4)
10. (4)(3)(2)(1)(0)
11. (0)(1)(2)(3)(4)
12. (4)(3)(2)(1)(0)
13. (0)(1)(2)(3)(4)
14. (4)(3)(2)(1)(0)
15. (4)(3)(2)(1)(0)
16. (4)(3)(2)(1)(0)
17. (0)(1)(2)(3)(4)
18. (4)(3)(2)(1)(0)
19. (0)(1)(2)(3)(4)
20. (4)(3)(2)(1)(0)
21. (0)(1)(2)(3)(4)
22. (4)(3)(2)(1)(0)
23. (0)(1)(2)(3)(4)
24. (4)(3)(2)(1)(0)
25. (4)(3)(2)(1)(0)
26. (4)(3)(2)(1)(0)
27. (4)(3)(2)(1)(0)
28. (4)(3)(2)(1)(0)

29. (0)(1)(2)(3)(4)
30. (4)(3)(2)(1)(0)
31. (0)(1)(2)(3)(4)
32. (4)(3)(2)(1)(0)
33. (0)(1)(2)(3)(4)
34. (0)(1)(2)(3)(4)
35. (4)(3)(2)(1)(0)
36. (4)(3)(2)(1)(0)
37. (4)(3)(2)(1)(0)
38. (4)(3)(2)(1)(0)
39. (0)(1)(2)(3)(4)
40. (4)(3)(2)(1)(0)
41. (4)(3)(2)(1)(0)
42. (4)(3)(2)(1)(0)
43. (4)(3)(2)(1)(0)
44. (4)(3)(2)(1)(0)
45. (4)(3)(2)(1)(0)
46. (4)(3)(2)(1)(0)
47. (4)(3)(2)(1)(0)
48. (0)(1)(2)(3)(4)
49. (0)(1)(2)(3)(4)
50. (4)(3)(2)(1)(0)
51. (0)(1)(2)(3)(4)
52. (4)(3)(2)(1)(0)
53. (0)(1)(2)(3)(4)
54. (0)(1)(2)(3)(4)
55. (4)(3)(2)(1)(0)
56. (4)(3)(2)(1)(0)

57. (4)(3)(2)(1)(0)
58. (4)(3)(2)(1)(0)
59. (4)(3)(2)(1)(0)
60. (4)(3)(2)(1)(0)
61. (0)(1)(2)(3)(4)
62. (0)(1)(2)(3)(4)
63. (0)(1)(2)(3)(4)
64. (4)(3)(2)(1)(0)
65. (4)(3)(2)(1)(0)
66. (4)(3)(2)(1)(0)
67. (4)(3)(2)(1)(0)
68. (0)(1)(2)(3)(4)
69. (0)(1)(2)(3)(4)
70. (0)(1)(2)(3)(4)
71. (4)(3)(2)(1)(0)
72. (0)(1)(2)(3)(4)
73. (4)(3)(2)(1)(0)
74. (4)(3)(2)(1)(0)
75. (0)(1)(2)(3)(4)
76. (4)(3)(2)(1)(0)
77. (0)(1)(2)(3)(4)
78. (4)(3)(2)(1)(0)
79. (0)(1)(2)(3)(4)
80. (0)(1)(2)(3)(4)
81. (4)(3)(2)(1)(0)
82. (0)(1)(2)(3)(4)
83. (0)(1)(2)(3)(4)
84. (4)(3)(2)(1)(0)

Scoring Directions for Group Effectiveness Exercises Based on "Quiz On Reviewing Key Ideas"

I. Score your own quiz using the scoring key that is provided. One person in the group should also score the group's answers.
II. Fill in the spaces below so that your group's score may be compared with the other groups' scores
  1. Highest individual score   _____
  2. Average of individual scores (total and divide by the
     number in the group)   _____
  3. Group consensus score   _____
  4. Group improvement score (subtract item 2 from item 3) _____

	Highest Individual Score	Average of Individual Score	Group Consensus Score	Group Improvement Score
A				
B				
C				
D				

Groups

A Partial Listing of Current and Past Normative Systems Applications

The Caring Community, a cultural change program for the development of *statewide community programs in the mental health field*

An analysis of *health cost management norms* in a large manufacturing corporation

A program for the *development of community skills* for the establishment of new cultures in a Canadian logging town and in a Canadian mill town

The identification of norms and the existing culture within a large diversified company, utilizing a *communication-feedback* process

An analysis of the *health-care culture* within a *Fortune* 500 company

Lifegain, a program to change the *health practice cultures* in business, family, and community organizations

A cultural analysis for an *equal employment opportunity* program in a business organization

A culture-based *first-line supervisory development system*

A culture-based *managerial development* system for corporate executives

A culture change program for *reducing shrink* (employee pilferage and waste) in retail companies

A culture change program for *reducing absenteeism* in a business setting

A culture change program dealing with *good manufacturing practices* in pharmaceutical companies

Building a new organization for a pharmaceutical manufacturer in the Commonwealth of Puerto Rico

A modification of norms affecting the creative process within a large *advertising agency*

The study and modification of cultural norms in a *large warehouse distribution center*

A modification of organizational norms in a multinational *soft drink corporation*

A comprehensive culture change program for a *large pharmaceutical corporation*

Cultural change in a *multilevel manufacturing operation*

The environmental care culture of a large company

Modifying the managerial and supervisory culture of an *agribusiness culture*

Developing positive cultures for the employment of *economically disadvantaged persons in business and industry*

A culture-based *new employee orientation system*

A culture-based change program for *American supermarket companies*

A study of positive and negative cultural norms in *European supermarket companies*

The use of positive norms within a *supermarket training system*

A self-study and the modification of cultural norms in a *state prison for women*

The modification of cultural norms affecting *buyer-seller relations in the food industry*

The modification of cultural norms in *union organizations*

A cultural analysis of *outreach programs* for the Senate Committee on Public Welfare

Analysis and change programs for *antipoverty agencies*

Analysis and change programs for *youth service agencies*

Analysis and change programs for *police departments*

A cultural analysis change program dealing with *drug addiction*

A culture-based program for *training juvenile court judges*

A culture-based *training system* for government employees

A cultural analysis of a change program dealing with *sanitation and bacterial control*

A cultural change program in a *state mental hospital and community services system*

A leadership development program for a *synagogue* board of trustees

A cultural analysis of change in a *suburban church congregation*

A cultural analysis of change in a *suburban family*

A culture change program dealing with *food waste* in the state of Pennsylvania

A cultural analysis and change program in an *urban welfare agency*

Changing *the litter culture* in American communities

A self-administered *environmental change program for European communities*

A cultural self-development program for *migrant workers*

Modification of win/lose cultures *between police and ghetto residents* in large cities

A culture-based self-change program for *college and university residential centers*

The study and modification of leadership norms in *teachers associations and professional education groups*

Conflict resolution in a *high school setting*

The creation of a positive learning culture within a *teacher aide training system*

A cultural analysis for large-city *boards of education*

A cultural analysis and change program for *college and university classrooms*

A leadership development program for a *parent-teacher association*

A cultural change program for *voluntary agencies in the field of mental retardation*

A cultural analysis of a high school *cross-country team*

A cultural change program for a *suburban school district*

A cultural analysis of a high school *football team*

The destructive elements of residential cultures within a *residential treatment center for delinquent youth*

The self-modification of cultures in *delinquency rehabilitation institutions*

The development of positive residential cultures within *Job Corps centers* for urban and rural youth

The social integration and English language development of *Puerto Rican children* in a large urban setting

Bibliography

SELECTED REFERENCES ABOUT NORMATIVE SYSTEMS

Allen, Robert F., "Changing Lifestyles through Changing Organizational Cultures," *Proceedings of Fourteenth Annual Meeting* (St. Petersburg, Fla.: Society of Prospective Medicine), October 1978.

———, "Commentary on Human Relations and Interracial Social Action: Problems in Self and Client Definitions," *Journal of Applied Behavioral Sciences*, Vol. 2, No. 1, 1966.

———, "The Corporate Health Buying Spree: Boon or Boondoggle?" *S.A.M. Advanced Management Journal*, Vol. 45, Nos. 2 and 3, Spring and Summer 1980.

———, "A Culture-Based Approach to the Improvement of Health Practices," *Proceedings of Thirteenth Annual Meeting* (San Diego, Calif.: Society of Prospective Medicine), October 1977.

———, "The Ilk in the Office," *Organizational Dynamics*, Vol. 8, No. 3, Winter 1980.

———, "Increasing Group Effectiveness through Normative Systems." (Morristown, N.J.: HRI Human Resources Institute, 1975).

———, "Keine Rolls fur Unbeteiligte," *Gruppendynamik*, Munich, Germany, No. 3, July 1970, pp. 270–271.

———, "Motivation through Normative Systems," *Journal of Dutweiler Institute*, Zurich, Switzerland, 1972.

———, *Normative Systems Programs in Union Organizations* (Morristown, N.J.: HRI Human Resources Institute, 1972).

———, "The Normative Systems Quality of Work Program" (Morristown, N.J.: HRI Human Resources Institute, 1975).

———, *When Are Results Not Results?* (Madison, Wis.: American Society for Training and Development Selected Papers, 1979).

———, and Harry N. Dubin, *Allen Adolescent Incomplete Sentence Test* (Washington: U.S. Office of Health, Education and Welfare and the Commonwealth of Puerto Rico, 1966).

———, ———, Saul Pilnick, and Adella C. Youtz, *Collegefields: From Delinquency to Freedom* (Seattle: Special Child Publications, 1970).

———, ———, ———, and ———, *From Delinquency to Freedom: A Report on the Collegefields Group Rehabilitation Program for Delinquent Youth* (Washington: U.S. Office of Education, 1966).

———, and Frank Dyer, "The Organizational Unconscious: A Here-and-Now Approach to Understanding and Dealing with It," *Personnel*, March 1980.

———, and Donald Gaal, *Integrative Management for Results* (Morristown, N.J.: SRI Scientific Resources Inc., 1968).

————, and Michael Higgins, "Ousting the Absenteeism Culture," *Personnel*, January–February 1979.

———— and Charlotte Kraft, "Building Wellness Cultures on a Community Level" (Morristown, N.J.: HRI Selected Papers, 1979).

———— and ————, "Changing Our Health Cultures: A Family Guide to Wellness and Positive Health," *Parents Magazine*, July 1980.

———— and ————, "Y Can Mobilize Communities toward Health," *Perspective: Journal—Association of Professional YMCA Directors*, Vol. 6, Nos. 2 and 3, Winter and Spring 1980.

———— and Shirley Linde, *Lifegain: A Cultural Approach to Positive Health* (Indianapolis: Charles Merrill, to be published).

———— and Richard Murphy, "Getting Started: The Development of a New Company," *Business*, Vol. 29, No. 4, July–August 1979, pp. 26–34.

———— and Saul Pilnick, "Confronting the Shadow Organization: How to Detect and Defeat Negative Norms," *Organizational Dynamics*, Vol. 4, No. 1, Spring 1973, pp. 3–18.

———— and ————, *Preliminary Report on Normative Systems in European Business Organizations* (Morristown, N.J.: SRI Scientific Resources Inc., 1970).

———— and ————, *The Rehabilitation of Delinquent Youth* (Seattle: Special Child Publications, 1968).

————, ————, and Colin Park, "The Accounting Executive's Shadow Organization," *Management Accounting*, No. 7, January 1974.

————, ————, and Frank Riesman, *A Report on Outreach*, prepared for the U.S. Senate Labor Committee, 1967.

————, ————, and Stanley Silverzweig, "Conflict Resolution—Team Building for Police and Ghetto Residents," *Journal of Criminal Law, Criminology and Police Science*, Vol. 60, No. 2, 1968.

————, ————, and ————, "The Influence of the Peer Culture on Delinquency and Delinquent Rehabilitation," *Psychiatric Outpatient Journal*, Spring 1970.

————, ————, and ————, *Normative Systems: An Approach to Increasing Organizational Effectiveness* (Morristown, N.J.: SRI Press, 1970).

————, ————, and ————, *Norms in the Supermarket Industry: A Self-Instructional Program* (Morristown, N.J.: SRI Press, 1970).

————, ————, and Richard Treat, *Guided Group Interaction in Job Corps Settings* (Washington: U.S. Office of Economic Opportunity, 1967).

———— and Joseph Rosner, *Social Integration and the English Language Development of Puerto Rican Children* (New York: Ford Foundation Files, 1954).

———— and Stanley Silverzweig, "Changing Community and Organizational Cultures," *Training and Development Journal*, Vol. 31, No. 7, July 1977, pp. 28–34.

———— and ————, "Group Norms: Their Influence on Training Effectiveness," *Handbook of Training and Development* (American Society for Training and Development, Spring 1975).

———— and ————, *The HRI Norm Indicator Series* (Morristown, N.J.: HRI Human Resources Institute, 1975).

—— and ——, *Minority Contributors to American History* (Morristown, N.J.: SRI Scientific Resources Inc., 1967).

—— and ——, "The Normative Systems Organization/Leadership Development Modules" (Morristown, N.J.: HRI Human Resources Institute and Hoffmann-LaRoche Inc., 1975).

—— and ——, "The Normative Systems Orientation Program" (Morristown, N.J.: HRI Human Resources Institute, 1975).

——, ——, and Marilyn Schneider, *Changing Our Litter Culture: Normative Systems Action Research Model for the Reduction of Litter in American Communities, Report of a Two-Year Project* (New York: Keep America Beautiful, Inc., 1974).

"ALP-Update," *Foodline*, Vol. 4, No. 1 (Coca-Cola Company Foods Division, January–February 1971) pp. 3–5.

"A 'Behavior Business' is Born," *Food Topics*, January 1967.

Blank, Joseph, "Migrants No More," *Reader's Digest*, July 1975, pp. 98–102.

"Building the Morristown High School Community," slide-tape presentation by the students of Morristown High School and the staff of HRI Human Resources Institute, Morristown, N.J., 1974.

Drury, Barbara, and Robert F. Allen, "Maximizing Employee Health by Changing the Corporate Culture," an address to the American Public Health Association, Nov. 2, 1977, Washington (Morristown, N.J.: HRI Human Resources Institute, 1977).

"An Experiment in Problem Solving through Personnel Involvement," *Chain Store Age*, supermarket editions, May 1970.

Garner, Phil, "A New Life for Migrant Workers," *The Atlanta Journal and Constitution Magazine*, Jan. 23, 1962.

Handbook for the Cultural Analysis of Groups, Organizations, and Communities (Morristown, N.J.: HRI Human Resources Institute, 1977).

Harris, Sara, and Robert F. Allen, *The Quiet Revolution* (New York: Rawson, 1978).

How to Reach Labor's Silent Majority, Industrial Bulletin of the New York State Department of Labor, March 1970.

Knebel, Fletcher, "The White Cop and the Black Rebel," *Look*, Feb. 6, 1968.

Kraft, Charlotte, "Changing our Litter Cultures," (Morristown, N.J.: HRI Selected Papers, 1979).

Larkin, Timothy, "Adios to Migrancy," *Manpower* (Washington: U.S. Department of Labor, Manpower Administration, August 1974).

"Maximizing Employee Health by Changing the Corporate Culture" (Washington: American Public Health Association, November 1977).

"Negro Arrests Cop: Role-Switching Games Aim at Ghetto Peace," *Wall Street Journal*, Midwest edition, Aug. 2, 1968.

New Employee Orientation System for Super Market Institute (Morristown, N.J.: SRI Scientific Resources Inc., 1968).

Normative Systems in the Food Industry, series of films produced by Fred Niles, Inc., for the Super Market Institute (Morristown, N.J.: SRI Press, 1970).

Normative Systems Programs in Business and Industry (Morristown, N.J.: SRI Scientific Resources Inc., 1970).

A Piece of the Action, a film report on the Agricultural Labor Project of the Coca-Cola Company, Atlanta Film Company, 1972.

Pilnick, Saul, and Robert F. Allen, "Guided Group Interaction," *1978 Yearbook of the National Association of Social Workers.*

———, ———, and Stanley Silverzweig, *The Peer Group in Adolescence* (Albany, N.Y.: State of New York, Division of Youth, 1968).

Polsky, Howard, *Cottage Six: The Social Systems of Delinquent Boys in Residential Treatment* (Poughkeepsie, N.Y.: Russell Sage Foundations, 1962).

A Project in Progress, series of status reports on the Agricultural Labor Project of the Coca-Cola Company Foods Division, April 1971 to September 1974.

Silverzweig, Stanley, and Robert F. Allen, "Changing the Corporate Culture," *Sloan Management Review,* Spring 1977, pp. 33–49.

——— and ———, *Proper Price Marking* (Morristown, N.J.: SRI Scientific Resources Inc., 1969).

——— and ———, *Employment of the Disadvantaged* (Chicago: Super Market Institute, 1968).

———, ———, and Saul Pilnick, *Customer Courtesy* (Chicago: Super Market Institute, 1967).

———, ———, and ———, *The SRI Organic Reading and Writing Laboratory* (Morristown, N.J.: SRI Press, 1966).

———, ———, and ———, *Teacher Aide Training Systems* (New York: The Macmillan Company, 1968).

Toward A Caring Community, film presentation on mental health services (Morristown, N.J.: HRI Human Resources Institute, 1977); available from the state of New Jersey, Department of Human Services, Trenton, N.J.

Index

Absenteeism, 248–249
Ackerman, Paul D., 29
Action tracking, 145
Addiction, 21, 27, 41, 131
Adolescence, norm pressure in, 26
Agendas, use of planned, 169–170
Alcohol use, 21, 41
Alcoholics Anonymous, 249, 254
Alger, Horatio, 100
Alienation, 84, 103
American Psychiatric Association, 32
Amish (community), 17
Analysis and objective setting phase (see Start-up)
Anomie, 18
Appalachian syndrome, 96
ARM (action research model), 214, 215, 218
Attica prison, 108
Authority figures:
    denial of feelings among, 66–67
    (*See also* Leadership)

Bannister, Roger, 86
Belief(s):
    institutional lack of, in change, 72
    norm influence on, 30
Benedict, Ruth, 103
Benson, Mark (pseudonym), 1–2
Bion, Wilfred, 75
Blake, Robert R., 123
Blame placing, norms on, 89–91
Blemish Game, 90
Blinders, 14–16, 142
    (*See also* Cultural norms)
Boy Scouts, 92
Brecht, Bertolt, 56
Bronowski, Jacob, 19, 102, 105
Brookings Institution, 78
Buber, Martin, 102
Bureaucratization, institutional, 68–69
Burn rate, 87–88
Business:
    cultural scripts in, 86
    as fertile ground for change, 240
    and individual development, 167
    information and communication systems in, 40
    keeping desired values in, 244
    MBO programs, 143*n.*, 237–238

Business (*Cont.*):
    migrant workers and, 199–210
    norm profiles for two businesses, illustrated, 150
    objectives in, 143–145
    orientation in, 44, 139
    simplistic solution in, 92
    supervisory norms in, 43
    systems change programs in: failure, 227–230
        success, 219–226
    systems introduction in new, 161
    workshop in, 156–160
Business management, 38

Calley, Lt. William, Jr. (Rusty), 53, 57–61
Caring Community programs, 235–236, 241
Ceilings on the mind, 24–25
Change, 107–108
    cultural obstacles to, 89–97
    and culture trap, 83–88
    instruments for planning (*see* Instruments)
    lack of belief in, in institutions, 72
    (*See also* Normative Systems)
Charlotte (N.C.), litter problem in, 211–218, 242
Chavez, Cesar, 108
Child labor among migrant workers, 121–122
Children:
    in burial clubs, 20
    creative, in schools, 70–71
        (*See also* Schools)
    cut off from human relatedness, 103
    destructive relationship between society and, 43
    history of childhood, 24
    and information and communication systems, 40
    norm pressures on, 26
    norms and long childhood, 18–19
Churches (*see* Religious institutions)
Clean Community System, litter problem and, 211–218, 242
Coca-Cola Bottling Company, Foods Division of, 199–201, 205, 210
Collegefields (N.J.) Delinquency Rehabilitation Program, 134, 187–197
Commitment:
    checklist on, 127

Commitment *(Cont.):*
  culture-based, sustained, as principle for
    change, 119, 125
  defined, 45
  individual, 248–249
  of leaders, 171
Communications [*see* Information (and
  communications) systems]
Community:
  and need for relatedness, 103–104
  Normative Systems in total development
    of, 239, 242
  sense of, 101–102
Competition:
  dealing with problem of, 45
  nonhelpfulness and, 67
  school and, 68, 76
Conceptualization problem, solutions and,
  86–87
Conditioning, 19, 133
Conflict resolution by cultural approach, 239
  (*See also* Cultural approach)
Conformity, 14–15, 101–102
Consultant's role, 156
Crash programs, cultural norm of, 93
Crime:
  retail store, 53–56, 150
  (*See also* Violence)
Cuiba Indians, 86
Cultural analysis, 4, 129–146
  handbook for, 263
  instruments for, 147–153
  (*See also* Start-up)
Cultural approach:
  conflict resolution by, 239
  to institutions, 72–78
  key hypotheses to change by way of, 2–3
  (*See also* Cultural norms; Normative Sys-
    tems)
Cultural barriers, 246–247
Cultural factors, influence of, 3–4
Cultural influences, 11–21
Cultural modification, 4
Cultural norm indicator(s):
  defined, 147–148
  family, 243–244, 263–269
  function of, 148
  leadership, 171–172
  organizational, 271–275
  reference group indicator, 150
Cultural norms:
  on blame placing, 89–91
  of crash program, 93
  current negative, 96–97
  in decision making, 94–95
  as fashions, 16–17
  of focus on individual, 95–96
  of helplessness, 93

Cultural norms *(Cont.):*
  in history, 20–21
  influence areas of, 36
    [*See also* Commitment; Information
      (and communications) systems; In-
      teractions and relationships; Model-
      ing behavior; Orientation; Rewards
      (and permissions); Training (and
      skills)]
  as laws, 17
  of losing clarity, 96
  as necessary, 18
  perceiving, 14–16
  power of, 23–24
  of proceeding uninformed and untrained,
    93–94
  quiz on understanding, 47–49
  of simplistic solutions, 91–92
  test showing influence of, 11–12
  as traditions, 16
  understanding, 13–14
  universality of, 25–27
  unsubstantiated promises as, 95
  in violence, 27, 29
  what norms are not, 18
  win/lose, 91
Cultural principles (*see* Normative Systems)
Cultural scripts, 86
Cultural values inventory, 150
Culture(s):
  building a new, 234
  defined, 3
  instruments for understanding (*see* In-
    struments)
  as trap, 83–88
  understanding and identifying, in work-
    shops, 161
Culture-based, sustained effort, 119, 127
  (*See also* Commitment)
Curie, Marie, 256
Cynicism as unproductive, 4

Dass, Ram, 46
Decision making, 163
  in institutions, 65–66
  norms of, 94–95
Dehumanization in institutions, 53, 57–61,
  69, 72
Delinquency, 130, 131
  Collegefields program on, 134, 187–197
  influence of norms on, 25
Delinquent culture, norms of, 189–190
Democracy, 24
  individual and, 100
  in people-involvement norms, 120–121
Democratic control in Normative Systems, 114
Dependence in institutions, 65–66, 74

Deviant behavior, 31–32, 37, 67
Dewey, John, 85
Dickens, Charles, 107
Dieting, 31, 93, 250–251
Direction, cultural norm of losing, 96
Disruption, change and, 108
Divorcees Anonymous, 253–254
Dix, Dorothea, 175
Drug addiction, 21, 27, 131
Drug culture, 56–57
Durkheim, Emile, 18

Education (*see* Schools)
Emancipation Proclamation (1863), 24
Environment, defined, 3
Eskimos, 41
Evaluation, renewal, and extension (*see* Sustaining change)
Exit interviews, defined, 152
Extension (*see* Sustaining change)

Family:
    commitment in, 45
    cultural change program in, 1–2
    cultural scripts in, 86
    interactions in, 42
    keeping values of, 242–243
    myth making in, 71
    and need for relatedness, 103, 104
    norm profile for, illustrated, 149
    systems introduction in, 161
    systems implementation and change in, 165
    training system in, 138
Family cultural norm indicator, 243–244, 263–269
Feelings, denial of, in institutions, 66–67
Ferdinand (King of Castile), 36
Field theory (Lewin), 246
Florida:
    litter problem in, 211–218, 242
    migrant workers in, 1, 199–210
Focused field observations, 152
Focused-theme depth interviews, 152
Food waste, 235
Fortune Society, 254
Four-minute mile, 86
Freedom, 1–5, 24, 257
    group/individual dichotomy and, 104
    real, defined, 165
    uniqueness and, 102
    (*See also* Change)
French Revolution (1789), 24
Freud, Sigmund, 3, 25, 88

Gandhi, Mohandas K. (Mahatma), 256

Garages, 33
General exploration interviews, 151
Genetics (field), norm influence on, 32
Geneva Conventions of War, 60
Genius, group activity and, 105
Ghetto, the:
    conflict of goals and abilities, 43
    conflict resolution in, 239
    drug-culture destruction of youth in, 56–57, 61
    interactions and relationships in, 42
    modeling behavior in, 39, 188–190
    personal counseling to remedy problems of, 95–96
Goal setting (*see* Objectives)
Government, negative norms and, 78
Grand Rapids (Mich.), 239
Great people, culture and, 88
Grid concept in problem confrontation, 123
Group(s):
    blind allegiance to, 101–102
    development of: in business, 224
        Collegefields, 191–192
        implementing change and, 166, 168–170
    effectiveness exercises for, 277
Group/individual dichotomy as unnecessary and unproductive, 99–105
Group interview discussion sessions, 152
Group norms (social norms):
    defined, 13
    [*See also* Cultural norms; Group(s)]
Groupthink, 101

Hairstyles, 12, 17
Handbook for Cultural Analysis (Human Research Institute), 263
Hard hats, 234–235
Harris, Arnold, 201
Harris, Sara, 201
Health, Education, and Welfare, U.S. Department of (HEW), 64, 188
Health practices, improvement in, 254
Health program, objectives in, 144
Helplessness, norm of, 93
Heroes, video, 47
Hersh, Seymour, 58, 59
Hierarchy(ies):
    destructive, 68
    of human needs, 134
Highlight tapes, 152
History:
    of childhood, 24
    norms in, 20–21
Hitler, Adolf, 113
Holly Ridge (N.C.), 218
Homosexuality, norm influence on, 31–32
Hopi Indians, 41

Hospitals:
  modeling behavior in, 135
  Normative Systems approach in, 241
  (*See also* Mental hospitals)
Houston (Tex.), 218
Human nature, concepts of, as culture trap,
    84–86
Human needs, hierarchy of, 134
Human Resources Institute (HRI), 140, 263
Human universals, 26

Ik (African tribe), 101
Implementation (*see* Installing change)
Indians (Native Americans), 20, 24
Individual(s):
  Buber on, 102
  destruction of, 53–61
    in crime, 53–56
    in drug culture, 56–57
    in war, 57–61
  development of: in business, 224
    Collegefields, 191–192
    implementing change in, 166–168
  focus on, as cultural norm, 95–96
  myth of isolated, 100
  Normative Systems applied by, 245–256
  as social solitary, 102–104
Individual/group dichotomy as unnecessary
    and unproductive, 99–105
Individualism, 69, 90, 103, 105
  cult of, 100–101
Industry (*see* Business)
Information (and communications) systems,
    40–42
  checklist on, 126
  norm of proceeding without sufficient,
    93–94
  in planned programs, 132, 136–137
  sound, as principle for change, 119, 121–
    122
Installing change (systems implementation
    and change; phase III), 116, 165–174
  in business: failure, 227–230
    success, 219–226
  in Collegefields program, 191–192
  in family, 165
  by group, 166, 168–170
  by individuals, 166–168, 247–248
  by leadership, 166, 170–172
    (*See also* Leadership)
  in litter program, 215–218
  among migrant workers, 205–209
  normative principles throughout, 173–
    174
  organizational structure and, 166, 172–173
    (*See also* Organizational structure)
  putting norms in practice, 166

Institutions, 63–79
  acquiescence in, 70–71
  bureaucratization in, 68–69
  change and inertia of, 85
  crucial questions about, 78–79
  culture-based approach to, 72–78
  dehumanization in, 53, 57–61, 69, 72
  dependence in, 65–66, 74
  failures of, 63–64
  feelings denied in, 66–67
  importance of, 64–65
  lack of belief in change in, 72
  myth making by, 71
  nonhelpfulness in, 67
  overprotection in, 66
  reality unrecognized in, 69
  sanctification of, 70
  separation of people in, 67–68
  size of, 69
  (*See also specific types of institutions*)
Instruments, 147–153
  additional, 149–152
  norm, 147–149
Intelligence, norm influence on, 30–32
Interactions and relationships:
  defined, 42–43
  in planned programs, 132, 137–138
  in war, 60
Interviews, defined, 151–152
Introduction of systems (*see* Involvement)
Involvement (systems introduction and in-
    volvement; phase II), 116, 155–164
  in business: failure, 227–230
    success, 219–226
  checklist on, 125–126
  in Collegefields program, 190–191
  by individual, 247
  in litter problem, 214–217
  of migrant workers, 204–205
  of people, as principle for change, 119–121
  reviewing key ideas in, 162–164
  workshops for (*see* Workshops in Norma-
    tive Systems)

James, William, 18
Jews, 21
John Brown's Body (Benét), 20
Jones, Jim, 101

Keep America Beautiful (KAB), 212, 218
Kennedy, John F., 39, 40
Kesey, Ken, 75
King, Martin Luther, Jr., 256
Ku Klux Klan, 53

Laing, R. D., 43
Language, 41–42
  dehumanizing, 53, 57–61, 69
Laws, norms and, 17, 18
Leadership:
  development of: in business, 224–225
    Collegefields, 191–192
    in implementing change, 166, 170–172
  Normative Systems applied by, 245
  and personal change, 248–249
Leadership norm indicator, 171–172
League of Nations, 94
Learning patterns, norm influence on, 30
Leaves of Grass (Whitman), 18
Lewin, Kurt, 246
Liberation movements, 32–33, 88, 95
Life-space, concept of, 246
Life-styles, unhealthy, 235
Lifegain health practices change program,
  162, 235
Lincoln, Abraham, 88
Litter problem, 2, 211–218, 242
Lobotomies, 21
Loneliness, 103

Macon (Ga.), litter problem in, 2, 211–218,
  242
Malcolm X, 39, 40, 245
Management by objectives (MBO), 143*n.*,
  237–238
Manson, Charles, 101
Marx, Karl, 84
Maslow, Abraham, 134, 244
Medicine:
  effect of training and skills on, 43–44
  norm influence in, 30–32
  preventive, 38
  (*See also* Hospitals)
Medina, Capt. Ernest, 58
Mental hospitals:
  bureaucratization in, 68
  dehumanization in, 69
  dependence in, 65, 74
  Dix and, 175
  effect of words "mental hospital" on func-
    tion of, 42
  failure of, 63–64
  as fertile ground for change, 241
  myth making in, 71
  and need for relatedness, 103
  nonhelpfulness in, 67
  norm influences in, 25
  normative look at, 72–76
  norms influencing treatment in, 20–21, 31
  overprotection in, 66, 93–94
  sanctification in, 70
  separation of people in, 67, 68
  study on, 75

Mental illness as chronic problem, 235
Migrant workers, 1, 199–210
Milgram, Stanley, 27, 29, 101
Military budget, 45
Minute Maid Company, 199–201
Misconceptions about cultural barriers, 246
Modeling behavior, 38–40
  in Calley, 58
  leaders as sources for, 171
  in planned programs, 132, 135
  in street culture, 188
Mondo Cane (film), 26
Mountain People, The (Turnbull), 101
Mouton, Jane S., 123
Murdock, G. P., 26
Murphy, Gardner, 246
My Lai massacre, 18, 53, 57–61, 156–157
Myths (and myth making), 71, 72, 85

Natural man, 84
Nazism, 21, 53, 101, 156
Needs:
  genuine and imaginary, 84
  hierarchy of human, 134
Negative norms:
  current, 96–97
  (*See also* Cultural norms)
Negative parenting, 42–43, 90–91
New programs, developing, 237
Nixon, Richard M., 37, 39, 101
Nobel, Alfred, 32
Nobel Prize, 32
Nonhelpfulness in institutions, 67
Norm influence areas, 261
  key, 250
    examples, 251–252
Norm profiles, 148
  illustrated, 149, 150
Normative behavior, defined, 25
Normative description inventory (NDI), de-
  fined, 150–151
Normative support and confrontation inven-
  tory, defined, 151
Normative Systems, 4, 113–117
  concept of, 114
  partial listing of current and past applica-
    tions of, 279–281
  phases of, 115–116
    illustrated, 115, 182
    (*See also* Installing change; Involve-
      ment; Start-up; Sustaining change)
  planned program as a key concept in, 114
  seven principles in, 119
    [*See also* Commitment; Culture-based
      sustained effort; Information (and
      communications) systems; Involve-
      ment; Objectives; Results orientation;

Normative Systems, seven principles in *(Cont.)*:
Systematic strategies and tactics; Win/win solutions]
uses of, 233–244
workshops in (*see* Workshops in Normative Systems)
Normative Systems model, 115–116, 181–183
Norms (*see* Cultural norms)
Nursing home, dependence in, 65

Oates, Joyce Carol, 100, 105
Obedience, study on, 27, 29
Obesity, 31, 93, 250–251
Objectives, 24
checklist on, 126
clear plans, tasks and, as principles for change, 119, 122–123
setting, 142–144
measurement of, 144–145
Observation techniques, 152
Openness to others, 255
Operant conditioning (behavior modification), 133
Organizational cultural norm indicator, 271–275
Organizational perception inventory (OPI), 151
Organizational structure:
development of: in business, 225
in Collegefields program, 191–192
making existing programs work in, 237–238
Normative Systems in total structure, 239–242
as "shadow trainer," 236–237
and systems implementation, 166, 172–173
Organizational support indicator, defined, 149–150
Orientation:
defined, 44
in planned programs, 132, 139–140
results: checklist on, 126
as principle for change, 119, 124–125
in street culture, 188
Overmedication, 66
Overprotection, 66, 93–94
Ownership, concept of, in Normative Systems, 114

Parenting, negative, 42–43, 90–91
Parents without Partners, 253
Participant observations, 152
Participation:
in analysis and objective setting, 131–132

Participation *(Cont.):*
in change, 120, 121
workshop, 155–156
(*See also* Workshops)
Pasteur, Louis, 256
Patients' Bill of Rights, 64
Patton, Col. George S., III, 58
Perception experiment to test effects of norms, 27
illustrated, 28
Perceptions of problems and ability to solve them, 86–87
Performance appraisal, 167–168
Performance improvement, 238–239
Piaget, Jean, 30
Pilferage, 53–56
Plan, using a systematic, 249–250
Planned agendas, use of, 169–170
Planned programs:
information in, 132, 136–137
interactions in, 132, 137–138
as key concept, 114
modeling behavior in, 132, 135
orientation in, 132, 139–140
resource allocation in, 132, 140–141
rewards in, 132–134
training in, 132, 138–139
Play, importance of, 254–255
Pleasure, importance of, 254–255
Policies and programs, formal, of total organization, and implementing change, 166, 172–173
Politics, 27, 29–30, 64
Positive norms of change, 162, 163
(*See also* Change)
Poverty, national programs to fight, 45, 78
Preventive medicine, 38
Prisons:
dependence in, 65–66
failure of, 63–64
myth making in, 71
and need for relatedness, 103
nonhelpfulness in, 67
orientation in culture of, 44
riots in, 108
Profit opportunities, 40
Promises, unsubstantiated, as norm, 95
Punishment and reinforcement in boot camp, 59
[*See also* Rewards (and permissions)]

Quiz:
on reviewing key ideas in Normative Systems approach, 162, 164, 277
on understanding cultural norms, 47–49